# U.S. and Soviet Aid to Developing Countries

# FROM CONFRONTATION TO COOPERATION?

Richard E. Feinberg
Ratchik M. Avakov

U.S.S.R. Contributors:
Elena B. Arefieva, Elena A. Bragina,
Andrei I. Chekhutov, Margarita P. Strepetova,
Nataliya A. Ushakova, and Leon Z. Zevin

U.S. Contributors:
Elliot Berg, W. Donald Bowles,
Gerald M. Meier, and Ernest H. Preeg

Series Editors:
Richard E. Feinberg
Valeriana Kallab

**Transaction Publishers**
New Brunswick (USA) and Oxford (UK)

ISBN: 0-88738-391-2 (cloth)
ISBN: 0-88738-879-5 (paper)
Printed in the United States of America

Library of Congress **Cataloging-in-Publication Data**

Feinberg, Richard.
 From Confrontation to Cooperation?: U.S. and Soviet Aid to Developing Countries

(U.S.–Third World Policy Perspectives: No. 15)
 1. Economic assistance, American—Developing Countries. 2. Economic assistance, Soviet—Developing Countries. 3. Technical assistance, American—Developing Countries. 4. Technical assistance, Soviet—Developing Countries. I. Avakov, Ratchik M.  II. Title.  III. Series.

HC60.F348   1991   338.9′1′091724—dc20     90-19831

ISBN: 0-88738-391-2 (cloth)
ISBN: 0-88738-879-5 (paper)

# U.S. and Soviet Aid to Developing Countries
# FROM CONFRONTATION TO COOPERATION?

# Acknowledgments

*U.S. and U.S.S.R. Project Directors:*
Ratchik M. Avakov
Richard E. Feinberg

*ODC Policy Perspectives Series Editors:*
Richard E. Feinberg
Valeriana Kallab


The Overseas Development Council gratefully acknowledges the support of The Ford Foundation, The Rockefeller Foundation, and The William and Flora Hewlett Foundation for the Council's overall program, including the U.S.-Third World Policy Perspectives series of which this book is part. This book project certainly would not have been possible without the three major seminars initially convened in Moscow and in Washington under the aegis of the American Council of Learned Societies and the Institute of World Economy and International Relations (IMEMO) of the U.S.S.R. Academy of Sciences and funded in part by the International Research and Exchange Board (IREX).

On behalf of the Council and all of the contributing authors, the series editors wish to express special thanks to the many experts—both American and Soviet—who offered comments and constructive criticisms on earlier drafts of the evolving book. Responsibility for the final content of the chapters rests, as is usual, with their authors.

Special thanks are also due to the translators, Arlo Schultz and William L. Gray Enterprises; to Danielle M. Currier and Jacqueline Edlund-Braun for their contributions to the editing and production; to Markus P. Goldstein for research assistance; to Catherine Bowen for library assistance; to John Kaljee for book design; to Joycelyn V. Critchlow for manuscript processing; and to Mid-Atlantic Photo Composition and Victor Graphics for book production.

# Contents

# Joint U.S.-U.S.S.R
# Overview

# From Confrontation to Cooperation? U.S. and Soviet Assistance to Developing Countries

Richard E. Feinberg and Ratchik M. Avakov

As early as 1986, the Overseas Development Council (ODC) of Washington, D.C., and the Institute of World Economy and International Relations (IMEMO) in Moscow undertook to study together the economies of the developing nations. The objectives were ambitious and multiple: to give scholars and policymakers the opportunity to exchange information and studies on a subject of global importance; to provide a forum for Americans and Soviets to learn more about their counterparts' views of the international economy; and, not least, to build new bridges between intellectuals in two capitol cities isolated from each other by the Cold War.

In pursuit of these objectives, three major seminars and a number of smaller sessions were convened in Moscow and Washington under the formal rubric, "Soviet-American Symposium on Problems of World Economic Development."[1] At the opening meeting, it quickly became apparent that each side had remarkably little understanding of its counterpart's national policies toward the developing world. In particular, neither was well versed with regard to the other's development assistance programs and strategies. It was therefore decided to devote a major segment of these exchanges to U.S. and U.S.S.R. experience with economic assistance to developing nations. Discussions of this theme led to the preparation—paralleling the evolution of *perestroika* and *glasnost*—of paired Soviet and American chapters on selected, mutually acceptable themes relating

3

to the two countries' economic assistance programs (military aid programs are not included in the analysis).

This book attempts a modest contribution to the restructuring of the code of conduct in Soviet-American relations. It is also the result of the restructuring itself. Not long ago—before April 1985—it would have been impossible to dream of preparing a joint Soviet-American book on such a sensitive political topic. Today, such collaborative efforts are spreading across a wide spectrum of issues of mutual concern.

The chapter in this volume entitled "Tripartite Projects: Proposals for Joint U.S.-U.S.S.R. Cooperation with Developing Countries" is an outgrowth of the deepening understanding of each other's assistance programs and capacities yielded by the present collaboration, as well as of the new opportunities that the dramatic improvement in U.S.-Soviet relations offered. The new world order, the transformed, less confrontational international space, sets a challenge of uniting efforts to overcome underdevelopment—notwithstanding short-term fluctuations in the overall U.S.-Soviet bilateral relationship. Taking for granted that bilateral relations may go through various stages, it is important to delink them, at least within certain parameters of tolerance, from a clear requirement of development cooperation. In their jointly authored chapter, W. Donald Bowles of American University in Washington, D.C., and Elena B. Arefieva of IMEMO put forward several reasons for the United States and the Soviet Union to cooperate in assisting developing countries. They propose specific areas of cooperation that draw on the strengths of the Soviet and American societies and that recognize the budgetary constraints facing both governments.

## The Background Papers

The Bowles-Ariefieva proposals grew out of the information and analyses presented in the other chapters of the volume, which were written separately by Americans and Soviets but prepared in close coordination to assure an integrated and comparative product. The first set of paired chapters provides provocative analyses of the changing conceptions among scholars and policymakers concerning the development assistance strategies that have marked U.S. and Soviet thinking and practice from the 1950s to the present. The second set of chapters describes in some detail each nation's major programs of development assistance as they have evolved over time. The final pair of chapters focuses on one specific program area that has been of central interest to both donors: the education and training of

Third World citizens. Together, the chapters provide the most extensive comparative discussion thus far available of the two countries'
development assistance programs.

### Development Strategies Reconsidered

Elena B. Arefieva and Elena B. Bragina trace the evolution in Soviet
thinking and practice regarding development assistance from the
earlier years of overwhelming emphasis on statism and heavy industry to current efforts to devise more balanced approaches that provide
more space for small-scale firms, the private sector, and agriculture.
They argue that the policies of the 1950s and 1960s, which fostered
such large-scale industrial and energy projects as the Aswan Dam in
Egypt, had their strong adherents not only in Moscow but also in the
recipient countries—and in some Western circles as well. These policies produced many positive contributions, if sometimes in a costly
manner that had distorting side effects. Today, the debates over the
proper mix of state and private firms, of import protection and open
trade, of factory and farm, are very much in flux. Soviet assistance
programs, however, still give considerable weight to government-
owned firms, import substitution, and industrial production.

Soviet thinking on development has been influenced by the disappointing performance of recipient nations and by the impressive
success of some capitalist-oriented nations, particularly in Asia. The
authors note that in Moscow "the prevailing view now is that the
concept of socialist orientation has failed, although the idea still has
many proponents in the Soviet Union." Central to the debate, of
course, is the experience of the Soviet Union itself, which is searching to redesign its own economic regime.

Arefieva and Bragina sketch the historic shift in Soviet thinking away from a world view that interpreted international economic
relations as being essentially conflictive and exploitative toward the
paradigm of interdependence and mutual benefit. They foresee a
"de-ideologization" of Soviet aid policies that will force a reallocation
of Soviet aid (away from Cuba, for example) and a greater emphasis
on Soviet commercial interests as well as on humanitarian objectives. Both purposes suggest Soviet participation in the multilateral
economic organizations, including the Bretton Woods institutions
and the General Agreement on Tariffs and Trade (GATT). The
authors proceed from the assumption that the more interdependent
the world economy, the higher the necessity to coordinate international economic activities of various countries, including measures
in the area of assistance to the South.

Elliot Berg elects to narrow his topic by defining foreign assistance in the traditional Western sense as loans and grants provided at concessional, below-market interest rates. Within the "development aid" portion of formal foreign assistance programs, he focuses on the most controversial thrust of the 1980s: policy-based lending. Berg explains Western disillusionment, first with earlier strategies that emphasized capital investments and import substitution industrialization, and then with the 1970s emphasis on poverty alleviation projects. The 1980s' preference for free markets, open trade, and private property arose as a reaction to these perceived failures—many of which are also recognized in the companion Soviet chapter.

Despite his adherence to the liberalization model, Berg expresses deep reservations about the "conditionality" process whereby Western donors, including the Bretton Woods agencies, have sought to foster liberalization in recipient countries. He notes that policy-based lending lacks the kind of "analytical scaffolding" that surrounds more traditional forms of resource transfer. For example, why do governments need to be bribed to adopt policies that are allegedly in their own self-interest? Nor is it clear just how aid money oils the reform process, and how donors should determine the necessary quantity of lubrication. Berg is also concerned about the frequent absence of genuine dialogue between donors and recipients and about the tendency of donors not to interrupt disbursements to poorly performing clients except when they are of little strategic interest (although the waning of the Cold War may dilute this economics/security trade-off).

The aid strategy debate has become more nuanced and less simplistically committed to liberalization than was sometimes the case in the 1980s. Berg notes the resurgence of concern about the social costs of adjustment and the renewed interest in directly attacking poverty even *before* the fruits of the free-market model have had the chance to ripen. In both the United States and the Soviet Union, the debates over development strategies—and how donors can best stimulate them—are again in full swing.

### Development Programs Described

While noting that Soviet authorities have released only extremely limited data on development assistance, authors Andrei Chekhutov, Nataliya Ushakova, and Leon Zevin provide the most complete data yet made available to the public. They caution, however, that Soviet and American foreign assistance data are not compatible because Soviet data include a number of items, such as trade subsidies and preferences, not included in the official aid statistics for the U.S. and other Western donors. Furthermore, Soviet bookkeeping typically suffers from double accounting, and many Soviet organizations have not always clearly distinguished between commercial operations and aid programs. Nevertheless, the authors cite OECD and U.S. government statistics to support the claim that the Soviet Union has been a major donor nation.

Looking at aid as a percentage of GNP, the authors discuss OECD estimates of Soviet aid that show a program that has been on a par with the average OECD donor. In aggregate figures, the OECD places 1988 U.S.S.R. assistance at net disbursements of $4.2 billion. The authors present Soviet figures placing aid at 11.7 billion rubles in 1987 and 12 billion rubles in 1988.[2] However, the recent devaluation of the ruble will decrease Soviet aid in dollar terms, and the severe economic crisis now gripping the Soviet Union is likely to compel sharp cutbacks in assistance programs.

In the paired U.S. chapter, Ernest Preeg provides a straightforward description of U.S. official development assistance (ODA), as well as brief presentations of such non-ODA programs as Eximbank credits and other trade-related programs. He finds that between 1970 and 1987, the value of U.S. ODA increased only marginally in real, inflation-adjusted terms, while U.S. ODA as a share of U.S. GNP declined from 0.32 to 0.20 per cent (U.S. ODA net disbursements fell to $7.4 billion in 1989, 0.15 per cent of GNP).[3] Preeg attributes this relative decline to overall fiscal constraints and to weak public support for aid.

Within the U.S. aid program, Preeg underscores three trends: 1) the proportion devoted to multilateral aid rose in the 1970s but in the 1980s returned to the 1970–71 level of about 20 per cent; 2) the quality of bilateral aid has been improved by the trends toward grants and untying: and 3) a rising proportion of U.S. aid has been disbursed as balance-of-payments support. Furthermore, the geographic distribution of U.S. aid has shifted in reaction to the growth performance and strategic importance of the various regions. Some Asian and South American countries have "graduated" to more commercially oriented trade and financial relations, while Sub-Saharan Africa's share of ODA has risen in response to the region's poverty problems. Security concerns have favored the Middle East and, in the 1980s, Central America.

Like Berg, Preeg underscores the shift during the 1980s toward policy-based lending, citing these principal U.S. objectives: support for macroeconomic adjustment; targeted assistance to the adversely affected and poorest segments of society through such programs as health delivery systems and primary education; and direct support to the private sector. Preeg also recognizes that the U.S. aid program has been criticized for its short-term political orientation, its nondiscriminating support for corrupt or ineffective governments, and cumbersome Congressional restrictions on aid programs. He notes that reformers are calling for more clearly stated objectives, a greater emphasis on development criteria, and a basic reorganization to simplify procedures and reduce bureaucratic inefficiencies.[4]

### Education and Training

Drawing on their own national experience, the designers of Soviet aid have placed a strong emphasis on education and on the role of the state in that process. Margarita P. Strepetova and Leon Z. Zevin stress that, for cost and cultural reasons, the Soviet Union has concentrated its efforts on technical-level training of workers in their own countries. These training programs have often been linked to the employment needs of large-scale Soviet-financed projects, and they typically occur at vocational training centers and schools constructed with Soviet assistance. Countries where Soviet educational efforts have been most active include Egypt, Algeria, India, Cuba, Mongolia, and Iraq. In those cases where training occurs in the Soviet Union, programs often include internships with major Soviet firms.

Strepetova and Zevin argue that the Soviet training programs have spurred the transfer of technology and industrialization programs of many nations. Moreover, even those persons who receive their training in the Soviet Union return home. While there is no *external* "brain drain" in that sense, they do express concern about an *internal* brain drain within developing countries—the migration of trainees to the private sector, which weakens the position of the public sector. Looking forward, Streptova and Zevin note that *perestroika* will intensify economic relations between the Soviet Union and developing countries and that more foreign personnel will have to be educated in the intricacies of evolving Soviet laws and institutions that impinge on Soviet international relations.

In the American chapter, Gerald Meier notes that historical experience demonstrates the economic value of education and training and recent empirical studies attest to high social as well as private returns to education, especially at the primary level of schooling. Less evidence is available for technical education, but in its case, too, satisfactory returns frequently have been reported.

Meier asserts that USAID programs make an important contribution toward removing deficiencies in the educational systems of the developing countries that limit their human resource development. The chapter reviews the guidelines for U.S. assistance to basic education programs. Vocational education and technical training for adolescents and adults, as well as scientific, technical, administrative, and managerial are all discussed. As in the case of the Soviet program, much of USAID's participant training is provided in the developing countries, but in recent years the United States has placed greater emphasis on making such training available in the United States. The evaluation of this program is especially important.

Unlike the Soviet programs, the USAID's programs emphasize the private sector. Meier notes, however that with the funding of basic education accounting for only some 34 per cent of USAID's total program, actual funding has fallen short of the professed interest articulated in USAID's policy statements. Funding of programs devoted to adult literacy and numeracy and to vocational training is also at a standstill. The differences between USAID's policy statements—with their overabundance of priorities—and actual funding result in large part from the politics of the funding process through Congress.

Meier is alarmed at the reduction of education budgets in many developing nations afflicted with severe financial constraints. To increase the flow and efficiency of resources devoted to education, he urges that the international donor community share its experiences and better coordinate its efforts on behalf of human capital enhancement in developing countries.

## Common Themes

Amidst the wealth of information presented in the volume, several rich veins of thought can be discerned that run through these six chapters. In both nations, foreign assistance strategies have their conceptual roots in domestic practices and ideologies. In addition, there has been a degree of parallel evolution in thinking about development. Today, in both the United States and the U.S.S.R., there is a certain loss of self-confidence within the development assistance community, and an open search for new directions. These new policies will have to operate within budgetary constraints—financial limitations that militate in favor of multilateral cooperation among donors.

Just as the foreign policies of nations are inevitably rooted in domestic politics, so are nations' foreign assistance strategies rooted in their economic structures and ideals. It is hardly surprising that early U.S. aid programs reflected such New Deal legacies as state activism and the importance of education and other social services and gave priority to the domestic economy over international trade.

In the 1980s, the Reagan administration pursued deregulation and privatization in both domestic and international economic programs. Similarly, Soviet development assistance strategy was determined by the state character of the Soviet Union's economy, and the domestic tilt toward industry over agriculture found its way into Soviet development theory and practice. In keeping with *perestroika*, Soviet thinking about development now looks more positively at the private sector and market relations.

Notwithstanding the tremendous differences between the two countries' development assistance programs, as mentioned earlier, the evolution of American and Soviet thinking has developed along some surprisingly parallel routes. In the 1950s and 1960s, both nations saw capital investment as the primary stimulus to growth, emphasized education and training, and looked favorably on import substitution industrialization strategies. To be sure, the motivations behind these overlapping perspectives were not always the same. The Soviets saw industrial protection as a method for achieving independence from a hostile capitalist world. For Americans, import substitution was intended to spur industrialization and employment creation, while an activist state was a useful corrective to the weak points in a still predominantly market economy.

This parallel evolution in thinking continued with the emergence of a common critique of excessive protectionism and statism and recognition of the deleterious consequences of neglecting agriculture and trade. Although by no means in full accord on an optimal development strategy, the U.S. and the Soviet positions on such issues as the role of the private sector, the value of international commerce and investment, and the need to balance industry and agriculture are undeniably closer today than ever before. However, while some U.S. theorists and practitioners have swung full force toward across-the-board liberalization, Soviet thinkers seem more comfortable seeking a middle ground that overcomes the sharp state-market dichotomies and finds harmony between the industrial and agricultural spheres. In neither country, however, is there a stable consensus on these highly controversial matters.

Although much has been accomplished in the Third World, the Soviet and American development communities have become less and less certain that they know how to foster prosperity abroad. It is hard to measure the efficiency of programs whose goals have often been inextricably muddled with commercial and strategic objectives. Furthermore, when aid programs were measured in capital transfers, and success was scored with such indicators as GNP growth, the number of students in school, or even caloric intake and mortality rates, evaluations were relatively easy. The factors now considered critical to development success—the structures of markets, the competitiveness of private firms, the efficiency of the civil service, the quality of education—are matters that must be worked on over long periods of time and require the dedication of the host society. As a result, the prevailing view in both donor nations is that external actors can typically influence events only at the margin and that the major effort must be made by the developing nation itself. Moreover, for the United States today—and probably for the Soviet Union tomorrow—foreign assistance is decreasing in relation to the volume of trade flows with developing nations. Thus, even within the sphere of international economic activity, the role of governments—and of official development assistance agencies—is declining relative to that of private decisionmakers and markets.

Budgetary pressures in both superpowers are another factor constraining foreign assistance programs. U.S. ODA has been roughly stagnant in real terms, and Soviet assistance has already begun to decrease. Certainly economic relations with the more advanced developing nations will increasingly be on a commercial basis, although governments may intervene with export credits, technical assistance and training, and support for foreign investment and joint ventures, while providing trading partners with secure access to their domestic markets (so long as they play by accepted rules). However, assuming that relations between the NATO nations and the Soviet Union do not revert to old patterns, foreign assistance programs may be less encumbered with Cold War security concerns and more focused on humanitarian objectives or other matters considered essential to the donors' national interest. High on this list of concerns is environmental protection, vital to both the United States and U.S.S.R. as well as to the global community. To prevent irreparable harm to our common planet, it is critical to design and support growth strategies that are ecologically sustainable and to negotiate international accords that foster collective action in the interests of world development in general.

In short, this volume appears at a time of fundamental rethinking in both countries of past development assistance efforts, catalyzed by the disappointing performance of many developing countries during the 1980s. Both donor countries are questioning old aid methods and are seeking new approaches that meet the needs of the 1990s. Indeed, both the United States and the Soviet Union now encounter great difficulty in defining clearly the purposes and priorities of their bilateral aid programs. In this context of reexamination and renewal, both American and Soviet authors point to the logic of multilateral cooperation in a world that is increasingly multipolar and pluralistic. The United States has pursued its policies of policy-based lending primarily through the international financial institutions, which the Soviet Union hopes to join. Currently the Soviet Union conducts programs with a variety of U.N. organizations (activities whose specifics lie beyond the scope of this volume). The Bowles-Arefieva chapter was conceived in this spirit of donor cooperation in the coordination of aid programs and policies.

## U.S. and Soviet Cooperation

Bowles and Arefieva note that Washington and Moscow already · have found common cause in seeking to help end civil conflict in some strife-torn regions of the Third World. The administrations of George Bush and Mikhail Gorbachev have cooperated to advance peace prospects in Southern Africa and Central America—and most recently in the Persian Gulf. They assert that the time is now ripe to extend this new spirit of cooperation into the economic sphere to help spur development in the world's poorer countries.

Bowles and Arefieva argue that both donor nations have knowledge and resources that can provide more benefits to the world's poor if joined together than if extended separately. Complementarities mean that acting together can produce a multiplier effect. Furthermore, superpower cooperation in economic development—itself a product of rapprochement—can enhance bilateral relations. Such cooperation among former adversaries in the pursuit of humanitarian objectives can even become a source of mutual pride for Americans and Soviets. In addition, as they work with Americans in development, the Soviets will be exposed to the theory and practice of contemporary economic thought; this integration of the Soviet Union into the global economy is an objective shared by both the U.S.S.R. and the United States.

Purposeful cooperation in development could serve as an antidote to the growing isolationist tendencies so palpable in both superpowers. Voices in Washington and Moscow are arguing that since much of the Third World no longer poses security threats, we should retrench. While a review of security-driven policies is indeed in order, both the United States and the U.S.S.R. still have a great stake in the economic progress of Asia, Africa, and Latin America. The relaxation of global tensions should result not in a loss of interest, but in a redirection of efforts. Instead of being theaters of conflict, developing nations can become arenas for cooperation between those nations and the superpowers. Interest in developing nations can be maintained through the power of a positive agenda.

### Concrete Proposals

Bowles and Arefieva propose specific areas of cooperation that meet stringent criteria. In these areas, projects should build upon existing bases of expertise, and they clearly must be economically justifiable and of value to the recipient nation.

Specifically, Bowles and Arefieva propose collaborative projects in eight areas: emergency assistance to combat natural disasters; reforestation; potable water supply; energy and other resource assessments; primary and secondary technical education; health care (in particular, ophthalmology); urban construction (light metal structures and waste disposal); and development studies. The projects are identified on a functional basis: the authors leave the selection of geographic sites to others.

The administrative design of cooperative projects can vary— from parallel efforts, in which each donor agency works separately on a designated portion of a project, to more integrated efforts, in which Americans and Soviets work side by side. The latter arrangements would be more administratively complex, requiring difficult technical and bureaucratic compromises; but in symbolic and human terms, they would yield the most exciting results.

### Financial Realism

These proposals are launched in full awareness of the budgetary squeezes that constrain policies in both Moscow and Washington. All of the proposed projects can be implemented at a modest level, while having the potential for more ambitious scaling up. In the United States, the post-Cold War cuts in military spending should eventually free additional resources for development assistance—in response to the redefinition of national security as essentially economic and social rather than primarily military. Even if the Soviet Union sharply reduces its overall foreign assistance budget, there can still be room for redirecting resources as proposed by Bowles and Arefieva. The Soviet public and parliament may well be more enthusiastic about these practical, humanitarian proposals than about, for example, the continuation of the large subsidy to a Marxist-Leninist Cuba. And even if the Soviet Union should itself become a recipient of external assistance, that would not be inconsistent with the simultaneous provision of assistance.[5] Just as it is rational for nations to simultaneously import and export according to comparative advantage and at the same time borrow and lend to satisfy their portfolio preferences, so is it rational for a nation to receive external support in areas of its relative weakness and extend support in areas of expertise. China, India, and such "newly industrializing nations" as South Korea have extended assistance to other developing countries at the same time that they have been aid recipients themselves.

U.S. and Soviet cooperation in development assistance cannot be held hostage to short-term oscillations in the temperature of the bilateral relationship. At the same time, sustained cooperation is of course contingent upon secular progress within the Soviet Union of *perestroika* and *glasnost*—of economic liberalization and political democratization. These reform processes create the diplomatic context for bilateral cooperation, while rapprochement in economic philosophy between the Soviet Union and market economies makes cooperation more feasible in third countries.

## Notes

[1]The larger seminars were held under the aegis of the American Council of Learned Societies and the U.S.S.R. Academy of Sciences and were funded in part by the International Research and Exchanges Board (IREX).

[2]These discrepancies result from several variables, including the Soviet practice of providing goods and services that are priced in non-convertible rubles and whose dollar price will vary depending upon the choice of exchange rates, the fact that repayments are usually not effected in currency but through the delivery of goods, and whether trade and other subsidies not typically included in Western ODA data are included. OECD estimates of Soviet aid are restricted to ODA flows and are based on both Soviet and recipient country statistics and on information obtained from certain OECD member embassies in the Third World.

[3]OECD Press Release SG/Press(90)34 of June 14, 1990.

[4]For example, see John W. Sewell and Christine E. Contee, "Foreign Aid and Gramm-Rudman," *Foreign Affairs*, Summer 1987.

[5]For an examination of the Soviet Union as a developing economy, and the conditions under which external financial support would be warranted, see Richard E. Feinberg, John Echeverri-Gent, and Friedemann Müller, *Economic Reform in Three Giants: U.S. Foreign Policy and the USSR, China, and India* (New Brunswick, N.J.: Transaction Publishers in cooperation with the Overseas Development Council, 1990).

# Policy
# Recommendations

# Tripartite Projects: Proposals for Joint U.S.–U.S.S.R. Cooperation with Developing Countries

## W. Donald Bowles and Elena B. Arefieva

The official text of the political declaration issued by the Group of Seven (G–7) industrial countries after their meeting in Paris in July 1989 urged cooperation between East and West "to find just solutions to conflicts around the world, to fight against under-development, to safeguard resources and the environment and to build a freer and more open world." In a letter addressed to President François Mitterand in his capacity as Chairman of the G–7 Summit, President Mikhail Gorbachev linked *perestroika* directly to wider Soviet participation in the world economy, and he urged "collective assistance for development." In effect, the concept of cooperation on assistance to developing countries now has support at the highest political and administrative levels both in the West and in the Soviet Union. This reflects a growing sense that Soviet and U.S. interests converge in the long run on peaceful alternatives to the political instability and economic deprivation that now characterize many developing countries.

## The Case for U.S.–U.S.S.R. Cooperation in Assisting Development

U.S. and Soviet scientists and others have met frequently in scientific and cultural exchanges, but the idea of the two countries mounting cooperative efforts to assist third parties is very new. In our view, the case for joint U.S. and U.S.S.R. efforts in the development cooperation field—efforts ranging from parallel, separately administered work to more closely integrated development projects or programs where these are desired by developing-country partners and feasible—is compelling on many grounds, a few of which are summarized here.

First, environmental problems, which spill across national borders and are also a major concern in developing countries, can be effectively addressed only through cooperative action. The importance of environmental issues was recognized most recently in the creation of a "fifth basket" of issues under the Helsinki Accord[1]— discussed initially in Moscow in May 1989 by U.S. Secretary of State James Baker and Soviet Foreign Minister Eduard Shevardnadze. This "basket" includes cooperative efforts to deal with environmental problems, drugs, international terrorism, and missile proliferation. The essential potential benefit from joint actions on the environment is that they could exceed those generated by each country acting individually.

Second, in the changing political atmosphere of the 1990s, one of the most persuasive arguments for joint action is that even if U.S.-Soviet relations improve only modestly in other areas, the relatively low strategic importance of cooperative assistance for development will permit progress in this area. Among other benefits, such cooperative efforts would serve to build confidence in the ability of the United States and the U.S.S.R. to work together—and to take on even more controversial matters.

Third, in the past, "security" concerns have provided a *negative* motivation for foreign assistance in both nations—leading to economic waste in assistance programs and support of regimes of dubious merit. Through increased cooperation, global security would in the future become more closely related to common approaches to international economic concerns, including successful development in the poor countries. In this setting, security issues could become *positive* motivations for foreign aid. Less emphasis on traditional geopolitical and military security might in turn improve the quality of aid, with humanitarian considerations and the sustainable development of natural resources becoming more prominent in the aid programs of both countries.

Fourth, a very strong case can be made that efforts to establish collaborative projects can be justified solely on the basis that they will bring U.S. and Soviet development specialists together—and in so doing provide training for both groups. Greater mutual understanding will at best improve the quality of assistance programs of both countries and at a minimum reduce misunderstanding of the intentions of each.

Fifth, joint U.S.-U.S.S.R. efforts would help the Soviet Union to better understand the requirements for participation in the world economic mainstream. Routinely, cooperative efforts would depend on more information from the U.S.S.R. on matters such as its international credit position, especially vis-à-vis developing countries, and the size and direction of its aid programs—all of which would also be essential ingredients of formal Soviet participation in the World Bank, the International Monetary Fund, and the General Agreement on Tariffs and Trade. Supplying such information would also be evidence of the Soviet Union's desire to be a member of the international economic community.

Sixth, joint U.S.-U.S.S.R. development efforts would be a reminder to the private sector in the West of the many opportunities for joint ventures with the Soviet Union at a time when the latter is actively seeking such ventures at home as well as abroad. Growing Western interest in such partnerships will in turn encourage Soviet authorities to clarify and codify regulations surrounding such enterprises.

In summary, the *benefits* to be derived from U.S.-U.S.S.R. cooperation on development assistance are both identifiable and important. But what are the potential *costs* of such efforts?

To begin with, cooperative activities are inevitably more complex than separate ones and therefore may result in higher costs. The complications will range from the difficulty of reaching agreement on going ahead with particular projects to developing criteria for their evaluation upon completion.

Cooperative efforts also may have a potential political cost, in that both the United States and the Soviet Union may prefer to be seen as acting independently in developing countries, with each representing a different worldview. In the past, each country has assiduously avoided "appearing in public" with the other because of the apparent political cost to be incurred among separate sets of allies.

In addition, joint action may be perceived by developing countries as an attempt by the United States and the Soviet Union to "gang up" on them. The colonial legacy—and some recent actions of each superpower—suggest to some in the developing countries that the embrace of a great power is one that smothers. From this perspective, the perceived danger of joint actions by the superpowers may be even greater. Indeed, the most serious concern of developing countries might well be that, with competition in the developing world no longer a pressure, the United States and the U.S.S.R. might agree to do very little—either jointly or separately.

In our judgment, the net economic benefits of joint U.S.-U.S.S.R. efforts could be substantial. The political costs and benefits are more difficult to assess. The alternative of continued totally separate efforts, however, seems inadequate to the development and environmental tasks at hand and incongruent with the professed political intentions of both the United States and the Soviet Union. Moreover, U.S.-Soviet development cooperation is something that could begin now.

Finally, it is important to emphasize that all of our suggestions in this paper are predicated on three assumptions:

(1) Without continued improvement in U.S.-U.S.S.R. relations, most if not all of our suggestions would become moot.

(2) We are in fact suggesting *tripartite* cooperation. While emphasis is given here to U.S.-U.S.S.R. initiatives, it should be understood that such actions would always include a third party: the developing country with which the project or program would be initiated.

(3) While our proposals make clear the importance of *concessional* assistance, severe budgetary constraints in both the United States and the Soviet Union suggest greater emphasis on ventures that pay their own way and on non-governmental sources of funding. An important possibility might be use of the "multi-bi" accounts administered by U.N. agencies. The United States or the U.S.S.R. could establish a trust fund with, say, the U.N. Environment Programme (UNEP) or the U.N. Development Programme (UNDP). Control over the activities financed would remain with the donor countries. In this way, both countries could contribute formally to multilateral efforts, and the sponsoring U.N. agency could act as a magnet for additional funds from other countries for the same purposes.

# The Feasibility of U.S.–U.S.S.R. Cooperation

On the grounds set out above, we are persuaded that the net political benefits of the tripartite projects that we propose would clearly exceed their costs. But are joint U.S.-U.S.S.R. actions *feasible*? We suggest that they are—and that they in fact already do exist in a number of areas. The change in the political course of the Soviet Union in international relations—based on the "new thinking" concept—opens wide the door of potential cooperation. In Soviet terminology, the foreign policy of the U.S.S.R. has become "de-ideologized." As a result, the emphasis in U.S.S.R. relations with developing countries is shifting away from political priorities toward economic ones, and away from military or ideological objectives toward global humanitarian goals less linked either to the concept of the class struggle or to the conflict between the two world systems.

Soviet analysts recognize that the West has only gradually come to accept these newly stated positions—in large measure because of the earlier Soviet worldview and actions taken in keeping with that perspective. Yet evidence of change can be found in the improved relationships between the European Community (EC) and the Council of Mutual Economic Assistance (CMEA),[2] and in warmer contacts between the U.S.S.R. and the United States, West Germany, the United Kingdom, and Japan. Further evidence of change is found in the decreased tension in international relations in general and in several attempts to settle regional conflicts (with U.S.S.R. participation) through negotiations (e.g., the Iran-Iraq Accord, the Geneva Accords on Afghanistan, discussions on Kampuchea). Although there is still considerable disagreement among Western leaders as to how to respond to these professed Soviet changes, there is at the same time a growing sense that the most productive response will be to test rather than to oppose their reality.

While significant differences remain, there has been something of a convergence of Soviet and Western views on the strategy of and policy toward development assistance, which in turn reflects changes in foreign policy and in the ideological emphasis of the two countries. Today, East and West both acknowledge the important role that markets can play in development, the critical needs of agriculture, the stimulating effects of exports, and the importance of limiting the sphere of government intervention. With some exceptions, the common goals emerging from this convergence are the alleviation of global poverty and the transfer of resources from developed to developing countries to help them overcome lags in education, public health, and technology—all with less regard than in the past to the sociopolitical path that they have chosen to pursue.[3]

Some joint U.S.-U.S.S.R. efforts already are in place. Currently, many cooperative agreements between the United States and the Soviet Union provide for the exchange of personnel, information, and technology in science, technology, education, and cultural areas, and the number of such agreements is increasing. Following a hiatus resulting from the Afghanistan invasion in 1979, steps have been taken to revive activity under four agreements reached in the early 1970s (on environment, medical science and public health, housing and construction, and agriculture). A 1983 agreement on cooperative study of the oceans has been renewed; a 1973 agreement on the peaceful uses of atomic energy and a 1972 agreement on the protection of the environment have been extended; and a new agreement on cooperative exploration of space for peaceful purposes was signed in 1987. In early 1988, a new five-year agreement on scientific cooperation was reached by the U.S. National Academy of Sciences and the U.S.S.R. Academy of Sciences. And in early 1989, an agreement was signed between the National Science Foundation and the U.S.S.R. Academy of Sciences on cooperation in basic scientific research.

How would planning for cooperative U.S.-U.S.S.R. efforts go forward? And what would be the scope and strategy of cooperation? The proposals below are intended to suggest some possible avenues to explore. A number of them would be appropriate for initial efforts (e.g., putting joint U.S.-U.S.S.R. studies of development on a permanent basis), while others would require more prior consultation. Some projects would be in fields in which each country has considerable scientific and institutional experience, and these could move ahead in advance of others. The important point is that the process of greater cooperation could begin once given the go-ahead by the political authorities of both countries.

The selection of priority projects, and the scope of those projects, would be part of the ongoing discussions that would be an essential component of all joint U.S.-U.S.S.R. efforts. And even if the issues chosen were global in scope (e.g., reforestation or other aspects of environment), the question of implementation in specific countries, or types of countries, would remain open. Some projects lend themselves to a global perspective and approach and would require more time to initiate. Other projects would be more specific, of a shorter gestation period, and could be made country- or region-specific.

A final note is in order on what is meant by a "joint" project. Such a project might simply involve the cooperation of research laboratories in the United States and the Soviet Union around a single issue, with the results made available jointly to a developing country. Or a joint project might entail the United States and the Soviet Union each taking a parallel "piece" of a development project, but with each country acting largely independently; overall project management could be in the hands of a third party—the recipient country or a multilateral agency. Alternatively, a joint project could be truly integrated—from its design through its implementation stage—with Soviet and U.S. aid personnel working closely together and managing it jointly together with a developing country. In effect, a joint project might be any combination of efforts that meet the requirements of a project.

In all cases, "joint" U.S.-U.S.S.R. projects are not meant to exclude the efforts of other nations or of multilateral agencies. On the contrary, the purpose of joint projects would be to widen donor cooperation in the pursuit of development—not to narrow it to an exclusive U.S.-Soviet "club." U.S.-U.S.S.R. cooperation must fit into the *global* development effort. In this context, it is important that the joint projects not be mere "additions" in a field that is already crowded with donors in some countries. Joint projects might sometimes be most appropriate as mergers of existing but separate projects, rather than as totally new projects.

## Potential Sources of Funding

Cooperative U.S.-U.S.S.R. development projects may well be feasible and desirable, but how can they be *funded*? Both the United States and the Soviet Union are today experiencing acute budget constraints. For a start, we suggest four potential sources of general funding. (Possible funding for specific types of projects is discussed in a later section.)

The first potential source is the savings to be realized from arms reduction. In both the United States and the U.S.S.R., there are of course those who suggest that there is no conceptual linkage between arms reduction and foreign economic assistance. Perhaps so—but a program of "disarmament and development" would have both symbolic and pragmatic value. It would highlight part of the human cost of arms expenditures, and it would provide a specific target for the use of savings derived from arms reduction; both are important to stimulating public support of foreign assistance. While the establishment of a program of "disarmament and development" is still under discussion in U.N. forums, and while official support for it lies in the future, the United States and the Soviet Union—the main participants in the discussions—could attempt this kind of linkage with some modest joint projects. (In the United States, precedents have been set in the reprogramming of funds from defense to assist economic reconstruction programs in Panama and Nicaragua.)

A second approach could be to raise funds for joint efforts by combining U.S. and Soviet budget resources traditionally allocated for bilateral aid. Even assuming that the total amount of Soviet aid does decrease, there is scope to use some portion of loans extended but not yet disbursed for joint U.S.-U.S.S.R. projects. This approach could in practice be supportive of the recent, broad commitment of Soviet aid agencies to improving the efficiency of projects—provided, of course, that parallel steps were taken to increase the efficiency of the U.S. inputs.

Cooperative assistance efforts will require considerable ongoing research on the potential for such assistance and its possible forms. Such activities can be financed from yet another source—both governmental and private institutions. Joint research might be conducted—in a context of cooperation with developing-country researchers and institutions—during reciprocal visits of researchers of the two countries to the United States and the Soviet Union.

Finally, another possible form of development cooperation could completely bypass traditional assistance sources. Joint companies could be established between a private U.S. business, an individual Soviet enterprise, and a third party (private or public) in a developing country. Such companies could operate on a commercial basis, or they could provide goods or services for local consumption partially subsidized from bilateral inter-governmental concessional loans. This potential form of financing seems most appropriate for the more advanced developing countries. For example, the newly industrializing countries (NICs) that have "graduated" from eligibility for concessional assistance might still benefit from capital inflows in this form to provide indirect support to their continued economic development. Setting aside individual differences in developing-country national strategies, cooperative U.S.-U.S.S.R. projects might be most appropriate in the export sector, in sectors particularly emphasized because of structural adjustment requirements, and in programs to promote efficient use and conservation of natural resources. It might—perhaps surprisingly—be quite feasible for the Soviet side to contribute to such projects in the form of debt-equity swaps. This would in effect be a kind of "conversion" (from military to civilian investments) in the aid area—since most of the debt owed by developing countries to the Soviet Union stems from armament supplies provided on credit.

Special note must be taken of the changed circumstances in which Soviet foreign aid will be channeled abroad, and in which the prospect for the expansion of concessional assistance from government funding is greatly limited by the extraordinary transition costs of economic restructuring. In operational terms, the problems are the government deficit and the shortage of almost all industrial and agricultural resources. This economic stringency is accompanied by an administrative constraint as well. Some of the enterprises that are expected to participate in the Soviet assistance programs are cost-accounting enterprises that must confine their activities to purely commercial transactions in the international market. This is one result of the current restructuring of Soviet external economic relations, under which these enterprises are to be self-financing, generating their own sources of foreign exchange through profitable exports.

In effect, these Soviet enterprises are expected to stand on their own financial feet, covering all expenses, and increasingly their capital costs, through sales. They are expected to earn a "profit" after expenses or suffer losses and eventual foreclosure. If such enterprises are to participate in concessional lending or grants abroad, they will require some form of state or private subsidy. In the U.S.S.R. private sector, the Peace Fund is emerging as the largest non-governmental funding source for concessional assistance. The central point here is that, under the current restructuring of Soviet external economic relations, Soviet enterprises shipping abroad are expected to earn foreign exchange through profitable exports. Concessional shipments will require some form of budget *subsidy*— either in initial allocations or in cost recovery.

Summing up, costs could be covered in a considerable variety of ways. Existing economic assistance projects in the areas we identify as potentially appropriate for joint U.S.-U.S.S.R. cooperation with developing countries clearly indicate that exploratory projects could be carried out at very modest costs. Thus costs cannot be considered a serious impediment to initiating cooperative efforts such as those we recommend. Beyond that, the suggested areas for cooperation of course also lend themselves to appropriate scaled-up efforts with higher price tags if all parties are interested.

# Guidelines for Choosing and Managing Projects

Even when all parties to a project agree on the desirability of the undertaking, unforeseen and often serious problems are inevitable. This is why pioneering efforts of this kind require not only top-level political support, but also the administrative and management support necessary to make such projects succeed. Support from international institutions might also be needed; appropriate U.N. agencies or the international financial institutions might be invited to be partners. Private U.S. firms and individual Soviet enterprises might, for example, cooperate in furthering a World Bank project. Cooperative U.S. and U.S.S.R. efforts might thus produce a positive resonance in individual governments, individual profit-oriented organizations, and international institutions.

An efficient process would be required for project generation and selection for implementation. As a starting point, before experience can provide a better guide, we suggest four essential steps in the identification of cooperative U.S.-U.S.S.R. development projects that could be offered to potentially interested countries:

(1) The "go, no-go" decisions on the central *idea* of cooperative U.S.–U.S.S.R. projects must be made at the highest political level in each country.

(2) A joint liaison office between the United States and the U.S.S.R. would need to be established with project recommendation as one of its tasks (see below, p. 37).

(3) While most of the cooperative projects we are suggesting could be carried out by a specific operational office within the foreign economic assistance apparatus of each country, there would need to be a coordinating office with the authority to cut across jurisdictional lines within each agency to ensure that the full measure of institutional resources will be brought to bear on the joint project. In effect, this should be a management coordinating group with the political "clout" to bend foreign aid efforts to meet these cooperative requirements.

(4) Evaluation methods must be part of the original project design. While contract evaluators could be used, tripartite evaluation would elevate the importance of evaluation and would bring lessons from past efforts into the design phase of new projects.

Perhaps the most important need in launching cooperative projects is administrative and management flexibility. In addition to the common problems encountered in formulating, implementing, and evaluating projects, there is another major complication. One of the partners, the Soviet Union, is undergoing comprehensive and continuous modernization, and this will affect many aspects of cooperation. Soviet foreign policy is moving toward a more businesslike approach to relations with other countries—away from ideology in the old sense and toward regularization of international relations. At the same time, the administrative and management structure of external economic relations is being changed to conform with radical internal economic reforms. There is every reason to expect that these changes will widen the potential for U.S.-Soviet participation in cooperative ventures to assist developing countries. These circumstances underscore the need for flexibility in project design.

Another factor in project selection is the imperative that the joint projects not only be helpful to developing countries but that they be widely perceived to be helpful. Therefore projects must not only contribute to increased productivity but also enhance welfare in the short run. The projects suggested in the discussion below seem particularly attractive on these grounds as well as for the following reasons:

(1) Many of the proposed projects' purposes are interrelated and mutually reinforcing;

(2) Because some of the projects are mutually reinforcing, the "whole" of U.S.-Soviet cooperative efforts might be greater than the sum of separate U.S. and Soviet efforts;

(3) Projects in the suggested areas have great potential to contribute to the satisfaction of basic human needs;

(4) The projects could contribute to broader distribution of real income;

(5) Many of the suggested projects would be especially beneficial to women in settings where they are relatively more disadvantaged;

(6) The proposed kinds of projects largely bypass issues of "capitalism versus socialism";

(7) Each of the proposed project categories has great positive symbolic value, illustrating the important point that the United States and the Soviet Union are interested in helping developing countries.

# Possible Areas of Cooperation

Each reader will see different possibilities for joint U.S.-U.S.S.R. actions to assist development in poor countries. Here we describe eight kinds of joint assistance activities that are in keeping with the common aims of Soviet and American assistance programs; that allow for building directly on the complementarity of each nation's capacities; and whose timely implementation is feasible.

### Emergency Assistance

Cooperative U.S.-U.S.S.R. assistance to developing countries for combating natural calamities—for example the provision of emergency food supplies during droughts and floods—can have both practical and symbolic importance. The United Nations has designated the 1990s as the International Decade for Natural Disaster Reduction, and disaster relief is a very promising avenue for U.S.-U.S.S.R. cooperation under multilateral auspices.

The United States and the Soviet Union are two countries with resources sufficient to meet serious disasters. While immediate reactions to disasters require complex planning and careful timing, these two countries acting together on a pre-planned basis could provide important backup for other national or multilateral endeavors. The U.S. support of Soviet emergency efforts in the wake of the disastrous earthquake in Armenia in 1988 suggests what can be done, as well as the improvement required in such cooperative undertakings. Joint efforts might be most effective in alleviating predictable disasters whose major emergency requirements can be foreseen—in cases such as the famines in Ethiopia and Sudan.

As a start, the United States and the U.S.S.R. could establish a small group of experts who would meet on a continuing basis (perhaps twice annually, in alternate capitals) to assess the essential kinds of short-term and long-term disaster relief needed and to develop a plan for coordinated actions appropriate for each case. Food emergency supplies might be a suitable program to begin with, since there is already some experience in this area. The plan should stipulate division of labor—for example, the United States might provide food, and the U.S.S.R. might provide transport or other services needed for the delivery of the food.

### Reforestation

In July 1988, in Oslo, the heads of major international aid organizations pledged to work toward more sustainable and environmentally safe development, including a halt to deforestation. Forestry is a theoretical and applied scientific field in which both the United States and the Soviet Union have a century or more of experience domestically, and in which both have experience in the developing countries. The problems in this field are widely recognized to be critical; extended tree loss is leading to soil erosion, diminished fertility, and climatic change—with particularly severe impact on large numbers of the poorest people in the less developed countries.

In 1987, the U.S. Agency for International Development (USAID) completed a Natural Resource Management Plan for Sub-Saharan Africa to clarify priorities for achieving sustained agricultural productivity and natural resource management on the drought-stricken continent. The plan emphasizes forestry, agroforestry, the maintenance of biological diversity, and soil and water conservation and management. Since the mid-1970s, Soviet assistance in reforestation has been provided in two ways. Some of it is channeled through the U.N. Environment Programme (UNEP), under the responsibility of the State Committee for Protection of Nature (*Goskompriroda*). Other assistance is provided through international projects of the Deserts Institute of the Turkmenia Republic.[4]

U.S. and Soviet scientists already have had some experience with cooperation on reforestation. A Soviet-U.S. Joint Committee for cooperation on the environment was created by the 1972 agreement on the environment noted above. Currently, a joint project on "Arid Ecosystems" is being established under the Committee's auspices that involves the cooperation of *Goskompriroda* with the U.S. Department of the Interior and Utah State University. One of the Committee's basic goals is the development of methods of reforestation and methods for the introduction of ecologically valuable desert plants. The results of this joint work are to be made available to UNEP and UNESCO as a common contribution. Work under the program is financed by the United States and the Soviet Union individually, while joint working groups are arranged on the basis of reciprocally financed working visits (with the United States paying dollar costs and the U.S.S.R. paying ruble costs). This project could be a model for other programs, and the findings (including those based on data gathered from space field surveys and deep ground exploration from space) could be helpful to each donor as well as to developing countries.

### Potable Water Supply

Although some progress was made during the U.N. International Drinking Water Supply and Sanitation Decade, which spanned the 1980s, the problem remains acute, especially in Sub-Saharan Africa. USAID has considerable experience with small-scale technology for water supplies.[5] The Soviet *Goskompriroda* also has international experience as a contributor to UNEP potable water programs. Moreover, the supply of potable water is an integral part of large-scale Soviet assistance programs in Syria, Afghanistan, and other countries. For example, the Soviet Ministry for Land Improvement and Water Economy has given assistance for the provision of water supply to Damascus, and presently its experts are engaged in the search for new underground water sources for that city. In Afghanistan, equipment was supplied from the Soviet Union for drilling wells and related work in order to provide water for pastures. Projects of this kind could be implemented by the same agencies for the provision of water supply to human settlements.

Other potential contributing institutions in the U.S.S.R. include the All-Union Research Institute for Designing Watering Projects. This institute could, for example, participate in establishing a consulting center for potable water issues somewhere in the developing world jointly with a U.S. firm. However, since the institute typifies the new Soviet cost-accounting enterprises whose continued viability depends on earning a profit, there would have to be some provision for concessional assistance in a joint venture if its services were to be provided to recipient countries on concessional terms.

Except in the case of border disputes over water sources, the provision of potable water is a development goal that can unite all parties. In cases where tribal or ethnic differences are important, the small-scale nature of the proposed projects and investment increments makes it possible to allocate the projects and funds to satisfy all groups. Since many projects would be very small, they could be managed by relatively less skilled individuals, or by individuals who work only at the local level. Private voluntary agencies are likely candidates for management; their involvement in this manner might help economize on the management resources of a joint venture.

## Energy and Other Resource Assessments

Joint U.S. and U.S.S.R. studies can be carried out to improve the methodologies of oil and gas resources assessment and to widen geological explorations. Many countries that spend large amounts of foreign exchange for energy imports have not explored their energy potential. In 1988, the U.S. Geological Survey expressed interest in methodological studies carried out at the All-Union Research Institute of Foreign Countries' Geology of the Soviet Ministry of Geology. The Institute has done studies in Argentina, Bangladesh, Brazil, Colombia, Namibia, the Philippines, Tanzania, and Thailand. As a result of a U.S. offer to collaborate with the Soviet specialists, a memorandum of agreement signed by the Geological Service and the U.S.S.R. Ministry of Geology (within the framework of the broader 1989 U.S.-U.S.S.R. "memorandum of understanding . . . on basic scientific research between NSF and the Academy of Sciences") provides, among other things, for further cooperation between the Institute and the Service.

A variety of funding arrangements would be possible for joint efforts in this area. Each party could simply fund its own studies, which would subsequently be exchanged or supplemented later by joint concluding work during short reciprocal visits. Alternatively, studies could be carried out on a contract basis—paid for by either the United States or the Soviet Union, which would then provide the results on concessional terms to a developing country. Another approach could be to establish a joint Soviet-U.S. company.[6]

Similarly, exploration and mining could be arranged for diamonds, quartz, coal, and other minerals and precious and semiprecious stones in developing countries that need such exploration (for example, Angola or Mozambique). An "easy" scenario might be an opportunity to develop minerals or stones resources in a country that lacks the capital for such an undertaking. Although private U.S. firms might be hesitant to enter alone, they might welcome going in on a joint basis with U.S.S.R. partners—to provide a kind of "Soviet protective umbrella" for the investment. A U.S. firm might think that if the return were sufficiently high (e.g., recoupment of principal after fifteen months), it would be worth the apparent risk. The U.S. firm might be encouraged to enter if the U.S. Overseas Private Investment Corporation (OPIC) either (a) provided some kind of investment guarantee—since private insurance might not be available for the risks of expropriation, loss of assets due to war, or inconvertibility; or (b) assumed a minority equity position along with the Soviets in a three-way ownership pattern. (As a matter of policy, OPIC would sell its share once market conditions were appropriate.)

### Primary and Secondary Technical Education

In 1987, the U.N. General Assembly designated 1990 as International Literacy Year and appointed UNESCO the lead organization for its observance. USAID has long been active in education, training, and technical assistance; today its emphasis is on the latter. Although the marginal social rate of return to primary education exceeds that at any other level,[7] particularly where illiteracy rates are high, USAID's projects in that area have steadily declined over the last decade (from almost one-third in 1980 to about 15 per cent in 1986), while total funding for all education subsectors almost doubled over those years.

The U.S.S.R. has also been active in this area, but its aid has been concentrated on secondary professional education—although in countries with very high illiteracy rates primary school levels have been assisted as well. The Soviet Union basically applies the experience it gained domestically in the 1920s. At that time, a special program was worked out for the whole country—with emphasis on Central Asia, where illiteracy was most widespread—under the label "likbez" (in Russian, *likvidatsiia bezgramotnosti,* or "eliminating illiteracy"). Contemporary Soviet assistance in illiteracy consists of the education of primary-school teachers within the framework of UNESCO programs and the construction of schools.

Most funding for joint U.S.-U.S.S.R. efforts in this area would need to be concessional, whether provided by governments or private organizations. U.S. and Soviet experts could jointly develop educational programs in consultation with individual developing countries, and then agree between themselves on the division of labor. One rule of thumb on financing might be that the more technologically advanced partner—the United States—would provide any sophisticated equipment or computers that might be required for the schools. A different division of labor would seem appropriate for upgrading and modernizing the polytechnical centers established by the U.S.S.R. in several developing countries. Such renewed (and possibly renamed) centers could be considered joint aid projects, with the United States now providing instructional staff (as well as equipment) to complement the earlier Soviet contribution of plant and equipment.

The professional mix of the training to be provided might at first be directed toward the training of workers in very broad categories of specialization: agricultural specialists, primary school teachers, nurses and medical assistants, workers for simple metal processing, etc. Such training could be arranged on the basis of additional equipment provided to the Soviet polytechnical centers, or the construction of new facilities. At a later point, when the market demand for specific sub-specialties became clear, narrowly defined courses could be established with short (three to six months) intensive programs.

Cooperative action could begin with an international conference on East-West/U.S.S.R.-U.S. cooperation on education in the developing world. The United States is the single largest donor in this field, and the Soviet Union, while a much smaller donor, has played a significant role in some countries. The conference could be designed jointly by specialists from the two countries and from a few developing countries. The subject is intrinsically important:

(1) Education is crucial to development;

(2) The focus on education would bring together two important providers of assistance in this area;

(3) The content would be treated in ways that transcend ideology; and

(4) The potential for cooperation rather than competition in this critical area has not been explored previously.

These four considerations suggest that this conference would be useful and would have wide support.

## Support for Health Care

Together, the United States and the Soviet Union have a wealth of experience in health care in developing countries. U.S. efforts are directed toward increasing life expectancy, and it is thought most efficient to pursue this goal by addressing the health problems of children and their mothers. Child survival and improved maternal and child health receive priority in USAID and of course in UNICEF programs. The U.S.S.R. also has health programs in the field, although they are less concentrated by type of program than the U.S. program.

A central problem of health-care delivery systems everywhere in the world is their financing and sustainability. The issue is both practical and symbolic. For example, clinics that provide prenatal care, or "barefoot doctors" who treat simple infections, are absolutely essential to health care systems, but their mission is so prosaic that they are difficult to sustain financially. Their clients can pay little toward the services rendered, and these activities lack the glamour to attract significant and sustained funding in the form of grants.

In seeking areas where the United States and the Soviet Union can cooperate to improve health care, basic financial considerations suggest that the activities undertaken should not only be essential but should have sufficient humanitarian and hence symbolic value to attract favorable international attention and hence funding.

One way to finance joint activities would be to establish joint enterprises between U.S. companies and U.S.S.R. cost-accounting enterprises to render services to developing-country populations on concessional terms. The firms would make a normal profit as commercial enterprises, but the local population would be granted services cheaply or free of charge. The difference—or subsidy—would be provided by special public assistance funds from either the United States or the Soviet Union or from non-governmental organizations in those countries.

This path might be especially suitable for increasing access to the treatment of eye diseases in developing countries. At least a third of all blind people in the world today could have sight restored by cataract operations. Moreover, a leading cause of blindness and nutrition-related visual impairment among children is vitamin A deficiency (xerophthalmia). Joint efforts to alleviate blindness could have great humanitarian appeal. Such projects are largely devoid of political content and attract great public attention. The nutrition side of the problem could be addressed by stimulating local governments and international organizations to provide minimal dietary requirements for children outside the context of joint projects, although local non-governmental organizations (NGOs) and volunteers (including physicians) would be logical partners.

The short-term goal of joint U.S.-U.S.S.R. efforts could be the creation of a minimum level of surgical facilities where these are lacking. Emphasis should be on working at the grassroots level as much as is technically and economically feasible. Priority could initially be given to children and mothers. A long-term goal could be the establishment of geographical zones free of operable cataract and glaucoma blindness.

Cooperation might proceed in two stages. First, the United States, the Soviet Union, and the developing country individually would evaluate what methodology and technology would be appropriate, as well as the specific equipment and personnel required for this kind of effort. No special funding would be required at this stage because each party would rely essentially on research already being funded in its own government medical research centers.

At the second stage, the construction and equipment of eye surgery centers would be carried out, and operations would begin. This work could be implemented on a contract basis, funded from a combination of government assistance and funds from potentially interested foundations such as, for example, Helen Keller International, Inc., of New York. Alternatively, a joint U.S.-U.S.S.R. venture might be established involving a U.S. private clinic and a Soviet cost-accounting enterprise. A joint venture might, for example, utilize the know-how developed by the eye-surgery enterprise run by Professor S. Fedorov (the "All-Union Inter-Industry Research-Technology Complex 'Eye Microsurgery' "), or it might build on the work of Professor M. Krasnov of the Institute for Eye Diseases. Minimal fees would be charged, and subsidies would be provided from existing national assistance funding (from the United States, the Soviet Union, or elsewhere), or from private groups around the world.

### Assistance for Urban Construction

Worldwide rapid urbanization necessitates civil construction on a massive scale. Yet construction is very material-intensive—dependent mainly on supplies of cement and concrete, bricks, timber, and metal. In developing countries, supply shortages often undermine municipal construction programs. In recent years, however, a widening range of projects has utilized light metal structures, which have several advantages. They are lightweight and transportable (buildings weigh one-fifth or one-sixth as much as those of similar capacity constructed in a conventional manner). They are capital-saving, with production and assembly costing 20–40 per cent less than conventional works structures. Such buildings are also multipurpose and can, to some extent, be reconfigured relatively cheaply. Light metal structures are equally suitable for the construction of all the kinds of projects so badly needed for urban development in the developing world: housing, factory buildings, warehouses, garages, workshops, sports projects.

Several U.S. firms specialize in such structures. A joint U.S.–U.S.S.R. venture could also utilize the know-how and materials developed by a Soviet firm, the All-Union Design, Production and Construction Trust for Special Light Structures (*Soyuzspetslegkonstruktsia*). A U.S. company could provide equipment for selected technological processes, as well as for necessary materials such as sealants, hermeticals, thermal insulation, and paints, which involve not more than 10–15 per cent of the total cost of such structures, but which are in short supply in the U.S.S.R..

A joint U.S.–U.S.S.R. major *regional* manufacturing plant in the developing world could be commercially profitable, since it could assist several neighboring developing countries either through direct sales to those countries at market prices or through sales to foreign assistance agencies. Such a joint venture could also operate on a concessional basis with developing countries if a subsidy covering the concessional amount were provided by an assistance agency.

A second area of urban development in which joint U.S.–U.S.S.R. efforts might be particularly appropriate is solid waste disposal. In the United States, a variety of techniques are used to burn waste that could be adapted to conditions in developing countries. Similarly, the U.S.S.R. could offer know-how and equipment it has developed (in, for example, Leningrad), with part of the more technical components provided by the United States. Technological change around the world has increasingly made such enterprises commercially viable. Joint U.S.-U.S.S.R. enterprises in this area could operate successfully in many different countries.

### Ongoing Joint Study of Economic Development

Initial steps in the search for U.S.–U.S.S.R. development assistance cooperation already have been taken. One example is provided by the U.S.-U.S.S.R. meetings that form the basis of this book—the joint symposia of Soviet and U.S. development specialists held in Moscow and Washington and sponsored by the Overseas Development Council in the United States and the Institute of World Economy and International Relations (IMEMO) in the Soviet Union. Another example is the relationship established by the Institute for African Studies of the U.S.S.R. Academy of Sciences and a group of experts from the Center for African Studies of the University of California in Los Angeles and the School of International Relations of the University of Southern California.

The focus of the ODC-IMEMO discussions is on issues of national development strategies in the developing world and the selection of assistance policies. The second group, in contrast, has been exploring prospects for assistance to specific sectors of African economies (for example, agriculture, mining, and research based on data from a space communication satellite). This African studies group has reached the same positive conclusions about the possibility of a joint approach to development as the policy-oriented group.[8]

We propose that such cooperative research on Third World development be institutionalized on a systematic and routine basis to ensure that two goals are accomplished. First, it is important that each side know what the other is thinking about, and that the actions of one in furthering development complement rather than conflict with actions of the other. Second, if the benefits of cooperative work are to be realized, there must be a permanent group or task force at work to explore potential forms of joint action. Two kinds of arrangements are necessary.

First, a workshop for development specialists from the United States and U.S.S.R. should be established on a permanent basis, and its agenda should be set up along the following lines:

- Annual meetings between a group of U.S. and Soviet development specialists and developing-country participants should alternate between Washington and Moscow. These meetings should include scholars and practitioners invited in relation to an agenda set the previous year. Their objective should be to make certain that the latest thinking on Third World development in the United States and the Soviet Union is apparent to the other side, with evaluation provided from the perspective of developing countries.

- Participation should assure some continuity as well as the involvement of new experts.

- To ensure that the annual meetings serve as a catalyst for future proposals, a permanent agenda item for each meeting would be "program development." A permanent subcommittee, with U.S. and U.S.S.R. members serving under a rotating chairmanship, would be charged with studying and making agenda proposals on a regular and timely basis.

- To make certain that the annual meetings consider future joint U.S.-U.S.S.R. actions, a permanent "task force" made up of U.S. and U.S.S.R. members would suggest and investigate possible future actions. Participation would provide for both continuity and new members, serving under a rotating chairmanship, which would be charged with bringing suggestions to the full annual meeting for discussion.

In summary, this workshop would be the basic building block for the extension of expert exchanges on Third World development in many different directions, including the creation of an ongoing task force specifically on joint projects. Over time, this arrangement will no doubt lead to proposals for exchanges of development experts (e.g., a "sabbatical" in which officials of one program could work in some capacity in the program of the other country), broader exchange training of students, institutional ties between academic programs and other organizations specializing in the development of the poor countries, proposals for joint projects, and joint U.S.-U.S.S.R. research projects in these countries.

A second suggestion is the creation of a liaison office between the United States and the Soviet Union specifically in the area of foreign economic assistance. On the U.S. side, this might be the Office of Donor Coordination within the Bureau for Program and Policy Coordination of USAID. On the U.S.S.R. side, it might be a similar group within the Ministry for External Economic Relations. Such an office would have three main functions. It would be charged with following in detail the foreign economic assistance program of the other government. It would ensure that this information would be widely disseminated within its parent agency. Finally, it would make project selection recommendations. Representatives from these offices would meet alternately in Washington and Moscow (on a financially reciprocal basis, with Washington paying dollar costs and Moscow paying ruble costs) to discuss areas of mutual interest in assistance programs and to attempt to define potential U.S.-U.S.S.R. joint efforts.

# Conclusion

Changes in the relationship between the U.S. and the U.S.S.R. will leave no part of the world untouched, and no areas watch the transformation with greater concern than the developing countries. Some new directions in development assistance are cited above, and many other similar projects can be suggested. These proposed projects can be based on the comparative advantages enjoyed by each country that form a basis for complementary action, as well as on the mutual interests of the United States and the U.S.S.R. in the peaceful development of less developed countries. The projects proposed are also fully within the capabilities of both countries.

There are of course numerous philosophical and practical obstacles to U.S.-U.S.S.R. cooperation. No doubt each nation will continue to support its "friends" in the developing world, with uncertain results all around. Cooperation will also depend on the capacity of each country to work with the other at the operating level—with all of the implicit administrative frustrations.

Most basically, U.S.-Soviet cooperation will clearly be linked to continued political calm and the expansion of bilateral economic ties between the United States and the Soviet Union. Under these conditions, trade will become more dependent on key economic criteria and less on non-economic restrictions. For example, the repeal or suspension of the Jackson-Vanik amendment to the U.S. Foreign Trade Act, linking most-favored-nation treatment to Soviet emigration policies, would send an important signal that the United States welcomes increased economic and financial ties with the Soviet Union—a signal that would be felt throughout the U.S. government and business community. Among othe things, its elimination would facilitate the financing and establishment of joint ventures in third countries.

Even assuming that relations between the United States and the Soviet Union continue to improve, however certain obstacles and difficulties will stand in the way of cooperative work and joint projects. There will be disagreements over the best economic strategy to follow, differences of views between the developing country and its U.S. and U.S.S.R. partners, between the U.S. and Soviet specialists, and among members of each group. Problems of accountability in foreign economic assistance may prove formidable, since two systems will be "mixing" resources to accomplish multiple and related goals. A single joint project failure may give those in each country who oppose this form of cooperation an opening to criticize the entire program.

At the same time, however, there are good reasons to forge ahead with joint efforts. They can enhance the human condition and improve the environment and productive base in developing countries. They can provide for greater understanding of development problems and suggest ways of linking forces to ameliorate those problems. They are forward-looking and intended to help developing countries improve their own lot. They can further improve mutual U.S.-U.S.S.R. understanding. And they can help move the Soviet

Union away from economic isolation and into the world economy—with closer ties to international trade and financial institutions.

In a word, these programs and projects fit the needs of developing countries and would be carried out on a tripartite basis with them; they are within the capabilities of the United States and the U.S.S.R., and they are proposed at a time when it is in the interests of both the United States and the Soviet Union to engage in activities that build confidence in and knowledge of each other's abilities and intentions.

## Notes

[1]The allusion here is to the four "baskets" of concern—arms control, human rights, bilateral relations, and regional conflicts—that are to be reviewed periodically in a process provided for by the Helsinki Accords.

[2]The starting point for the process of mutual recognition and movement toward cooperation of the two European organizations was the signing of the joint Declaration on Establishment of Official Relations between the EC and CMEA in June 1988.

[3]The new approach of the Soviet Union to the challenge of free choice of development orientation was emphasized in President Mikhail Gorbachev's presentation at the United Nations on December 7, 1988.

[4]The U.S.S.R.'s reforestation programs in developing countries have special significance in light of the concept of global ecological security set forth at the U.N. General Assembly in June 1988 by Soviet Foreign Minister Shevardnadze (the other four "securities" noted were military, economic, legal, and humanitarian).

[5]Although Soviet assistance has been focused on larger infrastructure projects, current thinking recognizes the importance of medium- and small-sized projects in a variety of fields; therefore, Soviet participation in such a joint project is consistent with present thinking.

[6]One consideration requires special attention. Since the resource under examination—energy—is exceptionally important, it must be clear that new knowledge of reserves in a developing country would not be used commercially unilaterally by either the United States or the U.S.S.R. This danger can be avoided by inclusion in the initial agreement of a provision for joint development of newly discovered resources consistent with the development plans of the developing country.

[7]See George Psacharopoulos, "Returns to Education: A Further International Update and Implications," *Journal of Human Resources,* Vol. 20, No. 4 (April 1985), pp. 583-604.

[8]Anatoly A. Gromyko and C. S. Whitaker, eds., *Agenda for Action: African-Soviet-U.S. Cooperation* (Boulder, Colo.: Lynne Reinner Publishers, 1990).

# I. Development Strategies Reconsidered

# Changing Approaches to Development Strategy and Development Assistance

Elena B. Arefieva and Elena A. Bragina

The formation of the Soviet state in 1917 brought about a fundamental change in the world economy and market: for the first time in history, a socialist country proclaiming international economic principles entirely different from those previously practiced became an actor in world economic relations. This introduced a new type of international economic relations among the nations of the world; after all, relations between a metropolitan country and a colony or between two countries with the same social and political orientation are one thing, but relations between countries that not only do not subscribe to the same social and political agenda but that also base their international actions on antithetical philosophies are quite another.

The leading countries that dominated the world economy and markets at that time could no longer ignore the new, complex, contradictory, conflict-ridden situation that was taking shape. The Soviet state, for its part, also had to adapt to the situation that accompanied the evolution of its economic system and its place in the international arena. In the process of expanding its foreign economic relations, the Soviet state made aid to other peoples the focus of its relations with other countries. The concept of Soviet aid, its principles, objectives, and main directions were of course formulated not all at once but over a period of years. Many aspects of the U.S.S.R.'s economic and scientific-technical relations with the developing countries improved, became more flexible, and adapted to

43

changing conditions, while other aspects were recognized as obsolete, erroneous, and unacceptable and were eliminated. This renewal process has been given substantial impetus in the present *perestroika* period of the Soviet Union's development.

## The Evolution of the Soviet Concept of Third World Development

From the 1950s on—the period of decolonization—economic relations with the developing countries became a major part of the Soviet state's foreign policy and economic relations. The scale and priorities of economic relations with the Third World were from the very outset determined by foreign policy objectives and the Soviet Union's own economic interests and needs. At the same time, the area of these relations to which this book is devoted—economic assistance in support of the economic and social development of Third World countries—also evolved under the powerful influence of another factor: these countries' need for foreign resources to accelerate their economic growth, to overcome their backwardness, and to gain equal rights to participate in the world economy and in the international division of labor.

In what ways have the goals, principles, and general concept of development assistance changed over time? Unfortunately, it is difficult to judge many important changes in strategy in retrospect. Collaboration with the developing countries, like other aspects of the Soviet Union's foreign economic relations, is an area that has traditionally been closed both to the general public and to scholars. We do not have at our disposal the complete statistical data required to evaluate even current trends—to say nothing of those of the 1950s and 1960s, when statistics were a product of the imagination of statistical agencies. The texts of strategic decisions by the government also were not published. Nor did the press publish discussions on foreign economic relations or foreign policy. It is therefore very difficult to present a full picture of the directions and shifts of policy in this area.

The officially proclaimed principles of Soviet economic assistance to Third World countries have remained the same since the 1950s. They are: equality, respect for sovereignty, non-interference in the internal affairs of other states, and assuring mutual benefits for both partners in development cooperation. Even though these principles could not be consistently pursued during the years in which assistance to Third World countries was in general dominated by political factors and ideological objectives (it should be noted that there was no fully articulated concept of assistance during that period), they nevertheless were among the bases of the U.S.S.R.'s relations with the developing countries.

In addition, however, Soviet relations with the Third World had another, quite contradictory aspect—one not made explicit either at the level of official politics or in public statements (even though the public was, as a result, deprived of a considerable portion of the national product). This was ideological expansionism, presented as the "enlightenment" of backward peoples that was to lead them toward socialist ideals. It was a philosophy expressive of a dogmatic system of thinking and an administrative system of social management.

At the same time, the Soviet Union's *economic* relations with the Third World have always taken into account a number of firm principles regarding the desirable direction of economic development:

(1) The idea that it is necessary to support the efforts of the developing countries to attain economic independence;

(2) The view that *internal* factors play an important part in accelerating the economic growth of these countries and in improving the system of their foreign economic relations; and

(3) The concept that the state and the public sector have a special role in building the economies of developing countries.

The interpretation and application of these principles are now undergoing comprehensive reassessment. Objective scientific analysis and an understanding of social and economic development of the Third World play a significant part in this process. This is not to say that there are necessarily direct correlations between research findings and the evolution of the forms and directions of assistance. In this connection, it is important to note that there are three different sources of influence on the formulation of the Soviet concept of economic and technical assistance to developing countries:[1]

(1) Scientific concepts—based on research on Third World countries' problems and devoted to the search for effective approaches to their development (with due regard to the necessity of improving the Soviet Union's foreign economic relations);

(2) The official position of state bodies on the directions of Soviet economic aid—which does not necessarily coincide with the recommendations of scientists;

(3) The actual practice of Soviet economic and technical assistance to developing countries—which is to a certain extent based on scientific recommendations, on practical possibilities

and constraints, and on cumulative experience—and (as is always true of implementation) not necessarily identical with officially proclaimed intentions.

The ideological and political bias of Soviet strategy toward the developing countries formulated in the 1950s and 1960s is quite apparent. In this initial stage, at a time when decolonization was generating numerous changes in political and world economic processes, the Soviet Union reacted positively to the upsurge of the national liberation movement and to the awakening national self-awareness of the peoples of former colonies and dependent countries. This position stemmed from Marxist-Leninist theory, in particular the principle of "proletarian internationalism." Supporting the national liberation movement was proclaimed to be the duty of a country where socialism had been victorious. The theory of the class struggle projected to the international level was the ideological basis of this concept. This theory pointed to an inevitable intensification of the opposition between the two principal forces—the international proletariat and "big capital." The Soviet Union's proletariat was assigned the mission of extending fraternal support to the international proletariat so as to hasten the worldwide victory of socialism, which was also considered inevitable.

But it would be a mistake to perceive the concept of "proletarian internationalism" as purely political and ideological. It also contained a strong ethical and psychological element. The idea of providing support was initially quite eagerly accepted by the Soviet people (most of whom had not known other ideological reference points than the official ones for many years). They went to the distant tropics to provide assistance, to restore or create from the ground up the economies of developing countries. While they thereby frequently subjected themselves to difficult living conditions and very limited earnings (not until the late 1960s was this system revised and improved), they were nevertheless confident of their international mission.

In the early years of Soviet assistance, the problems of economic effectiveness had not yet been practically addressed; the objectives of aid were vague, and the choice of partners was not always substantiated. Political objectives—both officially proclaimed and actually pursued—were included in their entirety under the heading of the class struggle. Contrary to the popular Western view of the military-strategic orientation of Soviet activity in former colonies, it should be emphasized that (strange as this might seem to Westerners) the reality was not a master plan to gain world dominance through rational actions, but rather a sum of quite random steps in support of the national liberation movement in places where it had been most successful. And even when such actions amounted to the export of revolution, the primary (never officially proclaimed) objective was world socialism—with Soviet dominance only secondary.

The ideological and political "conditionality" of foreign political relations with developing countries was particularly evident in aid to countries with a socialist orientation, whose peoples seem to need particularly large-scale support in the implementation of their economic programs. Moreover, the general trend showed that the poorest of the developing countries chose transition to a socialist orientation. Naturally, ideological support for their choice also required *economic* reinforcement. The flow of resources to these countries had to support the economic and political strategy that at the time seemed to correspond to the Marxist-Leninist conception of social justice.

It must also be acknowledged that the general confrontation between the two world social systems—socialism and capitalism—made its mark on the character of the U.S.S.R.'s relations with the developing countries. The national liberation movement and countries that had recently won their political independence were regarded as socialism's natural allies and as one of the revolutionary and anti-imperialist forces of modern times. The official premise was that these countries were lost to world capitalism and could not be a source of its rejuvenation.

Relations with the Third World were at the same time part of the quite contradictory general system of foreign political principles in which the policy of peaceful co-existence of the two systems was an important element. This policy, proclaimed by Nikita S. Khrushchev as part of his attempt to eradicate Stalinist stereotypes in domestic and foreign policy, later assumed the form of the policy of détente—which was implemented very inconsistently, given the absence of a clear articulation of the U.S.S.R.'s political and economic interests in the Third World.

It is important to emphasize that in the U.S.S.R., the formulation of a holistic concept of relations with the developing countries in fact began only in the last few years—with the advent of *perestroika*. The basic principles of this concept were proclaimed by Mikhail S. Gorbachev in his speech to the U.N. General Assembly on October 7, 1988, which repudiated the application of the class struggle principle in international relations, de-ideologized inter-governmental relations, and gave priority to general human values, the main objectives of which include mankind's survival in the nuclear age.

The same contradictory co-existence of the continuity and

change of models is seen in the purely *economic* part of Soviet relations with developing countries. At the same time, Soviet theory about Third World development, as well as the forms, methods, and scale of the Soviet Union's economic relations with the developing countries, all have been changing.

# New Directions in Soviet Theory About Development

The issue of "multivariant" development—which began to be addressed in the 1970s in the context of work on the theory of the economic differentiation of the developing countries—has been elaborated in the Soviet Union in recent years in works by orientalist sociologists and political scientists. Recognition of multivariant development has become part of the concept of "polymorphism" in Third World socio-economic development. The research conclusions drawn from this work have had a significant impact of the U.S.S.R.'s strategy of aid to the developing countries.

The thesis expressed in Communist Party documents of the 1960s regarding the possibility of choosing the path of development—capitalist or non-capitalist (subsequently increasingly replaced by the term "socialist orientation")—presupposed the eventual transition of the majority of the developing countries to non-capitalist development and the evolution of national liberation revolutions into socialist revolutions. Not until the early 1970s did Soviet scientific literature unequivocally state that the diversity of socio-economic conditions, class structures, and types of economic development in the Third World was leading to a wealth of diverse models of development, including the development of diverse political systems.

Historical experience provided more than enough evidence that most developing countries chose the bourgeois, non-socialist path of development. In these circumstances, the tasks of Soviet assistance naturally took on a different look than when the presumption was that developing countries required assistance in building the foundations of socialism. The main impact of such a change in concept was on the approach taken by the strategy of cooperation toward the state and the state sector in recipient countries. Recommendations to shift the emphasis in aid to take into account the role of private enterprise were first heard back in the early 1970s. But the most obvious change in emphasis has taken place during the period of *perestroika*—as a result of the re-examination of the overall attitude toward the "private production–state monopoly" dilemma. It should be noted that these changes likewise have been reflected in decisions relating to the U.S.S.R.'s own economy—in the development of the cooperative movement, in recommendations to introduce joint-stock property, and in the effort to attract private foreign investment. Particularly noticeable was the revival of non-state farms in Soviet agriculture, in which the interest of the farmer is directly linked to his right to lease or own the land.

Soviet economists no longer predicate their evaluation of the strategy of development of Third World countries on the premise that a large-scale state sector is absolutely essential. Of course centrally controlled state property is still perceived to be crucially important for the development of productive forces, especially where private enterprise is not sufficiently developed. But it must at the same time be acknowledged that private enterprise frequently has not less but more potential for the development of production.

Well into the 1970s, Soviet scholars considered industrialization and the creation of industrial production capacity the main driving force in Third World development. The forced transfer of resources from the agricultural sector to industry was considered essential for the development of the U.S.S.R.'s national economy; the importance of agriculture and animal husbandry for long-term economic development was underestimated. All this left its stamp on the conceptual model of Third World development. Insufficient attention to aid to the agrarian sector of the economies of developing countries is also the direct result of the Soviet Union's own lag in this area, which makes equipment and technology transfer difficult.

A further new direction of the evolution of Soviet concepts of the economic development of Third World countries—one that stems from their experience as well as from the U.S.S.R.'s own historical experience—relates to the view of the potential and limits of centralized planning and the role of the market, the pricing mechanism, and the credit system. Neglect of the principles of market regulation and their replacement by peremptory administrative methods in the management of the U.S.S.R.'s national economy were unintentionally transferred, if in somewhat milder form, to the concept of Third World development. Insufficient attention was paid by researchers to those aspects of the economies of the developing countries that are capable of accelerating the monetarization of their economy and of incorporating market stimuli in the regulation of the volume of production and the product mix.

The study of world economic relations in the 1970s and 1980s, analysis of Western economic research on the role of the international division of labor, and the movement of capital in the economy of the developing countries had a major impact on changes in the

Soviet concept of Third World development—and consequently on the structure of aid to these countries. The external economic relations of the developing countries came to be widely viewed more as a powerful factor in their economic growth than as a channel of exploitation by and a source of profit for the developed capitalist countries.

Recent research by Soviet scholars shows that "peripheral capitalism" is being drawn into the world capitalist economy not as a single, whole mass, but as numerous individual parts at different levels of economic integration. Contradictions between developed and developing countries in the world capitalist economy are supplemented by contradictions between national capitalism and various multinational groups of capitalists. The problem of the economic independence of the developing countries therefore emerges in a different light. Today it is more appropriate to raise the question of how these countries can attain equal partnership within the framework of the world capitalist economy than of how they can break away from it. This adds new dimensions to a number of questions of aid strategy—including the dilemma of import-substitution versus export-orientation.

These trends are of course reflected in Soviet analysis of the potential and limits of the "socialist orientation" model of development of Third World countries as an alternative to the capitalist path. In the past, the transition of individual socialist countries to the socialist orientation was equated with the expansion of the world socialist system, while their governments' declarations of the adoption of an ideological policy of building the foundations of socialism were considered an indicator of real change in the strategy of development. With the passage of time, however, the discrepancy between the model and their conditions—and between economic policy and such declarations—became apparent. The countries of socialist orientation began deviating from the declared path, and their adherence to it remained only in ideology. Thus, countries that are considered to be oriented toward socialism in recent years have been observed to depart to a certain degree from principles such as centralized planning and the dominant role of the state sector (Angola, Burma, Benin, Tanzania, Algeria, the People's Democratic Republic of Congo, Ghana), restrictions on foreign property (Angola, Burma, Benin, Tanzania), and a closed economy (Angola, Tanzania, Ethiopia, Benin, Algeria).

These conditions have led to a reassessment of the problems of socialist orientation; to getting rid of excessively general, declarative, and ostentatious statements; and to carrying out further theoretical and political analysis. The prevailing view now is that the concept of socialist orientation has failed, although the idea still has many proponents in the Soviet Union. Those who continue to adhere to the possibility of building socialism in the Third World argue that it is necessary to discuss it not in isolation from reality (as was the case in the past), but in full cognizance of all its contradictions and difficulties.

# The Relationship of the State and Private Sectors in Development Assistance Strategy

The Soviet strategy of assistance to developing countries was from the very beginning oriented toward the state sector, toward expanding the role of the state in the economy, and toward preferential relations with state organizations and enterprises. As already mentioned, this strategy was based primarily on the U.S.S.R.'s own development experience as a state economy. Consequently, the foreign state, rather than private capital, was the preferred and more familiar partner in economic relations. From the very first stages of economic and technical cooperation with former colonies that acquired independence, Soviet theoretical as well as applied research intended for the organizations responsible for aid policy and implementation emphasized differences between regulation and market aspects of the process of growth and the divergent roles and significance of the state and private enterprise in development strategy. The perception of these factors and modes as being in sharp opposition—as posing a dilemma of the state *versus* the private sector (a view that was to a certain degree promoted by Soviet researchers in the 1950s)—reflected the initially inadequate understanding of evidence to the contrary that was emerging from the experience of developing countries.

The actual experience of a number of developing countries was also influential in orienting Soviet foreign economic aid strategy predominantly toward state economic activity. More specifically, the following factors were of substantial significance in the formulation of the Soviet concept of aid to the state sector:

1. State regulation of economic policy became an important element in the promotion of change in the economy of a developing society, in the establishment of new links between sectors, and in the strengthening of their production relationships. The links formed between agriculture and industry and between the extractive and manufacturing sectors during the period of colonial dependence lacked dynamism. In this setting, the new structure of the economy took shape slowly, with great difficulty, many disruptions,

and much backsliding. Intervention by the state generally was an attempt to speed up and balance this process and to prevent excessive complications that threatened to disrupt both economic and social development.

2. The state sector in developing countries was viewed as the material base of the economy—making up for the many missing links in the production process and economic structures.[2] Indeed, the role of the state in the design and implementation of economic policy became one of the leading tenets of the ideology of development in Asian, African, and Latin American countries.

3. Long-range planning became a new element in the economic policy of the state.[3] More than three hundred long-term plans were formulated beginning in 1950. It is of course possible to point to the inconsistency of planning, to the weak impact of its economic levers on production, and to its insufficient effectiveness; nonetheless, planning was associated with state socio-economic policy and budget resources and therefore became an important part of economic development.

We also note that developing economies are in many ways a difficult setting for testing the relative developmental merits of either state planning or the market mechanism. These countries' state plans, with their limited influence on production, can hardly make up for the lack of a market mechanism in the economy. Nor can the market function effectively in a context of economic backwardness, a low degree of integration of the international and domestic markets, and the continued presence of non-monetized transactions in a number of sectors. What has evolved in developing countries is a variety of situations in which planning and market mechanisms co-exist in different and continuously changing combinations.

4. In the practice of foreign economic cooperation between the U.S.S.R. and developing countries, the potential influence of the state and centralized (administrative) methods of management on other sectors of the economy were exaggerated, while no systematic evaluation was made of the weakness of the position of local private enterprise in many developing countries. Although the state and private sectors also co-exist in the developed capitalist countries, these differ from the types of mixed economies that have emerged in the Third World. In developing countries, the state sector has expanded in two ways: through nationalization, especially in the initial stage, and as a result of new investment (which gradually became the basic form of its expansion).

Soviet assistance to the state sector was channeled primarily to production. Large enterprises in the manufacturing sector and in extractive industry were prominent among projects built with the economic and technical assistance of the U.S.S.R. The foreign economic organizations of the U.S.S.R. tried to take the development priorities indicated in the plans and programs of Third World countries into account in Soviet aid practices. Priority was given to large-scale construction within the framework of the state sector. It should be noted that this thrust of Soviet cooperation likewise influenced the content of the official assistance of Western countries, a considerable part of which was also directed to the state sector, particularly for infrastructure projects.

As already noted, Soviet aid strategy at the same time could not ignore the huge share of private enterprise in the economies of some developing countries and the dynamic combinations between state and private sectors.[4] State policy was also directed toward supporting local private enterprise.

This overall orientation of Soviet aid encountered serious problems connected with the low efficiency of many state enterprises compared to the private sector. (In this connection, however, it must be noted that state enterprises usually undertake the more complex or new types of production regardless of whether they are profitable or not, while private enterprises are attracted to the more profitable branches.) While the U.S.S.R. cannot fail to see this shortcoming, Soviet strategy nevertheless still proceeds from the premise that the state sector and relations with it cannot be evaluated solely on the basis of the profitability criterion. Projects that perform important socio-economic functions for economic development in general are carried out within its framework. Of course this does not mean that commercial characteristics are entirely ignored in the process.

This problem acquires special urgency in connection with the restructuring of economic principles and the work of foreign economic organizations in the context of current economic reform in the U.S.S.R. In essence, the discussion focuses on the need for the convergence of the domestic and the foreign economic mechanisms, and this requires a more flexible approach to the evaluation of the prospective development of Third World countries as a whole and in individual groups. Such an approach is also dictated by certain trends in the interrelationship of the state and the private sector in developing countries. We note, first of all, the trend toward the privatization of state enterprises, a reduction of the scale of the state sector, and increased state support for private enterprise. This process is directly connected with the growth of the foreign indebtedness of developing countries and with the low rate of structural change that exists in these countries alongside the increasing internationalization of their economies. Yet another thrust of development strategy is the intensification of the science and technology component in economic relations for the priority task of modernizing the economy.

# The "Dilemma" of Industrial vs. Agricultural Development

In the Soviet Union, industrialization was characterized by the priority for modern *large-scale industry* and by the creation of new enterprises primarily in branches of *heavy industry*—notably machine building, petrochemicals, and electrical engineering. High growth rates in industry became the decisive condition for eliminating unemployment by the year 1930. New industrial investment—which in the more backward regions in the eastern part of the U.S.S.R. (in the Central Asian and Transcaucasian republics) was financed from the state budget and employed specialists and skilled workers from Russia's leading industrial centers—was another aspect of Soviet industrialization that had an appreciable impact on Soviet aid strategy. Forced industrialization methods had, after all, enabled the Soviet Union itself to reinforce its economic independence in a short period of time, to overcome its technical and economic backwardness to a considerable degree, and to attain second place in the volume of world industrial output.

The collapse of the colonial system resulted in the emergence of a great number of independent Asian, African, and Latin American countries in the 1950s and 1960s. These countries were confronted with the task of undertaking profound socio-economic reforms that were in large measure identified in Soviet research with the early period in the development of the U.S.S.R.—with a need to resolve similar problems through the assignment of top priority to industrialization and the strengthening of the economic role of state. Yet it would be incorrect to view the priority given to industry in Soviet aid as something that was forced upon the developing countries from outside, against their own wishes and interests. The creation of an impressive national industrial sector became the foremost objective of a great majority of the developing countries for several basic economic, political, and social reasons:

(a) By analogy with the experience of developed countries, industry was considered the most dynamic branch of the economy—with high annual growth rates capable of reducing unemployment;

(b) The political slogan of industrialization was viewed as a symbol of independence in the economic sphere;

(c) The expansion of industry in the 1950s was primarily a result of the introduction of a number of preferential measures involving protection of the interests of national capital and the introduction of certain restrictions on foreign enterprises; and

(d) The 1950s and 1960s were marked by a drop in raw-material prices (the chief items of export from the developing countries), and by a deterioration of almost 15 per cent in the terms of trade in these commodities.

Governments saw the strengthening of domestic industry as one of the prospects for improving their positions in world economic relations through the export of finished products.

In the first programs of national governments and in their development priorities, there was a certain degree of obsessiveness with industry; the growth of this sector was perceived as an absolute good, and the expansion of industrial output was viewed as the one and only means of developing a backward economy. Top priority was given to mobilizing capital from external and internal sources and to attracting the foreign technology and experience that the developing countries lacked.

The formulation of the Soviet concept of industrialization for development was also very much influenced by the fact that India, which embarked on the expansion of national heavy industry, was among the first countries to receive Soviet economic and technical aid in the postwar period. India's leaders and members of the ruling party—the Indian National Congress—showed unflagging interest in Soviet economic restructuring methods. P. C. Mahalanobis, one of the founders of planning in India, was an advocate of assigning investment priority to heavy industry—a strategy reflected in India's Second Five-Year Plan.

In the late 1950s and early 1960s, the Soviet Union's technical and economic assistance was for the most part extended in the form of construction projects in India's machine building, oil refining branches, coal and oil-extracting industries, and ferrous metallurgy. Between 1960 and 1968, 65–75 per cent of the exports to India, Pakistan, and the United Arab Republic consisted of machinery and equipment needed to build up industry. As of the beginning of the 1960s, economic and technical aid agreements had been signed with fourteen developing nations. Cooperation with Egypt, Ethiopia,

Guinea, and Ghana was established for the first time. Ten years later, such agreements already had been reached with forty-nine countries—and by 1981, with sixty-five Asian, African, and Latin American countries.

In its content, Soviet assistance for strengthening the industrial potential of the developing countries went considerably beyond direct aid for the construction of industrial enterprises. It also involved participation in the construction of large infrastructure projects, including hydro-electric power plants and increases in irrigated agricultural area. This, for example, was the character of the construction of the Aswan Dam complex in Egypt, which was commissioned in 1964 and appreciably improved the nation's potential for producing grain. The Aswan Hydroelectric Power Plant became the most economical supplier of electric power, supplying one-fifth of the nation's needs.

Nevertheless, the realization of the industrial priorities of the national programs of the developing countries and the practice of Soviet assistance in the 1960s and 1970s demonstrated—despite some positive results—a need to reassess certain points regarding industrial development. Soviet researchers noted that industrialization requires enormous efforts; N. Shmelev, for example, characterizes the period of industrialization as a period of sacrifice, in a certain sense.[5] It should be noted that in the industrial countries themselves, rapid industrialization had not been accompanied by appreciable changes in consumption.

Moreover, the socio-economic features of Third World countries were not sufficiently taken into account in the formulation of the theory and practice of Soviet aid. These features were, above all, the inflexibility of traditional structures, unemployment—the magnitude of which was unparalleled in the industrialization of other countries—and a deep imbalance between industry and agriculture.

In the national planning process of the developing countries, basic investments were directed not to the entire industrial sector, with its complex structure of various types of production, but predominantly to the most modern branches of industry. Consequently, aid was likewise oriented toward these branches and toward large-scale projects that did not always have firm intra-industrial linkages and could not promote the integration of the internal market. This resulted in a considerable gap between industry and other sectors of the economy—especially agriculture.

We emphasize that the stimulus of a modern industrial sector, toward which Soviet aid was directed, introduced a certain dynamism in the development of Third World countries and proved the feasibility of the rapid assimilation of new products and of drawing local resources and national cadres into production. Large-scale development programs, especially in infrastructure and new industrial investment, raised the need for producer goods, means of transport, and special types of equipment. These types of products predominated in the structure of Soviet exports to most developing countries.

This orientation at the same time skewed the direction of large-scale industrial construction in ways that were not always justified from the standpoint of the demand of the internal market and potential for the sale of new products. A number of industrial construction projects were of a prestigious nature and demanded unjustified expenditures of resources. Economic effectiveness and feasibility occasionally yielded to political considerations and the pressure of various local groups in the developing countries. When Soviet foreign economic organizations encountered such phenomena, they did not always succeed in developing an appropriate approach combining economic and political principles.

The need for a closer interrelationship in the development of agriculture and industry, for their balanced development, and for a certain orientation of industry toward the needs of agriculture became obvious by the early 1970s. The prominent Soviet specialist on problems of industrial development of Third World countries, G. Shirokov, has noted that: "the elimination of the food shortage and the improvement of the supply of food to the population and of the supply of raw materials to industry in the present stage are also impossible without the substantial modernization of agriculture."[6]

Even though there has been some improvement in the growth of the absolute volume of aid to agriculture and to agro-industry, its share in the overall volume of economic and technical cooperation of the U.S.S.R. with the developing countries remains low—on the order of 5 per cent in the mid-1980s.[7] It must be noted, however, that the share of branches of the agro-industrial complex is higher (25–30 per cent) in economic and technical cooperation with many specific countries, especially those with a socialist orientation.[8]

The question of the relative shares of intensive and extensive factors in the formation of the industrial base in Third World countries—given the presence of traditional agriculture—was posed from a new angle in the 1970s. In our view, the development of industry on the basis of modern advances in science and technology does not preclude the simultaneous and prolonged existence of traditional industrial production that is extensive in nature and makes possible the use of unskilled labor and local resources on a large/larger scale. Governments of a number of developing countries are trying to use small-scale industry to slow down the rate of urbanization and to normalize production relations between industry and agriculture. This is also connected with deliveries of implements to the agricultural sector by small enterprises, and with the local processing of agricultural products. "The relative simplicity of the organization of small-scale industrial production creates a base for the partial resolution of the employment problem and for increasing commodity output in the face of limited capital expenditures."[9]

The influence of such a global phenomenon as scientific-technological progress on Third World development has been more clearly apparent since the 1970s. Its connection with industrial development has also been emphasized by A. I. Elianov: "The manifold increase in the industrial and thereby the general economic and technological potential is, in addition to everything else, an indispensable condition for the broader and more effective enjoyment of the achievements of the modern scientific-technological revolution by the developing countries."[10]

In recent years, there has been a serious re-examination of a number of concepts of development in Soviet research literature. The idea of closing the development gap—based on a certain degree of equating the development of Third World countries with models of the industrial West—proved to be a failure. Nor did the concepts of "alternative" development that replaced them correspond to the conditions that had formed in these countries. These concepts of course do contain useful points that could be used to develop new directions in the strategy of development more in keeping with rapidly changing conditions in both the world economy and national economies.

It appears that the increased influence of scientific-technological progress on the developing countries will intensify the need to search for alternative avenues of industrial growth—particularly in view of the ecological vulnerability of these countries. A new type of industrial progress, based on ecologically safer production facilities, will make the formulation of alternative variants of development an objective necessity.

Study of the relationship between economic growth and social progress cannot ignore all of the positive results that have been noted during more than three decades of the U.S.S.R.'s scientific-technological relations with developing countries. Soviet foreign economic organizations estimate that more than 80 per cent of all Soviet assistance to these countries goes to industry (together with power generation), including geological prospecting, and to the training of personnel for national industry.[11] Its distinguishing feature is the concentration of efforts on the most important projects in those branches of industry that are essential for the deepening and diversification of production relations in the national economy of new countries.

The early 1980s brought a noticeable deterioration of the economic plight of the developing countries under the influence of structural changes in the world capitalist economy and the mounting burden of debt. A number of completed industrial projects failed to produce the economic effect that was expected of them. The developing countries are adapting to structural changes in the world economy slowly and at great cost. They urgently require technical modernization of their economies, flexible economic mechanisms, new technologies, and more competitive industrial products in order to strengthen their position in the international division of labor.

The Soviet Union is encountering these new problems and difficulties that confront the developing countries in the process of formulating its concepts and programs of development cooperation, and its own new model of foreign economic relations opens up considerable prospects for the solution of these problems.

## The Choice Between Import Substitution and Export-Led Development

Within the framework of the strategy of development of Third World countries, the question of the limits to external influence on their economic growth is a source of constant debate. The choices between self-reliance and export promotion must, of course, take into account the increasing differentiation of the developing countries and the specific internal and external conditions of their development. Nevertheless, the general trend is to give preference to the thesis of maximum utilization of the *internal* potential for economic development. Up to the late 1970s, the dominant view among Soviet specialists was that the model of development of the U.S.S.R. and other socialist countries was widely applicable to the Third World. The negative, exploitative character of the entire complex of economic relations between the periphery and the center of the world capitalist economy was rigidly postulated.

In recent years, Soviet researchers, like specialists in other countries, have been more and more inclined to favor integrated strategies that combine the use of internal and external measures. It can be expected that this direction of economic thought, generated by the need to assess the outlook for opening up the Soviet economy, will grow stronger and will in the future influence recommendations on the strategy of cooperation with the developing countries. Scientific analysis of internationalization and transnationalization within the framework of the world capitalist economy—especially the study of the influence of imports of capital and technology to the developing countries and exports of industrial goods from them— also has a dual role in that it helps Soviet scholars to understand their own economy better as well as to put forward more updated aid recommendations.

In the late 1970s—after theorists had already broached the idea of *combining* export promotion with import-substitution—there was a slight shift in the U.S.S.R.'s economic aid to the developing countries toward export-oriented production. Import-substitution, however, continues to be the main approach in Soviet assistance. Experience shows that the concentration of aid projects in the basic import-substitution branches frequently has been justified in the long haul. It has made it possible to lay the foundation for various industrial sectors, including those oriented toward export, by providing domestic production with intermediate goods and equipment. The basic branches of industry are the very ones that make it possible to accelerate economic integration. They promote improvements in the balance of payments not by generating exports, but by limiting the need for essential imports of industrial inputs. Clearly such an approach can only be effective where the products of newly created import-substituting production facilities find a large market and do not encounter obstacles in the form of shortages of raw materials, spare parts, and skilled labor.

In this sense, the experience of assisting the developing countries in building power-generating facilities has been successful. Thanks to the energy systems built with the aid of the Soviet Union, developing countries have succeeded in substantially increasing their energy capacities, thereby avoiding the importation of energy resources; this was chiefly the case with energy systems that use hydro-power and other local sources. Other areas of Soviet aid for import-substituting sectors of industry that are presently recognized to have been effective are assistance in heavy machine building and ferrous metallurgy in large Asian countries. Aid to different developing countries in the traditional import-substituting branches (textiles and food) also continues to be considered useful.

Soviet aid practice is presently striving to use the results of scientific research to take into account the necessity for integrated development—for combining export promotion with import-substitution. The basic approach is to introduce more flexibility in directing aid to certain industrial sectors in countries whose economic growth depends heavily on the effective use of external factors while not diminishing attention to the basic sectors. Most common in this area are non-traditional forms of aid, including the repayment of credit by compensatory deliveries while orienting the output of enterprises toward the Soviet Union's needs. The organization of production facilities in developing countries that export their products to the U.S.S.R. may become the optimal way of securing their sales markets, and it may be an effective way to promote industrialization as well as resolve the balance-of-payments problem in Third World countries.

# The Soviet Union's New Model of External Economic Relations and Economic Aid to Developing Countries

The economic restructuring that was launched in the Soviet Union in the second half of the 1980s is also exerting a major influence on relations with developing countries. The internal radical reform of the economic mechanism is supplemented by the restructuring of the system of foreign economic relations. Relations with developing countries are first of all affected by the management changes augured by the structural reorganization of departments responsible for external relations, including the creation of the State Foreign Economic Commission of the U.S.S.R. Council of Ministers; by the merger of the State Committee for Foreign Economic Relations and the Ministry of Foreign Trade (MFT) into the Ministry of Foreign Economic Relations; and by the transfer of some branch foreign trade firms from the MFT to the appropriate ministries, which made those firms relatively independent from the central government.

Beyond that, the new economic independence of industrial associations and enterprises, which now operate on the basis of the principle of self-financing and have quite broad decisionmaking opportunities, is a matter of no little importance for their relations with developing countries. Moreover, since April 1989, ministries, associations, and enterprises have had the right to enter the foreign market on their own—to devise their own foreign economic strategy, and to enter into a variety of transactions with foreign partners. Simultaneously, steps were also taken to legislate interesting new forms of foreign economic relations—international cooperation of producers and joint ventures. Industrial enterprises are also able to undertake quite varied independent foreign economic activity.

These changes have not yet been fully determined, but their consequences for the general pattern of the U.S.S.R.'s relations with developing countries and aid to them clearly will be significant. The policy of opening up the Soviet economy and increasing the level of activity of foreign economic relations also points to steps to establish a new system of economic relations with developing countries. Under the new conditions of management and the foreign economic independence of ministries and enterprises, a broad system of commodity exchange between the Soviet Union and these countries can be created on the basis of production specialization that takes into account the comparative advantage of individual partner nations. It is important to emphasize that, despite the chiefly non-concessional, commercial nature of such economic relations (or relations that are only partially based on concessional aid), such transfers can, in the opinion of Soviet economists, provide direct support for the economic development of Third World countries. Without them, the developing countries' foreign economic problems are likely to intensify considerably in the next few years in light of the widening gap in technological levels between the center and the periphery of the world capitalist economy.

Thus, the restructuring of the Soviet Union's system of foreign economic relations is improving the prospects for shaping the U.S.S.R.'s division of labor with the developing countries in ways that would permit all participants in exchange to increase the efficiency both of production proper and of economic relations between them. Although such intensification of the division of labor would be based primarily not on economic aid, but on commercial relations, the Soviet Union views the new prospects as an important supplement to aid as such. The sale of the products of the most modern as well as the traditional branches of industry and agriculture of Third World countries (within the framework of intensifying the international division of labor) could make an appreciable contribution not only to increasing the inflow of foreign currency receipts, but also to the technological reform of specific sectors, to increasing labor productivity, and to lowering production costs. An important aspect of such an approach is that it also allows more flexibility in the selection of sectors and projects for direct aid.

As noted above, the Soviet Union's new system of foreign economic relations encourages predominantly non-concessional relations with foreign countries. At the same time, the U.S.S.R. does not yet propose to curtail the volume of concessional aid to the developing countries, and it unconditionally adheres to the necessity of fulfilling its aid obligations. Therefore the new ministry and Gosplan face the task of coordinating production enterprise targets for fulfilling orders for concessional aid to the developing countries with the principles of self-financing. This will probably require supplementing the existing system of state orders with an intermediate foreign trade credit link that will, incidentally, also undergo restructuring and will acquire new functions with the creation of the U.S.S.R. Foreign Economic Bank.[12]

At a later stage, and gradually, Soviet aid policy will have to be fully reassessed. The volume of resources allocated for aid purposes may eventually decrease if the purposes themselves undergo revision in accordance with the principles of the new political thinking. For the present, the essential principles are:

(1) De-ideologization of international relations; and

(2) Recognition of the Soviet Union's share of responsibility for *global* development.

The first of these two principles may influence aid policy through changes in the range of recipient countries. It is a well-known fact that about three-quarters of Soviet concessional resources goes to Cuba, Mongolia, and Vietnam; even the least-developed recipient countries have always been chosen on the basis of their adherence to socialist ideology. This practice is likely to be abolished.

Each of the three major recipients is of course a special case, but the Cuban example is to the point: it seems impossible to justify the fact that huge resources have been flowing to that country with a very low degree of effectiveness for the Cuban economy and with tangible harm to Soviet-U.S. relations. Moreover, the main component of Soviet aid to that country—trade subsidies making the prices of Cuban exports to the U.S.S.R. several times higher than they should be (compared to the world of market prices)—will have to be rejected if the U.S.S.R. is going to respect the trade rules operative under the General Agreement on Tariffs and Trade (GATT).

The Soviet Union will also need to restructure the distribution of aid resources in accordance with the second of the above-listed principles. The very fact of participation in the resolution of global problems means that the outflow of concessional capital from the country can diminish but cannot be terminated. Most likely, the purposes of aid will be changed—by cutting out ideologically based aid, but preserving, for instance, aid in support of humanitarian needs and purely economic growth to the least developed countries. Aid will definitely be provided for the reconstruction of Afghanistan's economy. Membership in United Nations institutions, where the Soviet Union intends to intensify its role, will also lead to a continuation of the U.S.S.R.'s donor function. The essential changes will be in the geographical distribution of aid—since aid will be freed of its ideological rationale.

It also should be emphasized that the U.S.S.R.'s new political thinking means revision of many aspects of the Soviet understanding of the *developed* countries' policies toward the Third World. The focus now is not so much on exploitation as on *interdependence*. And this makes it only natural for the Soviet Union to join efforts with the West in assistance to developing countries.

These actual and likely changes in Soviet aid policies do not, however, narrow the prospects for economic relations with the Third World in general. They may lead to further shifts of emphasis from concessional to commercial relations, with the latter becoming even more prominent. To be more specific, the Soviet Union now needs the Third World countries in a new role—as a source of high-tech goods, as well as a source of increased supplies of natural resources and labor-intensive consumer goods. To realize this objective, however, the U.S.S.R. has to overcome a number of obstacles.

The main problem is how resources can be secured for such an expansion of *commercial* relations with developing countries, which have long been important for both the Soviet Union and the Third World and which have become an important supplement to aid. Such relations are limited by the shortage of financial and material resources—a shortage that is becoming even more acute due to the restructuring of the Soviet Union's own economic mechanism. *Perestroika* stimulates the technological modernization of production. Consequently, enterprises that produce machinery and equipment are overloaded with orders from *Soviet* customers. The same modernization absorbs large amounts of financial resources; it becomes necessary to increase imports of investment goods from the developed capitalist countries, i.e., to pay in hard currency, which can be obtained only by increasing exports to *developed* countries.

The new model of the U.S.S.R.'s foreign economic relations has barely been introduced. It has not yet even passed through a "test" period. But the new principles inherent in it open up broad possibilities for strengthening cooperation with the developing countries. More active participation in world economic affairs is in the interest of both the Soviet Union and the development of the world economy. Soviet researchers place great hopes on the entry of the U.S.S.R. into international economic organizations: the International Monetary Fund, the World Bank, and the GATT. This would obviously make it possible to raise the discussion of aid to the Third World to a new level and to press it in the direction of practical and general solutions.

# Notes

[1]In the area of cooperation, there are probably differences in scientific concepts, official strategy, and actual practice in all countries of the world. In the Soviet Union, these discrepancies in the past have been particularly pronounced in the gap between propagandistic slogans of the nation's leadership on the one hand, and the real life and work of scientific and practical organizations on the other.

[2]G. K. Shirokov, *Promyshlennaia revolutsiia v stranakh Vostoka [The Industrial Revolution in Eastern Countries]* (Moscow: Nauka, 1981), p. 186.

[3]See, for example, S. A. Bessonov, *Natsional'nyye plany i ekonomicheskoe razvitie stran Afriki [National Plans and the Economic Development of African Countries]* (Moscow: Nauka, 1975).

[4]Experience indicates that the state sector made structural change through massive capital investments in modern branches of heavy industry. In the opinion of A. E. Granovskii, this created conditions for the autonomous development of the state sector, which could not, however, occur in isolation from the private sector. See A. E. Granovskii, *Nakoplenie i ekonomicheskii rost v Indii [Accumulation and Economic Growth in India]* (Moscow: Nauka, 1988), p. 251.

[5]See N. P. Shmelev, *Problemy ekonomicheskogo rosta razvivaiushchikhsia stran [Problems in the Economic Growth of the Developing Countries]* (Moscow: Nauka, 1970), p. 44.

[6]G. K. Shirokov, *Razvivaiushchiesia strany v mirovom kapitalisticheskom khoziaistve [The Developing Countries in the World Capitalist Economy]* (Moscow: Nauka, 1987), p. 120.

[7]*Delovoe sotrudnichestvo v interesakh mira i progressa [Business Cooperation in the Interests of Peace and Progress]* (Moscow, 1984), p. 191.

[8]*Razvivaiushchiesia strany vo vsemirnom khoziaistve [The Developing Countries in the World Economy]* (Moscow: Nauka, 1987), p. 159.

[9]E. A. Bragina, *Razvivaiushchiesia strany: gosudarstvennaia politika i promyshlennost' [The Developing Countries: State Policy and Industry]* (Moscow: Mysl', 1977), p. 173.

[10]A. I. Elianov, *Razvivaiushchiesia strany: problemy ekonomicheskogo rosta i rynok [The Developing Countries: Economic Growth Problems and the Market]* (Moscow: Mysl', 1976), p. 206.

[11]*Postroeno pri ekonomicheskom i tekhnicheskom sodeistvii Sovetskogo Soiuza [Built With the Economic and Technical Assistance of the Soviet Union]* (Moscow: Mezhdunarodniye otnosheniia, 1982), p. 145.

[12]This bank was created on the basis of the Foreign Trade Bank for the purpose of providing credit for all types of foreign economic activity of Soviet and foreign producers and trade enterprises in foreign currency, in transferable rubles (the unit of the Council for Mutual Economic Assistance), and in clearing-account currencies.

# Recent Trends and Issues in Development Strategies and Development Assistance

Elliot Berg

Systematic thinking about Third World development is relatively new, as are aid organizations and the accompanying community of practitioners. In most Western graduate faculties, "development economics" was not a recognized field of study until the 1960s, when the main flowering of bilateral, and even multilateral, development organizations also occurred. In 1960, the United States was responsible for over 60 per cent of worldwide official development assistance, while the World Bank was hardly active at all in the least developed countries.

During this less than half a century of development assistance, ideas about why countries are poor and about how to make them richer have changed frequently. In the 1950s and 1960s, academic writing stressed technological change and capital investment as strategic factors in economic growth. In the 1970s, poverty reduction and income distribution moved to center stage. And the 1980s have been marked by concentration on the importance of a more market-oriented economic policy environment. Aid agencies are often said to have followed these ideas in their lending programs—from technical assistance and capital transfers for infrastructure projects in the early days, to rural development and basic needs in the 1970s, to policy-based lending in the 1980s.

This neat progression of ideas and activities, with its implication of periodic consensus, is of course a great oversimplification. Even within development's mainstream, there has always been disa-

greement. And development theory has always had a lively frater-
nity of dissenters—an underground of institutionalists, dependency
theorists, and "de-linkers," as well as a parallel mainstream of
Marxist or neo-Marxist schools of various persuasions. Aid agencies
similarly have never been quite as susceptible to fads as they seem.
Policy reform was important in U.S. aid efforts in Latin America
and Asia in the 1960s; poverty-focused projects are not an invention
of the 1970s; and project aid in general has not disappeared, despite
the swing to policy-based lending in the 1980s.

The perception that there has been a linear evolution of ideas
about development strategy and action does, nonetheless, reflect real
tendencies. Income distribution and equity issues *were* more actively
debated in the 1970s than before or since, and there is no doubt that
the role of policy and the spread of policy-based lending have been
dominant features in the 1980s.

The new emphasis on policy and its embodiment in policy-
based lending represents in several respects an important break
with the past. It first of all reflects a theoretical shift, by increasing
the relative weight given to economic policy in explaining economic
growth. Second, it erodes some of the traditional rationale for foreign
assistance and presents new organizational challenges to aid agencies. Finally, it is strategy-specific; it is not policy reform in some
abstract sense that has been at issue in the 1980s, but *market-oriented* reform. Foreign assistance via policy loans is thus heavier in ideological and political overtones, and at the same time more dependent
on substantive policy consensus, than is project-focused assistance.

Some implications of these changes are explored in this chapter, which, after a brief survey of overall U.S. aid policies and programs, discusses some of the main factors behind the rise of policy-
based lending and its associated emphasis on market-oriented development strategies: the changed intellectual climate of the past
decade, the need for quick-disbursing budget and balance-of-payments support, and the need to find new sources of economic growth
in stagnant economies. The chapter concludes with an analysis of
some basic problems that the shift to policy-based lending has created for foreign assistance agencies and the foreign aid process.

Economic aid for development purposes is thus the main concern of this paper, the interplay between development aid and development strategies its central theme, and policy-based lending its
principal focus. Development aid, however, is only one element in the
much larger picture of U.S. economic relations with developing countries. Policy-based lending, moreover, is but one element in the
larger array of bilateral aid instruments and is, in fact, more the
instrument of multilateral financial institutions than of bilateral

donors. To place the analysis of development aid and strategies in an appropriate context, it is necessary to say a little about overall U.S. aid policies and programs.

## U.S. Economic Assistance: An Overview

The United States, like all industrial states, has a complex set of relationships—cultural, political, military, trade, investment, aid, and other—with the developing countries. Many of these interactions involve transfers of resources. By convention, however, we call only some of these transfers "economic assistance." U.S. universities, for example, subsidize foreign students to the tune of about $1.5 billion a year, according to one recent estimate.[1] This is so because university tuition in the United States is subsidized for all students, in that fees do not cover costs. This subsidized education for about 300,000 developing-country students is, however, not counted as "economic assistance." Nor is the $10 billion (including contributions to churches) that non-university, private voluntary agencies spend in developing countries.[2]

Foreign investment is also not counted as "assistance," nor is trade access. Where trade preferences are given, the value of the resulting subsidy to the recipient countries is often calculated, although it is not normally included in discussions of "foreign aid."

Many forms of valuable assistance for development are thus not included in the "formal" or conventional U.S. foreign assistance program. Moreover, the "formal" foreign assistance program has relatively little to do with aid for development. Table 1 gives the major components of the "formal" program between 1987 and 1990.

Of the $15 billion total in 1989, only $3.9 billion—the $2.4 billion in development assistance and the $1.5 billion allocated to multilateral institutions—is more or less unambiguously "development aid." The Economic Support Fund (ESF), which mainly provides balance-of-payments and budget support for political allies, is in principle a form of economic assistance (it cannot be used for military purposes), but much of it goes to countries that are not low-income: of $3.5 billion ESF in 1989, Israel received almost $1.3 billion; Egypt, $1.1 billion; and the countries where the United States maintains military bases (Philippines, Turkey, Portugal), about $1 billion.[3]

There is not much ambiguity about the military assistance component, which in 1988–90 accounted for some 37 per cent of all "formal" assistance. It is not "development aid." All resources are fungible, of course, and military assistance may in some circumstances substitute for local resources with positive effects on the

## Table 1.  U.S. Foreign Assistance, 1987–90, by Major Programs ($U.S. billions, constant 1989)

|  | FY1987 | FY1988 | FY1989 | FY1990 |
|---|---|---|---|---|
| Development Assistance | 2.4 | 2.5 | 2.4 | 2.3 |
| Economic Support Fund | 4.2 | 3.2 | 3.6 | 3.2 |
| Food Aid | 1.6 | 1.5 | 1.5 | 1.4 |
| Military Aid | 5.5 | 5.5 | 5.4 | 5.7 |
| Multilateral Assistance | 1.6 | 1.5 | 1.5 | 1.8 |
| Other Economic Aid | 0.7 | 0.6 | 0.7 | 0.9 |
| Total | 16.0 | 14.8 | 15.1 | 15.3 |

[a] Note: All figures represent obligations of U.S. assistance, unless otherwise noted.
[b] Estimate.
[c] President's request.

Source: U.S. House of Representatives, *Committee on Foreign Affairs, Report of the Task Force on Foreign Assistance*, February 1989 (The Hamilton-Gilman Report), p. 7.

local economy. But this is hardly assured, and other scenarios are at least as likely, so that aid to the military cannot be regarded as "development aid."

U.S. interests in the developing countries are multiple: economic, political-strategic, humanitarian, and cultural. The U.S. foreign assistance program reflects that multiplicity of interests. In recent years, as has happened periodically in the past, the foreign assistance program has become more heavily military and concentrated on a few strategically important countries. Of the $13 billion available for bilateral aid in 1989 ($15.1 billion minus $1.5 billion multilateral and $0.7 billion "other economic"), some 42 per cent was military. The country concentration is well known. Israel and Egypt alone received 47 per cent of all aid; Pakistan, Turkey, the Philippines, El Salvador, and Greece received another 32 per cent.[4]

Thus much of the formal U.S. foreign assistance program is not directly aimed at development; it is not "development aid" as considered in this chapter's later analysis. Moreover, one part of the U.S. program that is relevant to this analysis is not bilateral at all; it is the $1.5 billion that goes to multilateral institutions, mainly the World Bank.[5]

In the early 1960s, the World Bank's operations were one-quarter the size of those of the U.S. Agency for International Development (USAID). By 1988, World Bank commitments were four times those of USAID for development assistance and economic support. An increasing share of U.S. development aid now goes to international financial institutions. In 1970, the allocation for the multilateral banks was only 10 per cent of that for development assistance; in 1988, it was 80 per cent. With the encouragement of the United States and other bilateral donors, the World Bank has taken the lead in policy-based lending. This is partly because the Bank has the technical competence needed to formulate, negotiate, and monitor policy-based assistance. The World Bank has 760 economist positions, while USAID has 92.[6] But more important is the political dimension. Bilateral donors, including the United States, have a limited desire or ability to impose conditions on assistance to close political friends and allies. It has been politically more acceptable for all parties to have the technocratic multilateral institutions assume this task.

Some bilateral donors—notably the United States and France—have nonetheless introduced policy-based lending. But one obvious contradiction limits the use of this kind of assistance: sanctions for failure to adopt reforms tend to be applied only in countries where political and other interests are insignificant.

The following discussion thus addresses only one corner of a large tapestry—the "development aid" portion of the formal foreign assistance programs. And the analysis of policy-based lending encompasses the World Bank's policies as well as those of the United States.

# Reasons for the Rise of Policy-Based Lending and Market-Oriented Development Strategies

### The Changed Intellectual Climate

The recent changes in thinking about development strategies and aid policies have their origins in the discrediting of three key ideas: that economic growth depends mainly on investment; that import substitution can be the major source of sustained growth; and that because of ubiquitous failures in private markets, governments (a) should take major responsibility for mobilizing, allocating, and managing resources, and (b) are capable of doing so.

*Capital Investment, the Policy Environment, and Growth.* Until quite recently, most development theories made capital investment the main motor of economic growth. Poor countries became richer by saving and investing bigger shares of their national income. Institutions mattered, of course, and policy was rarely completely ignored. But capital investment was at the center of the growth process, as was reflected in the dominance of investment-driven growth models (Harrod-Domar) in the theorizing about development, in planning, and in determining aid "needs."[7]

This set of ideas began to change in the 1970s for many reasons. First, observation at the macroeconomic level strongly indicated that investment was only part of the growth story. Observed capital-output ratios varied enormously between countries and over time within countries. In numerous cases, relatively high investment rates were associated with low growth. Many African countries, for example, had comparatively high investment rates of 20–25 per cent of gross domestic product (GDP) in the 1970s, yet experienced little or no growth in output.

The macro-level observations were matched by observations at the micro level. Development practitioners saw innumerable cases of misallocation of investment—of ill-considered project selection and design, faulty implementation, neglected maintenance, and inefficient operation of completed facilities. And in country after country, they saw investment projects that were not necessarily poorly conceived, but that were frustrated by the inadequacies of the policy environment. Integrated rural development projects were the classic example: the impact of new rural roads, health facilities, subsidized farm inputs and credit, and better information were often nullified by low prices to farmers and poor marketing arrangements, which discouraged increased production. These on-the-ground observations were reinforced by the findings of scholarly research into the sources of growth in the industrialized world. Studies by E. P. Denison, Simon Kuznets, and others concluded that the contribution of investment to growth is not nearly as substantial as was usually assumed in the Harrod-Domar and similar models; according to their results, investment accounted for not more than 20–25 per cent of growth.[8]

All of this led, beginning in the late 1970s, to a stronger emphasis on the importance of policy. It has also led to intense debate about the relative weight to be given to policy factors in explaining economic performance, especially with respect to Africa. But while developing-country governments have little control over external factors uncongenial to growth, they can do something about reforming growth-retarding domestic policies. Along with the slowing down of world economic growth and the debt problem, this has given policy reform a new urgency and a much higher priority in the lending programs of development institutions.

***The Deficiencies of Import-Substitution.*** The intellectual pioneers of development economics were almost all skeptical about the feasibility and desirability of export-led growth.[9] The reasons for their skepticism are familiar:

- Developed-country markets grow too slowly to absorb developing-country exports at a rate sufficient to generate an acceptable pace of GDP growth.
- Protectionism in the developed countries makes market penetration too difficult and risky—even if income grows rapidly in the developed countries.
- Price elasticities for developing-country commodity exports are so low that increases in export volumes will in many cases risk reducing aggregate export earnings.
- Technological change works systematically against primary product producers—by spurring greater efficiency in raw material usage and by generating a growing supply of synthetics.

The intellectual attack on export-led growth strategies included other, perhaps less well known, arguments. Support for the protection of domestic industry in backward economies rested on many ideas, one of which was central in the literature of the 1950s and 1960s: that "surplus labor," or "disguised unemployment," was widely prevalent in developing countries, and that this justified many employment-generating industrial investments with economic rates of return that were dubious if based on market prices. Also, international trade was frequently seen as a zero-sum game, with the developed countries getting most or all of the gains from trade with developing countries. And the multitude of "dependency" theorists in the 1960s added their ideas and voices to the criticism of outward-looking growth.

Given this intellectual background, it is not surprising that import-substituting industrialization was the centerpiece of development strategies in the 1950s and 1960s. However, it was not ideas alone that pushed developing-country governments along the path of import substitution. Much of it was unplanned; it took place in response to periodic or persistent balance-of-payments crises. Also, it was not universal. Many economies—in Africa, the Caribbean, and Central America, for example—were too small and too dependent on imported inputs to go very far down that road. Nonetheless, import substitution was for over two decades the strategy of choice for many countries, particularly (but not only) in Latin America.

Whatever the theoretical appeal of such strategies, it was

apparent by the mid-1970s that *in practice*, import-substitution industrialization had grave deficiencies:

- High protection of domestic industries nurtured high-cost, inefficient industries. The guaranteeing of domestic markets and the stifling of competition tended to produce an inward-looking, dependent, inflexible industrial structure. Infant industries seemed rarely to mature, except in a few economies.

- Much of the import substitution that occurred was unplanned or poorly planned. Low-priority lines of production or nonessentials were often given relatively high effective protection. Considerations of comparative advantage received insufficient attention.

- Dependence on imports was not much reduced; only import composition changed. Dependence on inputs replaced dependence on finished goods. Import substitution led many economies to become more, not less, vulnerable to external shocks. Reduced capacity to import hit the economy harder than before.

- Import-substituting industrialization was in conflict with agriculture. The overvalued exchange rates associated with the strategy penalized the agricultural sector—the main source of exports in most developing countries. Farmers also suffered from inadequate supplies, higher prices, and lower qualities of agricultural inputs and consumer goods.

- The weak export performance induced at least in part by the priority given to import substitution led to administered allocation of foreign exchange, the growth of parallel markets, and widespread smuggling, with far-reaching macroeconomic consequences.

- Outward-looking economies in general seemed to have responded better to the crises of the 1970s. This is, of course, most evident in comparing East Asia with Latin America. But it is true also in Africa that those countries with good export performance (Kenya, Botswana, Ivory Coast, and Cameroon, for example) have tended to do well in other respects—GDP growth and evenness in income distribution, for example.[10]

The revealed failures of import-substitution strategies, coupled with the fact that such an orientation was never really feasible for small economies (such as most of those in Africa), account for the new emphasis on export promotion and the liberalization of import regimes in economic reform programs. Export promotion does not normally mean actively favoring exports; at a minimum, it means simply removing existing policy biases against exports. And export promotion has not always been associated with the liberalization of import regimes. A number of economies made a successful transition from import substitution to export promotion without reducing protective barriers (Taiwan and South Korea, for example). Import liberalization in any case does not mean removal of all protection for domestic industry, but rather a lower level and more rational structure of protection.

Most of the development community continues to be unconvinced about the generalizability and desirability of export-led growth and the associated liberalization of import regimes that would open up developing-country industrial sectors to external competition. It is only because the alternatives have proved so unpromising that the outward-oriented approach has won the measure of acceptance it enjoys. And the most ardent liberalizers allow that much scope exists for efficient import substitution.

*Public-Sector Failures*. Just as the intellectual climate between 1950 and the 1970s was generally negative about the potential of export-led growth and positive about import substitution, so too was it hostile to the view that market forces could be relied upon to generate rapid income growth and real "development." The state, almost everybody concluded, had to step in to correct the many failures and distortions of private markets:

- Entrepreneurs are often lacking, and markets for land, labor, and capital are highly imperfect.
- External market prices are often distorted by imperfections in world commodity markets.
- Indigenous private investors cannot mobilize enough capital to realize economies of scale, and it is socially and politically unacceptable to allow foreign capital to dominate basic industry.
- Income distribution is highly unequal in many developing-country economies, which results in market prices that give socially questionable demand signals.
- Unfettered free market growth leads to greater income inequality, given the unequal bargaining power between trader and farmer, employer and worker, rich and poor.

These ideas contributed to the growth in the role of the state after 1950, and especially after 1960. The share of government expenditure in GDP rose dramatically; in 1972, the International Monetary Fund (IMF) Yearbook recorded only 13 countries where central government expenditure was more than 30 per cent of GDP. By 1979 there were 39 such countries. The role of the state in directly productive activities also grew enormously during this period. In a sample of 24 developing countries in the early 1980s, state-owned enterprises accounted for 10 per cent of production and 30 per cent of investment. In countries as disparate as Brazil, Tanzania, Mexico, and the Ivory Coast, the number of state-owned enterprises multiplied by a factor of three or more between 1960 and 1980.[11]

And finally, state controls and policy interventions spread as regulatory systems became more dense, price controls flowered, and administered prices became much more common.

By the end of the 1970s, experience had made clear the many limitations and deficiencies in state economic interventions. Many developing-country public expenditure systems showed similar characteristics:

- Poor project-selection procedures, resulting in investment programs containing high proportions of low-priority, low-productivity projects;
- Higher priority given to spending for new public employment and salaries in general than for maintenance and operating costs, which condemned schools, hospitals, roads, factories to low-capacity, low-efficiency operation and/or quick deterioration; and
- Inadequate systems of expenditure control.

State-owned enterprises, once the hoped-for leading edge of development, most often proved to be costly burdens. Instead of generating surpluses for reinvestment and growth, they frequently became drains on budget and credit resources. There were and are, of course, many exceptions, especially in the middle-income and newly industrialized countries. Korean Steel and Singapore Airlines are state-owned enterprises, and many state enterprises in Brazil, Chile, and India are highly efficient. The poor financial performance of many others in the world, moreover, often resulted in part from the fact that they were also expected to help achieve desirable social objectives. Nonetheless, the performance of state enterprise sectors in most developing countries was far below earlier expectations. While they would continue to play a major role in the developing world, it was clear that reforms were essential in a great many countries.

The shortcomings of the endemic systems of economic regulation were also more in evidence by the late 1970s. Regulation and subsidy systems created to protect poorer consumers of food, fuel, health, education, and other goods and services often ended up in fact helping better-off people more, and they frequently absorbed large shares of available public resources. Regulations that were intended to protect vulnerable producers (guaranteed producer prices, single-channel marketing) often created, instead, state monopolies—with associated bureaucratic neglect or exploitation, illegal parallel markets, repressive controls over movement of food grains, rent-seeking and corruption, as well as higher and more variable food prices for consumers in least favored areas.

All of this led to a general awareness of the existence of "public-sector failures" equivalent to the private-market failures that for so long held the stage alone. It is extraordinary how asymmetrical the pre-1980s literature was—the failures of private markets were assumed to be general, while the failures of government were not considered worthy of attention. The unspoken assumption in this literature is that governments had the administrative capacity to do the many tasks that private actors failed to do. Accumulated experience has made it abundantly clear that many governments, particularly in the poorer, least developed regions, lack the capacity to perform the tasks urged on them by so many of the earlier theorists of development.

The days of blithe assumptions about state capacity to remedy private market failures are over. Development strategists now move, or should move, in a world more explicitly imperfect, where actions to overcome the inadequacies of private sectors and private markets have to be weighed against the limits of the government's capacity to act, limits that are most severe precisely where private markets function least well: in the poorest countries.

This more balanced vision, the result of thirty years of experience, explains why virtually all developing countries—like almost all developed countries—in the 1980s moved toward a greater reliance on private sectors and market-oriented policies. There are few developing countries where the following elements are not part of the policy reform agenda:

- Creation of a better environment—legal, administrative, political—for private investment.
- Deregulation and demonopolization, especially in the delivery of services.
- Rationalization of the state enterprise sector—rehabilitating strategic enterprises, selling or liquidating non-strategic ones,

and creating better incentives and a better mix of freedom and control for public enterprise managers.

- Rationalization of the foreign trade regime—creating lower, more uniform tariffs; removing price and institutional obstacles to exports; moving toward the creation of more competitive markets by liberalizing the import regime.

- Reduction in and better targeting of subsidies, and increased user fees in areas such as higher education and curative medical care.

## The Need for Quick-Disbursing Assistance

Policy-based lending was also introduced in the early 1980s (the World Bank's first structural adjustment loan dates from 1980) as a response to developments in the international economic environment that were harmful to developing countries. Higher oil prices, the slowdown of industrial economies, high rates of developed-country inflation and hence high import prices for developing countries, high interest rates, growing debt burdens, deteriorating terms of trade, and growing current-account deficits were creating severe balance-of-payments crises in the developing world. Quick-disbursing loans and credits were needed to reduce growth-inhibiting cutbacks in developing-country imports, and cash transfers or commodity programs that did not require the preparation of formal "projects," such as non-project policy loans, were more suitable for this purpose. Project loans for roads, factories, dams, educational improvements, etc., usually require lengthy preparation; inputs have to be defined, specific sites classified, project staff hired, etc. This almost always takes a long time.

Non-project lending was also aimed at another problem. In many developing countries, existing social and physical infrastructure was menaced by inadequate spending on running costs—a phenomenon exacerbated by declining public-sector revenues. It made little sense to provide capital assistance for new projects while completed facilities were underutilized.

These problems and the arguments for quick-disbursing balance-of-payments and budget support became more urgent as the decade unfolded and became a major rationale for shifting from project to non-project forms of aid. But non-project aid cannot be given without regard for the policy environment of the recipient country; to ignore policy issues would be to allow countries to postpone adjustment to changed external conditions or lead to disequilibria caused by inappropriate domestic policies.

## The Need for New Sources of Growth

The general slowdown of world economic growth after 1980, depressed commodity prices, reduced real resource transfers, and heavy debt burdens all led to slower developing-country growth. They also led to falling real public-sector revenues, fewer resources for development spending, and less opportunity to raise revenues by raising taxes. At the same time, demands were more intense on the public purse to finance newly built schools, hospitals, and roads; to subsidize the expanded state enterprise sectors; and to hire the growing numbers of graduates, as had become customary in many countries.

In Sub-Saharan Africa and much of Latin America, slow growth and recognition of the inadequacy of old solutions bred a willingness to entertain new strategies. But governments were also responsive to market-oriented policy ideas for positive reasons. Many political leaders and intellectuals recognized that private money, skills, and energies were a neglected but potentially potent source of new growth and dynamism.

Market-oriented policy changes can lead to faster output growth and more responsive economic structures in numerous ways. First, they can increase the volume of resources available for investment and services by reducing capital flight and attracting new foreign capital; by encouraging greater use of small-scale technologies that use little capital and few educated people (in transport and trade, notably); by inducing people to work harder and more fully drawing out energies that are underutilized or devoted, less than optimally, to the underground economy; and by attracting new financing for services and new suppliers of these services through higher user fees and the elimination of regulations that discourage private supply response. Second, not only are new resources generated in these ways, but resources (existing and new) will tend to be better used because of the greater focus on priority tasks in the public sector, greater competition from the private sector, reduced demand pressures on public-sector providers of goods and services, and productivity-raising competitive pressures, including those that derive from greater import competition. Third, internal specialization and trade are encouraged, with productivity-raising effects, by the removal of regulations, such as those aimed at regional self-sufficiency, and by new reliance on pricing systems that are based on costs. Finally, market-oriented policy reforms, and the more active private sector they promote, encourage the development of entrepreneurial capacities. In the poorest countries, where lack of entrepreneurship is often cited as a critical constraint to faster growth, reform-induced private-sector opportunities provide an indispensable training ground for entrepreneurs.

For all these reasons, growth rates are likely to rise and economies to become more flexible and dynamic when market-oriented reforms are introduced into systems needing reform—i.e., those characterized by extensive administrative regulation of the economy, legally created monopolies and monopsonies, high protection against competition from imports and other policy biases against exports, and extensive direct state participation in non-strategic, directly productive activities.

# Policy-Based Lending and the Aid Process: Some Problems

Policy-based lending gives rise to numerous new issues and problems, analytic as well as organizational. It challenges some of the traditional rationale for foreign assistance and forces aid agencies to change the way they do business. It exacerbates inconsistencies in the objectives of aid-giving states. It induces closer coordination within the donor community. And it poses with new urgency the conditionality question: how to assure that the resources transferred by policy-based lending lead to real "adjustment," and not simply to financing existing disequilibria.

### The Need for New Rationales and Organizational Responses

In the "traditional" intellectual and organizational world of development aid (before policy-based lending), there existed a nice harmony between thought and action. Poor countries had low savings rates, and, hence, low domestic capacity to invest. The main constraints to growth were shortage of capital and inadequate access to technology. The main economic rationale for foreign assistance and the chief business of aid organizations was therefore to supplement local savings, notably by financing the foreign-exchange costs of suitable investment projects. The policy environment was not ignored. Indeed, in some cases, it was at the center of the aid effort, as in the U.S. Alliance for Progress program in Latin America in the 1960s, and in South Asia during the same period. But generally speaking, policy concerns were muted.

"Traditional" aid thus defined operated in an analytic framework that provided an intellectual rationale for the aid relationship and practical guidelines for aid agencies. Since capital investment was the main motor of growth, simple economic models (e.g., variants of Harrod-Domar) were at hand to provide a macroeconomic framework for estimating needs, an "explanation" of how aid inflows affect output growth, and an instrument for measuring results.

At the microeconomic level, the centerpiece of "traditional" aid was (and is) the project, the elemental unit of development action—an activity with a beginning and an end, and with well-defined inputs and known costs and (usually) measurable outputs. From a project-centered perspective, each country is a locus of potential investments that either exist—i.e., are on the shelf already—or can be developed by proper preparation; only fiscal or foreign-exchange constraints prevent their execution. The function of economic assistance is then obvious: to release the binding constraint to faster growth, usually foreign-exchange availability, by financing the offshore costs of investment projects that meet the economic criteria of aid donors.

It is worth noting that "traditional" aid as discussed here refers to "development aid" only—resource transfers aimed directly at growth in income. The foreign assistance programs of the United States and most other aid-giving states have always had objectives other than economic growth, such as poverty alleviation and disaster relief. The analysis here is not relevant for these other aspects of the U.S. aid program.

This "traditional" approach, thus qualified, shaped the analytic tools that have dominated the development field since the 1950s. Because the project was the primary vehicle of development assistance, project evaluation became the best developed microeconomic instrument of the aid practitioner, just as investment-powered growth models absorbed most attention on the macroeconomic side.

Projects and capital investments were also the principal concerns of aid institutions. Within bilateral and multilateral aid institutions, the project was the backbone of the organization's structure. Project cycles regulated the flow of activity. The project focus also provided guidelines for basic management decisions, such as how much to lend (or grant) and for what purposes. Country allocations of course always depended on more than project considerations, but certainly the availability of "sound" projects was an important input in this decision, especially in the multilateral institutions. And although project "soundness" involved much more than determining an acceptable economic rate of return, the ideal of project soundness provided a conceptual anchor for aid organizations.

Policy-based lending lacks the kind of analytical scaffolding that surrounds "traditional" forms of resource transfer. On the organizational side, some of the implications are nonetheless clear. Aid agency demand for economists and for economic policy analysis has increased, both absolutely and relative to project staff and project-oriented activity. Since most of an aid organization's operational staff were non-economists who chiefly worked on projects while economists were preoccupied largely with general macroeconomic analyses, the shift to policy-based lending implied large-scale organizational adjustments. In the World Bank, these have occurred—although the relationship of its recent reorganization to the new needs of policy lending is not entirely clear. In USAID and in other bilateral agencies, economists and economic policy work are clearly more in evidence.

On the analytic side, what is called for are new rationales for that part of foreign assistance that is aimed at increasing growth rates and a stronger theory of policy reform. These are needed even to clarify everyday issues of foreign aid policy, such as how to determine which countries receive policy-based credits, how much they should receive, and how their performance should be evaluated. But now that the policy genie is out of the bottle, even more far-reaching questions arise, of which two are central. *First*, why do developing-country governments need aid money to change policies that are holding back their development? Why do they not simply adopt the reforms that experts tell them will both raise their current national output and their growth rate, thereby increasing the economic welfare of their people and brightening their future economic prospects? And how does aid money contribute to accelerating reform, which is after all the principal rationale for policy-based lending? *Second*, why does the availability of non-project aid money not simply allow governments to persist in the pursuit of policies and programs harmful to growth?

This second issue will be considered below, in the discussion of aid conditionality. With respect to the first, there is space here for only an outline of the issues.

There are, of course, many reasons why presumably beneficial policy and institutional reforms are not adopted.

*Vested interests stand to lose from proposed reforms,* and these people or groups are powerful enough to prevent their adoption. These vested interests can be of different kinds. The whole ruling class or ruling elite may be at issue; indeed, some of the classic writers on development adopt this position—Paul Baran, for example, and critics of the post-colonial elites, running from Franz Fanon to

René Dumont. Or sectional vested interests may be the principal source of obstruction: groups that enjoy special privileges (quasi-rents) under existing policies—for example, some civil servants, favored importers, or subsidized consumers. The presumption here is that no reform will automatically make everybody better off. It is further assumed that compensation of losers out of reform-induced income increases is either not desirable for "undeserving" losers or not easily accomplished for the deserving losers. Either way, the "reformers" are likely to generate opposition.

*Policymakers' preferences include other things besides economic growth.* At one end, this merges with the vested interest argument: Political elites may prefer the political (patronage) benefits accruing to them, in a system of direct administrative controls, over the alternative of reliance on more impersonal market processes that diminish their political influence. Ideological preferences could be included here; many governments do not wish to encourage the enlargement of the private economy, or fear policies that might make the distribution of income or assets more unequal. Others fear that the concentration of economic power in specific tribal or ethnic groups will follow deregulation, or that foreigners will become too powerful.

With respect to most policy issues that matter, *there is no intellectual consensus on either the nature of the problem at hand or the likely impact of given policy changes.* Put another way, most developing-country political authorities (and probably most developing-country technical people, including economists) do not agree with the views of, say, most World Bank or USAID economists on how markets and market institutions work in their countries, or on the likely impact of proposed reforms. This is especially true in key areas such as agricultural marketing, industrial policy, trade and exchange rate policies, and interest rate policy.

Another possible reason has to do with *time horizons; politicians in many developing countries do not have a long view, for various reasons, in many cases including the expected shortness of ministerial tenure.* Reforms may take too long to make the struggle for their adoption worthwhile—especially since the policymakers' enthusiasm for reform is often tepid, and they are often skeptical that results will be as positive as outside reform advocates claim.

How does aid money override these objections and obstacles to reform? Possible explanations are numerous. Policy-based loans can provide compensation, explicit or implicit, to soften the negative impacts of reform—e.g., by providing severance pay for discharged public employees, or by inducing additional support from donors.

Policy-based assistance also reinforces reform-minded individuals bureaucratically or politically.

These are plausible arguments, and there are others. But none of them is really solidly grounded in theory, and their empirical support is sketchy. The argument that policy-based lending strengthens national pro-reform forces, for example, can be easily, even plausibly, turned on its head: the position of local reformers can be easily undermined by their support of ideas and programs associated with the IMF or the World Bank. Moreover, analysis of precisely how aid money "lubricates" reform, how it overcomes the obstacles to change, is still sparse. It seems fair to conclude that the development community has only begun to elaborate a satisfactory rationale for foreign assistance based on policy reform—at least one that has the coherence of the rationale for "traditional" assistance, which was lighter on policy reform, project-centered, and focused mainly on the transfer of resources for investment and/or poverty alleviation.

### Donor Coordination

Policy-based lending creates a new need for donors to close ranks on policy conditions. This is part—a major part—of the reason for the proliferation of consultative groups, donor advisory bodies, and other coordination and information-sharing arrangements intended to assure that donors are fully informed of each others' programs and policy ideas. The hope is that donors will agree, for example, that only high-priority projects should be financed, or that if a lending agency such as the World Bank is pushing a specific reform (e.g., elimination of fertilizer subsidies), other donors will not adopt contradictory policies or programs.

These efforts at donor coordination have given rise to many difficulties, of which three stand out. First, it cannot be assumed that all donors have the same interests. In recent years especially, much assistance has been tied to trade credits. Dispassionate analysis might suggest that a purchase of diesel locomotives, buses, or sugar mills is not high enough in priority to be included in a public investment program. But commercial interests in the donor country may nonetheless triumph. This contradiction between donor commercial interests and the requirements of sound policy does give rise to some breaking of donor ranks, but such conflicts do not seem to be a severe or general problem, at least in the poorest countries, where policy lending is most prevalent.

More important in terms of difficulties are different perceptions of reality among donors. The Inter-American Development

Bank might finance an agricultural project that USAID or the World Bank judges to be uneconomic. This is not necessarily due to soft-headedness, bowing to political pressures, or poor project analysis; it is often because project evaluation is an art, not a science, and honest differences can exist about project "soundness."

Finally, donors differ among themselves on policy. At a high level of generality, agreement is relatively easy. Everybody favors "more efficient use of resources," an agricultural policy that provides "adequate incentives," or a "more competitive" industrial sector. But the more specific the policy issue, the greater the area of disagreement. The risk here is on the one hand that donor cacophony will confuse recipient countries, and on the other that donors will propose policies reflecting the lowest common policy denominator. There is also a danger that intra-donor dialogue becomes so urgent and so interesting that the participants talk too much to each other, forgetting the ultimate purpose of the exercise: working out *with host country authorities* appropriate solutions to the real problems of the host economy.

### The Conflicting Objectives of Bilateral Donor Policy

Richer countries provide economic assistance to poorer ones for many reasons: political, strategic, humanitarian, cultural, and/or historical, commercial. The allocation of bilateral foreign assistance reflects this mix of national objectives, as do all foreign economic policies. The bulk of U.S. and Soviet assistance goes to countries where each has strong political and strategic interests. Historic links, cultural factors, and commercial objectives are probably more important for France and Britain; humanitarian considerations dominate Nordic aid.

Whatever the mix of national interests being served by bilateral aid to developing countries, policy reform and policy-based lending complicate matters substantially. What is to be done when a country that is important for political or strategic purposes, or is the focus of humanitarian concerns, is unwilling to adopt suitable economic policy reforms? It is hard to envisage many cases where the policy reform objectives would not be toned down or abandoned altogether. This suggests, somewhat ironically, that only where a bilateral donor's political/strategic interests are not great is a hard line on policy reform viable. Since each bilateral donor tends to concentrate its aid in countries where its national interests—political/strategic or other—are greatest, this is a quite damaging general constraint on the effective use of bilateral policy-based lending.

### The Conditionality Dilemma

Policy-based loans or grants require some form of conditionality. Without it, governments can persist in the inappropriate fiscal, monetary, exchange-rate, and other policies that may be the source of their structural problems. In fact there is a strong likelihood that this will happen. An influx of balance-of-payments support, for example, buoys up the exchange rate, contributing to overvaluation. Similarly, budget support from donors removes some of the pressures to increase domestic savings rates by raising taxes. It also allows favored public expenditures of low economic or social priority to continue or expand.

The problem on the spending side is acute. For various reasons, strong propensities exist in most developing countries, but particularly in the least developed, to use public resources less than optimally from an economic efficiency perspective. This is so for several reasons. First, political leaders have many objectives besides economic growth: political stability, regional balance, social equity, indigenization of the economy, etc. They allocate resources accordingly. Their perceptions of spending priorities therefore differ substantially from those of lending agency staffs and managements.

Second, the public expenditure process is often weakly structured. Procedures, data, and manpower for investment project selection are inadequate. Many investment and other expenditure decisions are thus made with imperfect, sometimes nonexistent, analysis and evaluation. The results are operating budgets loaded with salary costs and little for government workers to work with, inadequate maintenance, and many low-priority or wasteful development projects. The unconditioned budget support provided by policy-based lending allows such spending to go forward.

Another factor leading to conditionality in policy loans is bureaucratic and political. The managers of aid agencies have to show their political constituencies that they are not simply throwing money away. After all, with old-fashioned project loans one bought roads and bridges and diesel locomotives. But what, legislators like to know, are we buying with policy-based lending? The answer: policy reform; and the proof: explicit conditionality.

For these reasons, policy conditionality, including (in the case of the World Bank) donor review of public investment programs, has become standard fare. The process of defining and negotiating the specific policy conditions to be included in policy loans has had important benefits—not the least of which is a vast broadening of the scope of the policy debate as well as a great improvement in its quality.

But policy conditionality has also given rise to severe problems. First, explicit conditionality has become excessive. World Bank conditional loans nowadays can include over a hundred specific conditions, and an IMF agreement, twenty or thirty. Bilateral donors are increasingly including policy covenants in their loans. "Cross-conditionality" is frequent.

Some of this conditionality is unnecessary. One agreement repeats conditions imposed in other agreements. Often the conditionality is fictional and cosmetic; governments long ago agreed to do what is asked, and may have already completed actions specified in new agreements.

Moreover, much of the conditionality is inappropriate. Conditions on institutional reforms are of this kind. There is little point in "requiring" governments to improve their planning and budgeting system or their management of state-owned enterprises. Most governments want to make these improvements. But improvement is slow and difficult for reasons inherent in underdevelopment—shortages of basic data, blocked information flows, shortages of trained analysts, and weak accounting, auditing, and personnel systems. None of this has much to do with conditionality.

Conditionality is inappropriate, too, when it covers policies for which theoretical support is lacking or highly contested. For example, economists can propose border parity as an agricultural pricing principle. But the impact of higher-than-parity prices is uncertain and disputed and therefore not appropriate for conditionality. It should rather be considered more experimentally and dispassionately.

Explicit conditionality is also largely ineffective. Bilateral donors are rarely ready to sacrifice their other interests by cutting off aid to a friendly country because it violates policy conditionality. Even the main conditional lender, the World Bank, rarely invokes sanctions for non-compliance. Overall assessment of performance is difficult and subjective. How does the evaluator weigh good performance in one area (say, reduced budget deficits) with clear non-compliance in another (say, agricultural marketing liberalization)?

Finally, and most important, explicit policy conditionality is often counterproductive. All parties want an agreement and want it to stay on track. When drafting it, they smooth over differences, invent words of art, and otherwise arrange to produce a document that will be acceptable to their respective constituencies. If, later, there is non-compliance, it is minimized, or the requirement is waived in order to let disbursement proceed.

What frequently results from the conditionality exercise, then, is game playing—not joint problem solving. The latter requires true dialogue—i.e., open discussion of disagreements and hesitations, mutual efforts at genuine persuasion (including study, analysis, and debate in a non-contentious atmosphere), and joint efforts to discover technically and politically acceptable policy solutions.

In the last few years, more and more practitioners have come to share this view that conditionality-laden policy-based lending does not yield real dialogue and is counterproductive. But there is little agreement about what form of conditionality is appropriate. One proposition is that explicit conditionality should be drastically reduced or even eliminated, keeping only IMF-type macroeconomic conditionality. There will always be *implicit* conditionality in any case—the understanding by all parties that future levels of assistance will depend on present willingness to modify failed policies. But forms of conditionality that will avoid game playing and encourage true dialogue remain to be defined.

# Conclusion

This chapter has sketched out some of the factors behind the rise in policy-based lending and the widespread turn toward market-oriented development strategies in the 1980s, as well as some of the problems associated with these approaches. A few concluding observations can be made regarding results and prospects.

First, the generally uncongenial international economic environment since 1980 has made it difficult for even effective reform programs to show much in the way of better growth performance. The depression in world commodity markets was particularly damaging to the poorest regions, which are heavily primary-product exporters, and which have been the setting of most of the formal structural adjustment programs of the 1980s.

Second, the intellectual foundations for market-oriented strategies are coming under renewed attack. Some writers say that the agricultural prescriptions are all wrong—prices matter less than technology; relevant elasticities are too low; export-led growth is a pipe dream for primary-product producers such as the African countries.[12] Others say that the promotion of import liberalization and privatization derives from a misreading of history.[13] So the analytic foundations of market-oriented strategies, which were never unanimously accepted in the development community, are being more vigorously contested than in the recent past.

Alternative approaches to aid strategy are also surfacing—or resurfacing. Ideas close to those of the basic needs approach of the 1970s are being proposed by such agencies as United Nations Children's Emergency Fund (UNICEF), and even within the World Bank, concern over social costs of adjustment, food security, and direct poverty reduction is loosening the attachment to market-oriented strategies. The faith in growth through policy reform, the romance with free market ideas, is thus being newly challenged before the results of this policy reform—in most of the Third World—have even had a chance to appear.

## Notes

[1]U.S. Agency for International Development (USAID), *Development and the National Interest: U.S. Economic Assistance into the 21st Century*, A Report by the Administrator, February 1989 (Washington, D.C.: USAID), p. 70. (Hereafter cited as the Woods Report.)

[2]Ibid., p. 61.

[3]U.S. House of Representatives, Committee on Foreign Affairs, *Report of the Task Force on Foreign Assistance*, February 1989, pp. 21–22. (The Hamilton-Gilman Report.)

[4]Ibid., pp. 13–26.

[5]The following paragraphs draw heavily from the Woods Report.

[6]The Woods Report, p. 23.

[7]For a useful summary analysis and a review of the relevant literature, see R. F. Mikesell, *The Economics of Foreign Aid* (Chicago, Ill.: Aldyne, 1968), pp. 30–38 and 70–104.

[8]Simon Kuznets, *Modern Economic Growth: Rate, Structure, and Spread* (New Haven, Conn.: Yale University Press, 1966); *Population, Capital and Growth: Selected Essays* (New York: W. W. Norton and Co., 1973); and E. F. Denison, *Why Growth Rates Differ: Postwar Experience in Nine Countries* (Washington, D.C.: The Brookings Institution, 1967). For a recent review, see Dennis Anderson, *Economic Growth and the Returns to Investment*, World Bank Discussion Paper No. 12, 1987.

[9]See Ragnar Nurkse, *Problems of Capital Formation in Underdeveloped Countries* (New York: Oxford University Press, 1953).

[10]See Dharam Ghai, "Successes and Failures in Growth in Sub-Saharan Africa: 1960–1982" in Louis Emmerij, ed., *Development Policies and the Crisis of the 1980s* (Paris: OECD, 1987).

[11]See Elliot Berg and Mary Shirley, *Divestiture in Developing Countries*, World Bank Discussion Paper No. 11, 1987.

[12]See Michael Lipton, "Limits of Price Policy for Agriculture: Which Way for the World Bank?" *Development Policy Review*, Vol. 5, 1987, pp. 197–215.

[13]Colin I. Bradford, Jr., "Trade and Structural Change: NICs and Next Tier NICs as Transitional Economies," *World Development*, Vol. 15, No. 3, March 1987, pp. 299–316.

# II. Development Programs Described

# Economic Assistance to Developing Countries

Andrei I. Chekhutov, Nataliya A. Ushakova, and
Leon Z. Zevin

The beginning of a new decade traditionally provides an opportunity
for analysis of the results of past policy and prospects for the future.
In Soviet foreign policy, the present divide between decades marks
the most serious appraisal of experience gained during the entire
post-World War II period. This appraisal is an integral part of the
current radical restructuring of the Soviet economy, which can be
characterized as a transition from a command and administrative
model of development to a regulated market system.

## Special Characteristics of Soviet Economic Assistance

Soviet economic assistance up to the present has pursued three basic
objectives. The first is the participation of the U.S.S.R. in developing
the economy of the recipient country. With the aim of securing self-
sustained growth, the Soviet Union has sought to improve the economic potential of developing countries and to stimulate both the
productive energies of the people and a more equitable sharing of the
benefits of development. In keeping with this objective, a portion of
Soviet economic cooperation has been extended on concessional
terms or free of charge.

The second objective has been to strengthen the whole system
of economic cooperation between the U.S.S.R. and the recipient coun-

try so as to promote both the growth and efficiency of the Soviet economy and the economic potential of the developing country. In keeping with this objective, the main form of Soviet aid has not been a hard-currency cash flow, but a transfer of supplies of materials, know-how, and appropriate services. This is consistent with a broad interpretation of the international concept of aid contained in U.N. documents.[1]

A third objective of Soviet aid has been to give priority to particular developing countries in the provision of assistance. These have included the socialist developing countries,[2] other countries of geo-political importance to the U.S.S.R., countries in urgent need of defending their independence, and countries interested in establishing good relations and cooperation with the U.S.S.R. Thus, political and ideological motives have been important in Soviet aid, with economic factors sometimes relegated to second or even third place.

### Official Estimates of the Amount of Soviet Aid

This combination of objectives has been reflected in official Soviet aid disbursements. To date, this aid has included the following components:

(1) Concessional credits—provided primarily in the form of Soviet goods and various types of services, but partly also in convertible currencies—offered on conditions that conform to internationally accepted criteria for preferential treatment;

(2) Outright grants of machinery, equipment, materials, manufactured goods, and foodstuffs, as well as services;

(3) Subsidies involved in the partial compensation of Soviet specialists working in developing countries;

(4) Preferential prices (the difference between the world price and the transaction price) extended to developing-country imports of Soviet goods and services as well as to developing-country exports of goods and services to the Soviet Union; and

(5) Complete or partial payment for the technical training and education of developing-country nationals either in the Soviet Union or in the developing nations themselves.

Unfortunately, Soviet statistics on assistance have been extremely limited in the past. Only data on total amounts of assistance extended to developing countries have been released for public use so far.

According to Soviet government data for the period 1976–1980, all of the aid components enumerated above, minus debt payments, totaled about 30 billion rubles. For 1981–86, the figure was about 63 billion rubles. Thus, the average annual amount of net aid, calculated according to the U.S.S.R. definition and in current prices, increased from 6 billion rubles annually in the period 1976–1980 to 10.5 billion rubles annually from 1981–86. In 1987, the figure was 11.7 billion rubles; in 1988, 12 billion rubles; and in 1989, 12.5 billion rubles. For the three years 1987–89, this represented 1.4 per cent of an average annual GNP of 864 billion rubles.[3] If one takes into account the financial terms, more than 80 per cent of all aid commitments were extended on a grant basis in 1987 and 1988.[4] The total grant element for all Soviet aid reached over 90 per cent with the inclusion of some concessional credits.[5]

It should be noted that these figures provide only a general representation of the scope of Soviet assistance. Moreover, the data are given in prices that do not account for inflation, which was over 40 per cent during the period of 1971–1988 according to calculations of the U.S.S.R. State Committee of Statistics.[6] (The index of GNP deflators for the United States, 1971–1988, was 2.56, indicating a growth rate of prices of 156 per cent.)

### Comments on Differing Estimates and Comparability of Soviet Aid

It would be unfair to draw a direct comparison between the amounts of Soviet and U.S. aid for several reasons. *First,* some components of Soviet aid—i.e., those numbered 3 and 4 in the above list—are not used by Western nations in their aid policy. These components differ from Western practice and obviously should be taken into consideration in attempting any monetary comparison of Western and Soviet foreign aid. Understanding Soviet methods of extending and calculating foreign aid has increased in recent years. In 1987, for example, the OECD Development Cooperation Directorate commented that, in addition to recognizing the differences between the Soviet and Western methods, it should be noted with respect to preferential trade prices (item 4 in the list of Soviet aid components provided earlier) that:

> There is no reason to doubt that these price subsidies have a tremendous positive effect on the balance of payments (of the recipient nations) and at the same time are a real burden to the Soviet economy. It makes practically no difference either to the Soviet Union or to the recipient nation whether all the oil is supplied at half the price of the world market, or whether half

of the oil is paid for at world market prices and the other half is supplied free of charge.[7]

*Second*, comparisons of Soviet and Western aid in terms of aid per GNP must consider a special feature of Soviet bookkeeping. According to Soviet economist D. Valovoi, repetitive inclusion of the cost of labor and semi-finished products equaled 37 per cent of Gross Production (Social Product) in 1965; 42 per cent in 1975; and 39 per cent in 1985.[8] This gives an upward bias to GNP estimates. We do not have any information at our disposal on the percentage of repetitive accounting in Soviet aid programs. But it is logical to conclude that this practice significantly affects the calculation of Soviet aid and its comparability to that of other nations.

*Third*, one must also consider the fact that many Soviet organizations have not always clearly distinguished between commercial operations and aid programs to developing nations in their accounting procedures. For example, important Soviet aid programs run by the now abolished U.S.S.R. State Committee on Economic Relations were financed mainly through concessional state credits. But some of the goods and services supplied were repaid by developing countries with regular commercial trade shipments or with convertible currencies.

*Fourth*, additional difficulties in comparing the levels of Soviet and U.S. assistance arise from different ways of calculating the exchange rate of the ruble in relation to the dollar. At the present Soviet official exchange rate, the ruble is generally considered to be overvalued.

It should be noted that critics of Soviet official assistance statistics do not dispute that the U.S.S.R. is in the ranks of the major donors. This is evident in both the OECD and CIA data shown in Table 1. OECD appraisals are significant in that while they rely upon the Western method of calculation and thereby omit some components included in Soviet calculations, they show the dynamics of Soviet assistance over the long term. Calculated on the basis of OECD data, the average annual growth of the U.S.S.R.'s net aid disbursements between 1970 and 1988[9] in current prices was 9.7 per cent, or 1.5 times that of the United States.[10]

CIA calculations of Soviet aid differ from OECD estimates in that they include preferential prices (aid component 4 in the list above) for *some* countries (Vietnam, Cuba, Mongolia, Laos, Cambodia, and North Korea). It can be seen from the CIA data for 1985–86 shown in Table 1 that if one took these CIA aid figures and used the OECD (rather than the CIA) estimates of the Soviet GNP, the U.S.S.R.'s aid efforts measured as a percentage of its GNP would greatly exceed not only the corresponding 1985–86 average indica-

## Table 1.   Western Estimates of Soviet Aid to Developing Countries (U.S. $ millions and percentages)

| | 1970–71[e] | | 1975–76[e] | | 1980–81[e] | | 1985–86[e] | | 1988 | |
|---|---|---|---|---|---|---|---|---|---|---|
| | $ mil. | % GNP | $ mil. | % GNP | $ mil. | % GNP | $ mil. | % GNP | $ mil. | % GNP |
| OECD Estimates, Net Disbursements | 1,994[a] | 0.15[b] | 1,794[a] | 0.16[b] | 2,247[a] | 0.25[b] | 3,195[a] | 0.32[b] | 4,210 | — |
| CIA Estimates, *Gross* Extensions to Non-Communist Less Developed Countries | — | — | — | — | 1,730[d] | 0.17[c] | 3,123[d] | 0.14[c] | — | — |
| CIA Estimates *Net* Extensions to Communist Less Developed Countries[d] | — | — | — | — | 5,809[d] | 0.34[c] | 6,546[d] | 0.29[c] | — | — |

[a] U.S. $ millions at 1985 prices and exchange rates.
[b] Based on OECD estimates of Soviet GNP, which differ from those of the CIA.
[c] Based on CIA estimates of Soviet GNP, which differ from those of the OECD.
[d] Includes direct economic aid on a net basis and the indirect effect of price subsidies on Soviet imports and exports.
[e] Annual averages.

[Editor's Note: OECD and CIA estimates of Soviet aid are based on different definitions of aid and different calculation methods for Soviet GNP. In addition, CIA uses different methods of calculation for Soviet aid to Communist and Non-Communist Less Developed Countries; therefore the two categories cannot be added to obtain total Soviet assistance to all less developed countries.]

Sources: Organisation for Economic Co-operation and Development (OECD) estimates from *Development Cooperation: 1987 Report* (Paris: OECD, 1987), p. 55, and ibid, *1989 Report*, p. 176. Central Intelligence Agency (CIA) estimates from CIA *Handbook of Economic Statistics, 1989* (Washington, D.C.: NTIS, U.S. Department of Commerce, 1989), pp. 31, 174, and 178.

tor for the United States (0.23) but even that for all OECD nations (0.35).[11] Moreover, to compare the burdens that different donors bear in providing assistance to developing countries, it is useful to take into consideration not only the volume of aid and GNP of the donor but also the donor's level of per capita income. According to estimates by Soviet economist B. Bolotin, during the mid-1980s, the national per capita income in the U.S.S.R. was 68 per cent of the average for all Western nations and 56 per cent of U.S. income.[12] In other words, for each Soviet citizen, the burden of extending assistance to developing nations greatly exceeded the burden on each citizen of the United States and of other Western nations.

### Direction of Assistance

The largest recipients of Soviet aid have been (a) the Council of Mutual Assistance (CMEA) developing countries Vietnam, Cuba, and Mongolia; (b) other developing nations with special relations with the U.S.S.R.; and (c) neighboring developing countries. In the first half of the 1980s, developing nations neighboring on the Soviet Union received more than 40 per cent of all Soviet economic and technical assistance to non-socialist developing countries.

The least developed of the developing nations also have received considerable attention in Soviet aid programs. In keeping with U.N. and UNCTAD resolutions, the Soviet Union has expanded economic and technological assistance to these countries, especially in recent years. This assistance was valued at 6 billion rubles in 1981–85; 2 billion rubles in 1986; 1.5 billion rubles (or about 0.20 per cent of the Soviet GNP) in 1987; and 1.8 billion rubles (or 0.21 percent of Soviet GNP) in 1988.[13] This assistance was extremely concessional. This included long-term debt repayment plans and, in some instances, interest-free loans and grants. In December 1988, President Gorbachev announced before the U.N. General Assembly the U.S.S.R.'s intention to grant a debt moratorium of up to 100 years on debt owed by the least developed countries and in some cases to write it off altogether.

# Credits in Soviet Economic Assistance

Credit relations between the U.S.S.R. and developing countries had their beginnings in the 1930s. Credits were first offered to Turkey in 1934 and to China in 1938. During World War II, credit relations with developing countries were curtailed. After the War, not only did severed credit relations have to be renewed, but a new system of credit cooperation needed to be put into place to respond to the emergence of dozens of newly independent nations.

There have been four stages in the development of credit relations between the U.S.S.R. and developing nations. During the *first stage*—from the late 1940s through the 1950s—the volume of credits from the U.S.S.R. was small. Economic relations with socialist developing countries had not been developed, and credits to non-socialist developing nations amounted to 130 million rubles.[14] (During this period, the U.S.S.R. essentially bought more from the non-socialist developing nations than it could sell to them.[15]) This was due to the fact that the Soviet economy was dealing with the consequences of war and was concentrating its main efforts on its relationship with the socialist countries of Eastern Europe. As of the mid-1950s, economic and credit agreements had been concluded only with Afghanistan, Vietnam, India, the Korean Democratic People's Republic, and Mongolia.

The *second stage*—from the beginning of the 1960s to the mid-1970s—was marked by a sharp increase in economic relations between the Soviet Union and developing countries. In this period, developing nations became important markets for Soviet exports. Due to credit offered, Soviet exports grew significantly. Throughout the entire 15-year period, increases in exports averaged 17 per cent annually. The developing countries' share of total Soviet exports rose from 10 per cent in 1960 to 21 per cent in 1975. Their role as importers of Soviet machinery and equipment (largely on concessional terms) increased even more significantly—from 16.5 per cent to 31.5 per cent.[16] By the end of the 1960s, the gross accumulated volume of Soviet credits to non-socialist developing countries alone had reached 4.5 billion rubles.[17]

In the mid-1970s, a definite shift in Soviet credit policy marked the beginning of a *third stage* in the provision of Soviet credits to developing countries. First, there was a slowdown in the rate of increase in credits extended. Yet the amount of credits continued to increase to more than one billion rubles annually in the second part of the 1970s, and to two billion rubles annually in the first part of the 1980s. Second, the concentration of credits to a particular group of recipient nations continued to intensify. Third, there was a change in the direction of Soviet credits. Credits to non-socialist developing nations began to increase at a rapid rate, especially during the second half of the 1970s. Within this subgroup, there was also a shift among the recipients of Soviet credits in favor of the petroleum-importing countries—and among them, of the least developed countries. Fourth, in total volume of credits extended to developing nations, there was an increase in the share of credits offered by state enterprises on semi-commercial terms. These credits carried higher interest rates and shorter repayment periods than credits disbursed on softer assistance terms.

The *fourth stage* in Soviet credit relations with developing countries began in the mid-1980s and was linked to a sharp decline in the export potential of many developing countries and a significant worsening of their hard-currency situation. Deliveries from developing nations to the U.S.S.R. tapered off and stopped altogether by the mid-1980s. This resulted in the rapid development of a positive balance of trade between the U.S.S.R. and developing nations that required increased credits, the annual value of which according to some estimates exceeded 3–4 billion rubles in the second half of the 1980s.

Information published by the Soviet Ministry of Finance indicates the substantial contribution that has been made by the U.S.S.R. to the financial needs of developing countries. At the same time it stresses the importance to the U.S.S.R. of its credit relations with developing countries and the particular interest of the U.S.S.R. in a reasonable solution of debt problems of developing countries. An overall picture of the debt obligations of developing countries to the U.S.S.R. is presented in Table 2.

If one categorizes developing countries according to their per capita income, the share of low-income socialist and non-socialist countries in the Soviet portfolio is about 42 per cent, and that of the least developed countries is about 15 per cent (for OECD countries, corresponding figures in 1987 long-term debt claims were 23.7 per cent and 2.9 per cent). Another noteworthy aspect is the preferential treatment of debt relief operations by the Soviet Union. The average rate of debt reschedulings in Soviet assets is 17.9 per cent, but for the least developed countries, this figure is 20.5 per cent.

The Soviet system of credits differs in a variety of ways from other countries' credit relations. First of all, although the role of credits in the Soviet Union's complex of economic relations with developing nations is important, it is subordinate to the broad objectives of Soviet assistance (e.g., promoting self-sustained growth in developing countries and strengthening the U.S.S.R.'s relations with developing countries). These objectives determine the basic parameters of Soviet credit relations: for instance, the branches of production to which credits are directed, their volume, their distribution among different recipients, their mainly bilateral character, their fairly long-term character and predictability, and the terms for their repayment. All of these are determined by the importance attributed to economic cooperation as a whole.

Soviet credits are distinct in that they have been offered at rel-

**Table 2.    Debt of Developing Countries to the U.S.S.R., Outstanding and Disbursed,[a] as of November 1, 1989 (millions rubles and percentages)**

|  | Debt | | Debt Restructuring | |
|---|---|---|---|---|
|  | *(mil. rubles)* | *(% share)* | *(mil. rubles)* | *(% share)* |
| All Developing Countries | 79,197 | 100.00 | 14,241 | 100.00 |
| Socialist Developing Countries[b] | 37,157 | 46.9 | 6,429 | 45.1 |
| Non-Socialist Developing Countries | 42,040 | 53.1 | 7,812 | 54.9 |
| Least developed | 10,848 | 13.8 | 2,913 | 20.5 |
| Other low-income | 12,260 | 15.8 | 97 | 0.7 |
| Middle-income | 18,932 | 23.5 | 4,802 | 33.7 |

[a]The amounts include economic and military debt as of November 1, 1989.
[b]The group comprises Cuba (15.5 billion rubles), the Korean People's Republic (2.2 billion rubles), Laos (0.8 billion rubles), Mongolia (9.5 billion rubles), and Vietnam (9.1 billion rubles).

Source: *Izvestiya*, March 1, 1990.

atively low cost by international standards (see Table 3). Due to the low cost of Soviet credits, between 1981 and 1985, payments by developing countries to the U.S.S.R. for credit use were 2.7 times lower than the flow of new Soviet credits. Due to differences in interest rates, the share of interest payments in developing-country total repayments on their debt to the U.S.S.R. was 17 per cent, which is approximately 2.5 times less than the average share of interest payments in the total repayments to all foreign creditors.[18]

In deciding its credit policies, the Soviet Union stresses the importance of meeting international obligations. But at the same time, it takes into account the state of bilateral payments as well as the overall currency and financial position of the developing countries. Soviet credit policies take into account the payment difficulties of some developing nations and the practical impossibility of a full settlement of their former debts. These policies recognize that what the severely indebted developing countries need is not just par-

**Table 3.   Comparison of Interest Cost of Credit Obtained by Developing Countries (percentages)**

| Sources of Lending | 1974[a] | 1977[b] | 1980[c] | 1982 | 1986[d] |
|---|---|---|---|---|---|
| Developed Market-Economy (DAC) Countries | 5.2 | 6.3[e] | 10.2[e] | 11.4[e] | 7.2[f] |
| Official Development Assistance | 2.4 | 2.1 | 2.3 | 2.1 | 2.2 |
| Other Official Debt | 6.0 | 6.0 | 7.1 | 5.6 | — |
| Officially Guaranteed Private Export Credits | 6.6 | 7.5 | 8.5 | 8.9 | 8.6 |
| Other Private | 9.0 | 8.1 | 11.5 | 13.1 | 7.0 |
| International Private Bank Loans | — | 7.9[g] | 15.0 | 16.3 | 8.6[h] |
| Private Bonds | — | 5.2 | 7.5 | 8.1 | 9.0 |
| Multilateral Organizations | 5.2 | 5.2 | 6.25 | 5.9 | 1.7[i] 8.8[j] |

| | | | | | |
|---|---|---|---|---|---|
| **European Centrally Planned (CMEA) Countries** | 1.9 | 1.6 | 2.7 | 2.6 | 2.8[l] |
| OPEC Countries | 6.9 | 4.0 | 4.8 | 4.6 | — |
| Remaining Developing Countries | 9.4 | 4.6 | 3.8 | 2.8 | — |

[a]Percentage of debt at end of 1973.
[b]Percentage of average of disbursed debt at end 1976 and at end-1977.
[c]Percentage of end-1979 debt.
[d]Annual interest effective payments and other charges as a percentage of long-term disbursed debt at the beginning of the year.
[e]Developed countries (DAC) and capital markets.
[f]Percentage of total developing-country long-term debt disbursed at the beginning of the year.
[g]Total bank loans, including loans through off-shore centers, but excluding export credits and bonds.
[h]Percentage of floating-interest debt at the beginning of the year.
[i]Concessional.
[j]Non-concessional.
[k]U.S.S.R. accounted for two-thirds to four-fifths of all credits offered.
[l]U.S.S.R. only.

Sources: OECD, *Development Co-operation: 1976 Review* (Paris: OECD, 1976), p. 254; OECD, *Development Co-operation: 1979 Review* (Paris: OECD, 1979), p. 257; OECD, *External Debt of Developing Countries: 1982 Survey* (Paris: OECD, 1982), p. 30; OECD, *External Debt of Developing Countries: 1983 Survey* (Paris: OECD, 1983), p. 64; OECD *Financing and External Debt of the Developing Countries: 1986 Survey* (Paris: OECD, 1986), p. 76; and UNCTAD Document TD/341, July 16, 1987, p.3.

tial measures to decrease the burden of their indebtedness, but serious debt relief to allow them to mobilize their domestic resources and to carry out necessary programs of structural change. The Soviet Union has made specific recommendations to provide for a long-term moratorium on and even forgiveness of past debts for the least developed countries.

# Soviet Economic and Technical Assistance

### General Description

The Soviet Union's main form of resource transfer in support of Third World development has been "economic and technical assistance"—the supply of credit, machinery, and technical know-how for specific projects. This type of assistance encompasses conducting preliminary research, including technical and economic feasibility studies for the construction of projects; conducting geological prospecting operations and engineering surveys; developing factory designs; providing technology and technical documentation; exporting accompanying licenses; supplying construction equipment and materials; training local personnel; and financing business travel by Soviet specialists who provide assistance in completing building, assembly, and adjustment operations, and, if necessary, in the operation of the project. Most operations within the framework of Soviet economic and technical assistance have been provided in the form of bilateral government agreements with credits extended on concessional terms.

The Soviet Union began to broaden bilateral economic and technical ties with developing countries in the mid-1950s. Since the signing of an agreement on economic and technical cooperation with Afghanistan in January 1954, the number of the Soviet Union's partners in Asia, Africa, and Latin America has steadily increased.

Between 1961 and 1970, the average annual increase in the volume of economic and technical assistance (according to available data) was over 11 per cent; between 1971 and 1980, it was 13 per cent; between 1981 and 1985, over 8 per cent; and between 1986 and 1988, somewhat more than 7 per cent.[19]

One can get an idea of the increase in the scale of cooperation by looking at the dynamics of the deliveries of complete equipment[20] to developing countries; these rose almost 3.5 times between 1970 and 1987 and presently comprise more than 11 per cent of the Soviet Union's total exports to these countries and 45 per cent of the exports of technical/machinery products.[21] Between 1985 and 1988,

## Table 4. The Dynamics of Soviet Economic and Technical Assistance to Developing Countries[a] (cumulative totals as of years shown)

|  | Agreements | | | Estimates | |
|---|---|---|---|---|---|
|  | 1960 | 1970 | 1980 | 1985 | 1989 |
| Number of partner nations | 18 | 45 | 70 | 72 | 73 |
| Asia | 13 | 22 | 24 | 24 | 24 |
| Africa | 4 | 20 | 34 | 36 | 36 |
| Latin America | 1 | 3 | 12 | 12 | 13 |
| Number of projects built, under construction, or planned to be built | 613 | 1,417 | 2,834 | 3,308 | 3,673 |
| Asia | 481 | 920 | 1,072 | 2,027 | 2,207 |
| Africa | 121 | 327 | 503 | 616 | 649 |
| Latin America | 11 | 167 | 459 | 665 | 727 |
| Number of above projects in operation | 112 | 827 | 1,578 | 2,103 | 2,492 |
| Asia | 96 | 561 | 1,084 | 1,405 | 1,876 |
| Africa | 16 | 169 | 286 | 334 | 348 |
| Latin America | — | 97 | 208 | 364 | 468 |

[a]In accordance with U.N. classification, "developing countries" includes the market-oriented developing countries as well as the following socialist developing countries: Vietnam, Cuba, the People's Republic of Korea, Laos, and Mongolia.

Sources: Y.N. Grekov, A.I. Kachanov, D.I. Sukhoparov, and T.V. Teodorovich, *Ekonomicheskoye i technicheskoye sodeistvyie SSR zarubezhnym stranam* (Moscow: (1987), p. 239; and *Narodnoye khozyaistvo SSSR v 1988*, (Moscow: 1989), pp. 655, 656.

the exports of complete equipment from the Soviet Union to developing countries showed a slight average yearly decrease of 1.1 per cent—after a sharp increase of 17.95 per cent in the period 1976–1980 and a moderate increase of 3.7 per cent in 1981–85. More detailed information on complete equipment deliveries to developing-country partners appears in Table 5.

Table 6 also gives a picture of the significance of economic and technical assistance provided by the Soviet Union to improve the economic potential of developing nations.

Of the entire volume of Soviet economic and technical assistance, two-thirds has been distributed to non-socialist developing countries and less than one-third to five socialist developing countries (Cuba, the Democratic People's Republic of Korea, Laos, the Mongolian People's Republic, and the Socialist Republic of Vietnam).

Turning to the qualitative aspects and results of this aid, it should be noted that cooperation with the Soviet Union and other socialist nations opened up alternative options for developing countries in selecting suppliers of machinery and equipment, design, and technical documentation, as well as in obtaining credits and loans. Moreover, most Soviet economic and technical assistance has been provided for strengthening the production potential of developing nations and for establishing and developing their industrial sectors. Dozens of projects built with Soviet assistance have played a key role in strengthening the economic base of the recipient countries, in facilitating their assimilation of modern technology, and in helping them alleviate their pressing social problems.

The history of Soviet economic and technical assistance as an independent area of economic relations with developing nations can be roughly divided into four stages: the first stage from the mid-1950s to the mid-1960s, the second from the mid-1960s to the mid-1970s, and the third from the second half of the 1970s to the mid-1980s. A fourth stage, characterized by new trends and ideas, began in the mid-1980s.

### The Development of a System of Mutual Cooperation

During the *first stage* of the U.S.S.R.'s economic and technical assistance program, from the mid-1950s to the mid-1960s, Soviet assistance was aimed at increasing newly independent countries' self-sufficiency and overcoming the one-sided orientation of their foreign economic relations.[22] Economic and technical assistance was viewed primarily as a necessary material condition for the more complete realization of the principle of proletarian internationalism. Eco-

Table 5.    Exports of Complete Equipment[a] from the U.S.S.R. to Developing Countries, 1960–1987 (millions rubles and percentages)

|  | Total[a] | Asia | Africa | Latin America |
|---|---|---|---|---|
|  | (mil. rubles) | (percentages) | | |
| 1960 | 72.7 | 80.2 | 19.8 | — |
| 1970 | 577.0 | 73.5 | 15.7 | 10.8 |
| 1975 | 738.7 | 73.5 | 14.2 | 12.1 |
| 1980 | 1,686.3 | 62.3 | 16.8 | 20.9 |
| 1981 | 1,610.6 | 61.0 | 18.7 | 20.3 |
| 1982 | 1,865.8 | 59.4 | 23.0 | 17.6 |
| 1983 | 2,067.8 | 57.3 | 23.7 | 19.0 |
| 1984 | 2,067.7 | 60.2 | 20.2 | 19.6 |
| 1985 | 2,018.7 | 65.9 | 16.2 | 17.9 |
| 1986 | 2,083.4 | 69.1 | 12.6 | 18.3 |
| 1987 | 2,248.5 | 70.5 | 11.0 | 18.5 |
| 1988 | 1,952.0 | 69.8 | 9.6 | 20.6 |

[a]The data does not include deliveries of equipment and materials transfered on a grant basis, the contract price of producing engineering designs and technical documentation, business trips by Soviet specialists to the joint project sites, and training and education of foreigners at Soviet enterprises and organizations.

Sources: *Vneshnyaya torgovlya SSSR: Statisticheskiy Sbornik* (Moscow, Mezhdunarodnye otnosheniya for corresponding years); *Vneshniye ekonomicheskiye svyazi SSSR v 1988: Statisticheskiy Sbornik* (Moscow: Finansy i Statistyka, 1989), pp. 47–48.

nomic characteristics of assistance, while important, did not yet play a decisive role.

Legal and institutional mechanisms for economic and technical assistance were established during this period. Economic interaction became more reliable and predictable in character, foreign aid was linked more effectively to domestic efforts in developing countries, and planning instruments were institutionalized.

During this first stage, economic and technical assistance served mainly as a channel for the transfer of resources to weaker partners. Its structure was determined mainly by the national development priorities of the recipient countries. Thus, in the mid-1960s, industry accounted for 72 per cent of economic and technical assistance; agriculture for 6 per cent; geological survey operations for 9 per cent; transportation and communications for 8 per cent; and sci-

**Table 6.    Capacity of the Projects[a] Built, Under Construction, or Planned by the Soviet Union in Developing Countries**

| | 1970 | 1975 | 1980 | 1984 | 1985 | 1989 |
|---|---|---|---|---|---|---|
| Power stations, set capacity (millions kilowatts) | 8.3 | 16.5 | 25.7 | 30.0 | 37.0 | 40.9 |
| Coal mined (millions metric tons) | 15.3 | 29.5 | 66.8 | 87.0 | 119.0 | 122.0 |
| Coke (millions metric tons) | 7.2 | 11.8 | 20.3 | 22.0 | 22.0 | 22.0 |
| Iron ore mined (millions metric tons) | 11.2 | 14.0 | 18.0 | 22.0 | 22.0 | 22.0 |
| Cast iron (millions metric tons) | 10.5 | 15.8 | 27.0 | 27.1 | 27.1 | 27.1 |
| Steel (millions metric tons) | 14.2 | 19.0 | 28.8 | 30.2 | 32.0 | 27.0 |
| Rolling of ferrous metals (millions metric tons) | 12.8 | 15.4 | 22.9 | 25.0 | 25.0 | 21.0 |
| Oil, refined (millions metric tons) | 14.6 | 25.6 | 23.9 | 29.0 | 30.0 | 39.0 |
| Mineral fertilizers (millions metric tons) | 1.2 | 1.6 | 1.3 | 1.4 | 1.4 | 1.3 |

| | | | | | | |
|---|---|---|---|---|---|---|
| Metallurgical, mining, hammer-welding, press lifting, and transportation equipment (thousands metric tons) | 150 | 155 | 155 | 192 | 192 | 192 |
| Cement (millions metric tons) | 1.8 | 5.0 | 6.4 | 6.7 | 6.4 | 6.4 |
| Frame and panel housing construction, (millions square meters) | 2.7 | 3.8 | 4.8 | 4.8 | 4.8 | 5.2 |
| Grain elevators (capacity) (millions metric tons) | — | — | 2.1 | 2.1[b] | 2.2 | 2.1 |
| Extent of railroads[a] (kilometers) | 3,667 | 3,832 | 5,429 | 5,631 | 6,094 | 6,094 |
| Extent of highways (kilometers) | 1,948 | 2,024 | 2,450 | 2,694 | 2,694 | 2,852 |
| Irrigation and reclamation of lands (millions hectares) | 1.8 | 2.3 | 2.2 | 2.2 | 2.3 | 2.5 |

[a]Including expansion and modification.
[b]1987.

Sources: Authors' estimates based on "Narodnoye khoziaistvo SSSR," *Statisticheskiy Sbornik za 1975–1988* (Moscow: Finansy i Statistika); "Sotsialisticheskaya Respublika Vietnam," *Spravochnik* (Moscow: Nauka, 1976 and 1981); "Koreiskaya Narodno-Demokraticheskaya Respublika," *Spravochnik (Moscow: Nauka, 1975 and 1985);* "Respublika Kuba," *Spravochnik* (Moscow: Nauka, 1974, 1981, and 1984); "Narodnoye khoziaistvo MNR za 65 let, 1921–1986," Yubileiniy Statisticheskiy Sbornik, Ulan Bator, 1986; "Postroyeno pri ekonomicheskom tekhnicheskom sodeistvii Sovetskogo Soyuza" (Moscow: Mezhdunarodnye otnosheniya, 1982); *Statisticheskiy yezhegodnik stran-chlenov Soveta Ekonomicheskoi Vzaipomoshchi* (Moscow: Finansy i Statistyka, 1981).

ence, culture, education, health, and other areas for 5 per cent.[23] These proportions have remained much the same to the present.

In the 1950s and 1960s, economic and technical assistance was provided, in widely varying levels, to countries including Afghanistan, Syria, Egypt, Iraq, the People's Democratic Republic of Yemen, and India. Soviet deliveries of construction and transportation equipment as well as Soviet expertise in the technical and administrative management of projects helped these nations overcome inadequacies related to insufficient resources in their own construction and engineering organizations and a lack of trained personnel. In some countries, such cooperation has led to the development of national construction firms.

### Diversifying the Forms of Assistance

During the *second stage* of Soviet economic and technical assistance, which began roughly in the mid-1960s, Soviet organizations started to pay greater attention to the costs and benefits of assistance to developing nations. The main emphasis shifted principally to ways of improving efficiency and to transforming a unilateral transfer of resources into an equitable and mutually beneficial cooperative relationship between partners. The basic concept and thrust of economic and technical assistance at this stage remained basically unchanged. But emphasis shifted to finding more flexible and varied forms and mechanisms of economic and technical assistance to assure that the entire system of economic collaboration with developing countries (including both trade and other economic relations) helped the Soviet Union to attain or approximate internationally acceptable norms of profitability. This point of view was widely discussed in the Soviet economic literature of the mid-1960s.[24] It was also suggested that the elements of "pure" aid (grants) and concessional resource flows be maintained and even increased where necessary—specifically in cooperation with the less industrialized socialist nations and the least developed nations of the Third World.

Increased attention to the *economic* aspects of assistance helped strengthen cooperation efforts. It established a premise for transforming these aid efforts from a number of construction projects in developing nations into a system of long-term, stable, and to a certain degree *planned* measures affecting various sectors of the economy. In the developing countries, this approach helped bring about closer coordination of domestic efforts in working with this aid. It also increased the socio-economic efficiency of cooperation projects; raised the productivity of the domestic labor force; strengthened the integrative processes within the national economies; and involved developing countries more actively in the international division of labor.[25] In extending aid to Mongolia, Vietnam, and Cuba, additional instruments, such as preferential prices for exports and imports and very favorable terms of credit, were also made available.

The strengthening of economic trade relations between the U.S.S.R. and developing nations and an increase in the duration of long-term agreements led to changes in the international division of labor among countries at varying levels of development and different social structures.[26] This trend also had a definite effect on the development of Soviet cooperation. New forms of assistance were developed during this period, including cooperation on the basis of compensation, joint ventures, and tripartite assistance. Although in quantitative terms these types of cooperation did not predominate in Soviet economic assistance relations with developing nations, in qualitative terms they were indicative of the changing character of these relations.

*The Contract Form of Assistance.*[27] Although the first twenty-six projects in the social and industrial sphere in fourteen developing nations were built by the Soviet Union on contract terms, i.e., a turnkey basis, at the beginning of the 1960s, contract terms were not a dominant form of assistance at that time. Even in 1970, contractual agreements comprised only 4 per cent of the total amount of economic and technical assistance to developing nations.[28] The only exception was Mongolia, where this form was prevalent in the 1960s and remains so to the present.

The percentage of contracts in the entire volume of Soviet economic and technical assistance to the developing countries increased from 15 per cent in 1975 to approximately 42 per cent in 1980, and in some countries from 50 per cent to 100 per cent.[29]

Contract terms have been most frequent in assistance relating to the construction of power generating plants, metal and cement factories, gas and oil pipelines, and mining enterprises. As of the beginning of 1987, contract terms had been used to build and put into operation hydroelectric, thermal, and nuclear power plants, ferrous metal plants capable of producing approximately 2.5 million tons annually, and gas and oil pipelines totaling 2.5 thousand kilometers.[30]

The active use of the contract form of assistance between 1976 and 1980 gave some Soviet foreign trade organizations too optimistic an opinion of this form of assistance. By the end of the 1970s—and especially by the beginning of the 1980s—contracts experienced difficulties relating both to their nature and to the inexperience of Soviet organizations. In particular, this can be explained by a declining interest in developing countries due to the creation and expansion of their own construction and assembly base. This meant less demand for such Soviet exports of equipment and services. The debt crisis in developing countries was another problem affecting contract agreements in the 1980s.

While problems have been encountered and the expansion of contractual cooperation slowed in the first half of the 1980s, the Soviet Union continues to be interested in this form of economic and technical assistance.

*Compensation Agreements.* The Soviet Union was among the first to introduce compensation agreements as an international form of assistance. In this form of assistance, credits granted by the Soviet side to cover the cost of the provision of equipment and services necessary for building new projects are repaid by the output of the projects built with Soviet assistance or in part by the output of other enterprises (partial compensation). As of the end of 1980, the U.S.S.R. had more than forty compensation agreements with developing countries.[31]

The advantages of compensation agreements have been: the long-term nature of such agreements (in some cases 25 or even 30 years); the possibility of maneuvering mutual deliveries without diverting significant resources from other sectors of the economy; the promotion of the export capabilities of developing countries; their stability (fixing the volume of deliveries); their large scale (especially when developing natural resources); their assistance in the establishment of regional-industrial complexes in a poorly developed economy; and the possibility of obtaining credits, technical assistance, and other forms of assistance without having to resort to scarce convertible currency resources.

In the Soviet Union, compensation cooperation is understood in the broader sense—not only as supplying a product within the framework of credit payment and receiving goods in return, but also as an active means of stabilizing economic relations and increasing the effectiveness of economic and technical assistance to Third World nations. The importance of this form of cooperation can be assessed by looking at the Soviet Union's purchase of products on a compensation basis.

More than one-half of the products imported under compensation agreements have been foodstuffs. This form of cooperation stimulated the creation in developing nations of stable food industries capable not only of satisfying domestic demand, but also of exporting their excess production.

Approximately one-third of the total volume of supplies from cooperation projects have been fuel and raw materials products.

# Table 7. Soviet Imports of Various Goods from Projects Built in Developing Countries with Soviet Assistance

|  | 1976–80 | 1981–85 |
|---|---|---|
| Oil (millions metric tons) | 23.4 | 17.1 |
| Natural gas (thousands millions cubic meters) | 40.0 | 11.8 |
| Coal (thousands metric tons) | 441.0 | 1,588.0 |
| Bauxite (millions metric tons) | 11.6 | 11.8 |
| Cast iron (thousands metric tons) | 526.0 | 467.0 |
| Commercial timber (thousands cubic meters) | 761.8 | 737.1 |
| Natural rubber (thousands metric tons) | — | 54.1 |
| Nitrogenous fertilizer (thousands metric tons) | 230.0 | 267.0 |
| Raw sugar (millions metric tons) | 16.9 | 18.0 |
| Tea (thousands metric tons) | 16.5 | 22.2 |
| Coffee (thousands metric tons) | 3.1 | 13.3 |

Source: Y.N. Grekov, A.I. Kachanov, D.I. Sukhoparov, T.V. Teodorovich, *Ekonomicheskoye i tekhnicheskoye sodeistviye SSSR zarubezhnym stranam* (Moscow: Mezhdunarodniye otnosheniya, 1987), p. 107.

Large-scale agreements along these lines have provided the Soviet economy with a reliable source of raw materials in short supply. Compensation cooperation has also developed in the manufacturing sector, including machine building, but it is not as widespread as in other sectors.

The effectiveness of compensation cooperation to a large extent depends on the proper organization of the project to avoid having to postpone credit payments and prevent closing down due to non-profitability. The situation has been less than ideal in this respect. This is sometimes because Soviet organizations are not always able to completely live up to their obligation to deliver spare parts for their technology.[32] The further development of collaboration on a compensation basis requires the solution of a broad range of complex problems. In our view, however, most of these problems are organizational in character. The prospects opened up for the Soviet Union and its partners in the Third World by collaboration on a compensation basis are attractive enough to stimulate the mobilization of efforts for its further development.

*Other Forms of Assistance.* A definite shift (although insufficient in scope) took place during the 1970s in the use of joint enterprises with the participation of the U.S.S.R. in developing countries.[33] During the first postwar years, such joint ventures were established in non-manufacturing sectors. Joint ventures, for example, involved joint fishing companies and expeditions. Many were aimed at facilitating the export of Soviet machine-building products to developing-country markets.

In the early 1970s, joint enterprises started to appear in the industrial sector. However, they were not widespread. In spite of the fact that such enterprises operated successfully in Iran, Afghanistan, and Mongolia as early as the 1920s and 1930s (and also from 1949 to 1957 in Mongolia), heated arguments took place over whether or not widespread application of this type of cooperation would be right and advisable. The opponents of joint ventures considered them to be a form alien to a socialist economy and an instrument of exploitation. Nevertheless, the foundation for developing joint enterprises was laid down, and by the end of the 1970s, there were some tangible results. The joint company Vietsovpetro, which conducts geological surveys and oil drilling for oil on the continental shelf in the southern part of Vietnam, was established in 1981. The partners were the state bodies of both countries, and the capital was shared 50:50. Later in the 1980s, an agreement was reached to set up the first joint enterprises in the manufacturing sector; a Soviet-Korean textile enterprise in the Democratic People's Republic of Korea and a poultry equipment manufacturing factory in India. In the latter, 60 per cent of the shares were to be held by an Indian company, and 40 per cent by a Soviet public enterprise.[34] There are plans to establish joint enterprises in some other countries in the agricultural sector.[35]

The decree issued by the Presidium of the Supreme Soviet of the U.S.S.R. in January 1987 established legal guidelines for developing nations to participate in joint ventures inside the U.S.S.R. This process, which allows Soviet state and cooperative enterprises to work with the developing-country state organizations and private firms, is gaining in popularity.

### Strengthening the Long-Term Character
### of Assistance Programs

In the second half of the 1970s, economic and technical cooperation entered its *third stage*. By this time, economic and technical assistance was marked by inertia—reflecting worsening economic stagnation in the U.S.S.R. The magnitude of the aid program continued to increase, but the rate of growth slowed in comparison with the previous period.

Attempts to reinvigorate Soviet assistance during this period related primarily to the further development of different types of assistance and of a legal mechanism for cooperation to give it longer-term stability. It was during this period that the majority of *long-term programs* (for ten or more years) were signed for economic and technical cooperation with India, Angola, Mozambique, Ethiopia, Libya, Turkey, Algeria, Mongolia, Vietnam, Cuba, and other developing nations.

These programs were a step forward compared to the earlier long-term cooperation agreements in that they encompassed a broader spectrum of sectors and industries— including non-traditional ones, such as engineering services and scientific and technical research between the Soviet Union and Third World countries. The programs provided for determining those sectors of industry in developing nations that could be expanded or modernized with an orientation toward long-term export to the Soviet Union. Such provisions even involved the decision not to build new enterprises or to expand production of the same products in existing factories in the U.S.S.R.

Yet another form of economic relations with developing nations that emerged in the late 1970s and early 1980s was *multilateral cooperation*—primarily with the participation of the Council for Mutual Economic Assistance. Although CMEA signed agreements on cooperation with two developing countries, Iraq and Mexico, as early as the mid-1970s, these were only partially implemented (only in the case of Iraq). In the 1980s, similar agreements were signed with Nicaragua (1983), Mozambique (1985), Angola, Ethiopia, the Democratic Republic of Yemen (1986), and Afghanistan (1987).

*Trilateral cooperation*—involving the participation of Soviet organizations, developed capitalist countries, and organizations and companies in developing nations—has also been developed. By the mid-1980s, the Soviet Union had concluded trilateral cooperation agreements in almost fifty developing nations. These included the participation of more than two hundred firms from developed capitalist countries.[36] There also have been some trilateral agreements in third countries with Indian companies and with Brazilian firms.[37]

In the late 1970s, economic and technical assistance programs between the Soviet Union and the developing nations began to suffer from problems and difficulties resulting from the general state of the world market and depressed economic conditions in trading-partner nations. In addition to the negative impact of external factors, there were also shortcomings in the forms and methods of cooperation: a certain lack of flexibility and dynamism, and insufficient interest on the part of Soviet enterprises in the manufacture of export products. Economic interaction was frequently determined by current demand and shortages without taking into account long-term trends in demand on either side. There was also evidence of stag nation in the Soviet Union's foreign trade mechanism. In particular, manufacturing enterprises were isolated from foreign trade activity because exports and imports were carried out by specialized foreign trade organizations under the control of the Ministry of Foreign Trade. Consequently, even the advantages of existing complementarities between the economic structures of the U.S.S.R. and less developed countries were not fully realized.

External factors and internal structural problems have resulted in a decrease in the Soviet Union's share of the trade (exports plus imports) of the developing countries (excluding Vietnam, the People's Republic of Korea, Cuba, Laos, and Mongolia) from 15 per cent in the mid-1970s to 11.3 per cent in 1988.[38] In the mid-1980s, the U.S.S.R.'s participation in trade with Third World nations (again excluding the five above-mentioned nations) comprised only 2.2 per cent and has remained practically unchanged.[39]

One of the barriers to greater economic relations between the U.S.S.R. and developing countries was the continuing concentration of assistance in the areas of metallurgy and energy. These two areas comprised more than half of all aid. The key contribution of these sectors in establishing a strong national economic structure, overcoming the lack of integration of the national economy, and helping to solve employment problems is beyond dispute. But it is also true that these are capital-intensive sectors with long repayment periods.

The main point is that this existing structure does not take into account the changes occurring in the national strategies of developing countries. Today the most important questions are those concerning agricultural development (especially agribusiness), and the encouragement of small and medium-scale enterprises that utilize local raw materials and uncomplicated and capital-saving technology. Small- and medium-scale enterprises are also capable of assuring the rapid recovery of invested money. The short lead times involved in constructing these enterprises result in increased business and increased production and provision of services. However, despite the benefits, expansion of aid to small- and medium-size enterprises has been hampered not only by insufficient economic incentives for and the inexperience of Soviet organizations in assisting in the promotion of such business, but also by the inertia of the Soviet foreign trade mechanism, which from the very outset has been oriented toward large-scale projects.

Other hindrances to increased cooperation with developing countries include the disproportionately small amount of cooperation on geological surveying operations—accounting for only 4–5 per cent of the total volume of the Soviet Union's economic and technical assistance to non-socialist developing nations.[40] Projects to build *social* infrastructure also have received little attention.[41]

Economic and scientific-technical cooperation between the U.S.S.R. and developing nations has been based on and mainly prompted by the mutual complementarity of economic structures—i.e., raw materials and foodstuffs of developing countries in exchange for Soviet industrial products and some other raw materials. Such a pattern of *inter*-sectoral cooperation cannot ensure the rapid rate of expansion for the long term and cannot be extended to new economic sectors. Therefore it is necessary to promote *intra*-sectoral specialization and cooperation, mainly in machine building, agribusiness, and consumer goods manufacturing industries. Overcoming manifold problems of cooperation in these sectors of industry would be a powerful impulse to expanding the volume of mutual trade and to diversifying the entire system of economic interaction.

The existing mechanisms of cooperation, mainly founded on bilateral relations and operating within the framework of inter-governmental agreements, initially fulfilled all the goals set for them. However, they did not—indeed could not—anticipate future changes brought about by the *internationalization* of economic life—particularly the expansion of multilateral forms of cooperation, including cooperation between nations with different types of socioeconomic systems. The Soviet Union did not significantly develop these forms of cooperation with the majority of Third World nations. Moreover, Soviet state organizations as well as Soviet enterprises were slow to cooperate with other socialist countries in implementing projects in developing nations. Trilateral agreements were also slow to develop.

The most general cause of these considerable shortcomings in the Soviet Union's sphere of foreign trade and aid is the fact that for decades, this sphere (like the entire economy of the country) was in the grip of administrative-command methods of management. Inadequate experience and information, lack of qualified personnel, and the weakness of incentives that might have offset the greater risks of operating in unfamiliar markets were also contributing factors.

### Changing Prospects for Economic and Technical Cooperation

A comparison of this chapter with several aspects discussed in Chapter 1 could create the impression that these chapters contradict one another; but the contradiction is only apparent. Chapter 1 describes changes in the *strategic* approach to cooperation with developing countries—changes that reflect the new political thinking and radical changes in the economic life of the U.S.S.R. But it should be noted that many of these changes have yet to be implemented. Throughout the course of *perestroika* in the Soviet Union, a new social policy is being formulated, and major political transformations and radical structural changes are taking place. Yet so far only the first steps have been taken in the transfer from administrative command methods to economic management and regulation. Clearly there will be a tremendous lag between the onset of radical economic reform in the Soviet Union and its complete manifestation in the sphere of foreign economic relations—although some changes (several of which are mentioned below) are already taking place.

The new concept of aid includes as one of its most important components both humanitarian and *global systems problems*, the solution of which to a great extent depends on improvements in the international political climate, the strengthening of mutual trust among governments, a decrease in the arms race, and progress on disarmament. All of this indicates why Soviet aid programs contain elements of both the traditional and the innovative. As economic reforms take place inside the country and as the political climate in the world improves, new approaches to cooperation with developing countries may prevail.

The mid-1980s clearly did mark the beginning of a new stage in the area of economic and technical cooperation between the Soviet Union and developing nations. In the period ahead, economic relations between the Soviet Union and developing countries will be characterized more and more by increasing interdependence and a search for ways to unite, not separate, nations and people. This new approach can already be seen in negotiations with several developing countries with which economic relations were until relatively recently non-existent or severely limited by political and ideological factors (for example, Iran, Pakistan, and the Republic of Korea).

In the context of the increasing internationalization of economic life, cooperation with countries in the Third World is not viewed as a closed system, but as an integral part of the world economy. These postulates of the new thinking, as well as the shift of the Soviet economy itself toward intensive development and radical reforms in the economic mechanism require numerous corrective measures in the system of economic and technical cooperation. The strategy of cooperation needs to be re-examined in the context of the fundamental principles of the new thinking in Soviet foreign policy.

Efforts to intensify the development of the Soviet economy and the U.S.S.R.'s more active participation in the international division of labor require, first of all, very rapid expansion of those sectors of the economy that promote scientific and technical progress, especially machine building. With respect to foreign trade, this means increasing exports of machinery and equipment, with the long-run goal of turning them into the U.S.S.R.'s major export commodities. The different levels of development characterizing the U.S.S.R. and its developing-country partners suggest a special role for less developed countries as markets for Soviet machines and equipment. Experience confirms that frequently stable Soviet exports and imports of the products of the machine-building industries begin with the provision of economic and technical assistance to developing countries in the creation of these industries.

Cooperation with developing countries in the machine-building industry will involve assisting the expansion of small and medium-size businesses in countries that are technically well equipped and capable of swiftly altering their production. Since the majority of these businesses tend to be privately owned, it is obvious that business contacts with these nations' private sectors will have to expand.

Another possible change in the structure of Soviet economic and technical cooperation is linked to an increase in participation in the agricultural sector and agribusiness, especially irrigation and the production of fertilizers, tractors, other agricultural machines, etc. This area could be enhanced by cooperation between organizations in the U.S.S.R. and those in other countries—e.g., Bulgaria, Cuba, Hungary, all of which have a wealth of experience in the development of agribusiness, including experience in Third World nations.

The new concept of economic and technical cooperation opens up possibilities for bringing together various types of material and intellectual resources of smaller enterprises and scientific and engineering organizations in the U.S.S.R. that presently participate little or not at all in foreign trade activity. Such contacts could be permanent in form—for example, joint-stock (public) companies—or they could involve temporary consortia active in a particular cooperation project. Economic cooperation with developing nations in these new areas would help diversify relations with these countries, establish direct links between enterprises and organizations, and increase the stability of trade relations.

The realization of a new model of economic cooperation with developing nations presupposes the necessary coordination of this model with internal economic processes in the U.S.S.R.—especially those related to fuel-energy, foodstuffs, machine building, and manufactured consumer goods. The division of labor with developing countries needs to enable the Soviet Union to concentrate on producing goods at home for which there are favorable conditions, while enabling partners in the developing world to expand their exports of manufactured goods and semi-finished products on a reliable basis. This could be accomplished by establishing joint ventures and enterprises, including those on the territory of the Soviet Union. There is a view that it would be better to establish joint industrial ventures in the relatively more developed countries because of their experience in developing these types of relations with Western countries. In our opinion, at the initial stages of establishing this form of relations, which is new to Soviet organizations, the most successful joint industrial ventures would be with countries that have the most experience in trade and economic cooperation with the U.S.S.R.

A decree adopted by the Soviet Council of Ministers in 1988—"On Further Development of Foreign Trade in Government, Cooperative, and Other Social Enterprises, Unions and Organizations"—and later official measures greatly expanded the number of organizations in the Soviet Union that could be opened up for foreign trade participation. As of mid-1990, over 14,000 Soviet enterprises and organizations have gained the right to operate independently in foreign markets, to form joint ventures, and to establish direct links with foreign enterprises and firms. The new measures should give a new impetus to the establishment of joint ventures, international associations, and organizations in developing countries and in the Soviet Union. The possibilities of developing this type of cooperation are great, especially for the establishment of ventures producing consumer goods and foodstuffs.

Joint ventures and enterprises between the U.S.S.R. and *developing* countries—located on the territory of either partner—are one of the most promising forms of expanding the volume of mutual cooperation and improving its structure and efficiency. The scale of this form of cooperation depends on the manner in which the legal basis for such ventures is worked out—allowing them more flexibility, relaxing the legal restrictions, and creating other more favorable conditions. Clearly most important are the actual prospects for the increased economic autonomy of Soviet enterprises and organizations that will operate on the basis of joint ownership.

# Conclusion

Taking into account the turbulent processes at work in the economic, political, and social life of the Soviet Union, it is very likely that the expansion of economic interaction with the developing countries will in the very near future encounter considerable difficulties. It is our view, however, that this slowdown will be of a temporary nature. Long-term interests on both sides will promote the expansion of mutual trade and its diversification, as well as the growth of other forms of economic cooperation.

## Notes

[1] Article 22 of the "Chapter of Economic Rights and Duties of States" states: "The flow of development assistance resources should include technical assistance."

[2] In Soviet statistics, these countries are Cuba, the People's Democratic Republic of Korea, Mongolia, and the People's Republic of Vietnam. The People's Republic of China is not included in this group.

[3] *Narodnoye khoziaistvo SSSR, 1988*, (Moscow: Finansy i Statistika), 1989, p. 5; *Kommunist* (Moscow), No. 11, 1990; p. 80.

[4] Statement by the head of the U.S.S.R. delegation at the 36th session of the Board of the U.N. Conference on Trade and Development (UNCTAD), October 6, 1989.

[5] For an example of the method of calculation, see the annual reports from the Development Assistance Committee of the OECD. The degree of concessionality or grant element is calculated on the basis of annual interest of the credit, payments per annum, discount rate, grace period, and the life of the loan. According to the OECD Development Assistance Committee's criteria for aid, there must be a grant element of 25 per cent or more.

[6] *Kommunist* (Moscow), No. 3, 1990, p. 27.

[7] OECD, *New Trends in U.S.S.R. Aid*, OECD Document DCD/87.14, November 5, 1987.

[8] D. Valovoi, "Ekonomika v chelovecheskom izmerenii," Moscow, 1988, p. 287. In 1985, Gross Social Product was equal to 1.8 of GNP.

[9] See Table 1.

[10] Authors' calculations based on OECD, *Development Cooperation: 1975 Review* (Paris: OECD, 1975), p. 217; and OECD, *Development Co-operation: 1989 Review* (Paris: OECD, 1989), p. 279.

[11] Authors' calculations based on OECD and CIA data in Table 1.

[12] *MEIMO* (Moscow: Institute of World Economy and International Relations), No. 11, 1987, p. 150.

[13] Statement by the head of the U.S.S.R. delegation at the 36th session of the Board of the U.N. Conference on Trade and Development (UNCTAD), October 6, 1989.

[14] D. D. Degtyar', *Plodotvornoye sotrudnichestvo* (Moscow: Mezhdunarodniye otnosheniya, 1969), p. 7.

[15] See *Vneshnyaya torgovlya SSSR za 1918–1966 gody* (Moscow: Finansy i Statistyka, 1967); *Vneshnyaya torgovlya SSSR za 1959–1963 gody* (Moscow: Finansy i Statistyka, 1965).

[16]*Vneshnyaya torgovlya SSSR za 1922–1981 gody* (Moscow: Finansy i Statistyka, 1982).

[17]D. D. Degtyar', op. cit., p. 7.

[18]UNCTAD Document TD/341, July 16, 1987, p. 3.

[19]Estimated by Y. N. Grekov, A. I. Kachanov, D. I. Sukhoparov, T.V. Teodorovich, *Ekonomicheskoye i tekhnicheskoye sodeistviye SSSR zarubezhnym stranam* (Moscow: Mezhdunarodniye otnosheniya, 1987), p. 239.

[20]In Soviet foreign trade statistics, the delivery of "complete equipment" means the provision of the set of machines and equipment necessary for erecting a production unit (whether a factory, a workshop, or a production line).

[21]"Vneshniye ekonomicheskiye svyazi SSSR v 1988," *Statisticheskiy sbornik* (Moscow: Finansy i Statistyka, 1989), pp. 8, 11, 14, and 46–48.

[22]See, for example, N. S. Semin, *Strany SEV i Afrika* (Moscow: Mezhdunarodniye otnosheniya, 1968).

[23]D. Degtyar', *Plodotvornoye sotrudnichestvo*, op. cit., p. 28.

[24]See, for example, *Problemy sotrudnichestva sotsialisticheskikh i razvivayushchikhsya stran* (Moscow: Nauka, 1960); L. Z. Zevin, *Noviye tendentsii v ekonomicheskom sotrudnichestve sotsialisticheskikh i razvivayuschikhsya stran* (Moscow: Nauka, 1970); *Ekonomicheskiye otnosheniya sotsialisticheskikh gosudarstv so stranami Afriki* (Moscow: Nauka, 1973).

[25]For detailed information see: *Sotsialisticheskaya ekonomicheskaya integratsiya i sotrudnichestvo s razvivsayushchimisya stranami* (Moscow: Nauka, 1975); L. Z. Zevin, *Economic Cooperation of Socialist and Developing Countries: New Trends* (Moscow: Nauka, 1976); N. P. Shmelev, *Sotsializm i mezhdunarodniye ekonomicheskiye otnosheniya* (Moscow: Mezhdunarodniye otnosheniya, 1979); *Sotsializm i perestroika mezhdunarodnykh ekonomicheskikh otnosheniy* (Moscow: Mezhdunarodniye otnosheniya, 1982).

[26]See *Strany SEV i razvivayushchiyesya gosudarstva: 80-e gody* (Moscow: Nauka, 1985; Mirovoye sotsialisticheskoye khozyaistvo, Voprosy politicheskoi ekonomii Moscow, 1988, Chapter 19.

[27]With this type of assistance, the contractor has responsibility for completing the project as a whole and its parts according to the timetable. In this form of cooperation, the Soviet side usually provides credits, delivers machinery and equipment, and sends specialists to assist the local partner. The right of ownership is transferred to the customer when the project is completed and ready for operation (acceptance on turnkey terms). The services of Soviet specialists, the cost materials, amortization of construction equipment, and means of transportation are included in the total cost of the contract project, not paid for separately.

[28]*Vneshnyanya torgovlya*, No. 11, 1986, p. 2.

[29]*Postroyeno pri ekonomicheskom i tekhnicheskom sodeistvii Sovetskogo Soyuza* (Moscow: Mezhdunarodniye otnosheniya, 1982), p. 259; and Y. N. Grekov et al., op. cit., p. 89.

[30]*Vneshnyaya torgovlya*, No. 11, 1986, p. 2.

[31]*Postroyeno pri ekonomicheskom i tekhnicheskom sodeistvii Soveskogo Soyuza* (Moscow: Mezhdunarodniye otnosheniya, 1982), p. 155.

[32]*Izvestiya*, August 29, 1987.

[33]E. Y. Obminskiy, *Razvivayushchiyesya strany i mezhdunarodnoye razdeleniye truda* (Moscow: Mezhdunarodniye otnosheniya, 1974).

[34]*Pravda*, December 19, 1987.

[35]*BIKI*, February 2, 1989.

[36]*Vneshnyaya torgovlya*, No. 3, 1984, p. 27.

[37]*Izvestiya*, December 9, 1984.

[38]"Vneshnyaya torgovlya SSSR v 1975," *Statisticheskiy sbornik* (Moscow: Mezhdunarodniye otnosheniya, 1976), p. 14; and "Vneshnyaya torgovlya SSSR v 1987," *Statisticheskiy sbornik*, (Moscow: Mezhdunarodniye otnosheniya, 1988), p. 8.

[39]*Monthly Bulletin of Statistics*, Vol. XXXIX, No. 6, June 1985, Sp. Table B, pp. XVIII-XIX.

[40]Delovoye sotrudnichestvo v interesakh mira i progressa (Moscow: Izdatelstvo politicheskoi literatury, 1984), p. 190.

[41]For detailed information see: *Sotsializm preobrazuyet strukturu proizvodstva* (Moscow: Nauka, 1982); N. A. Ushakova, *Strany SEV i razvivayushchiyesya gosudarstva sotsialisticheskoi orientatsii: ekonomicheskoye sotrudnichestvo* (Moscow: Nauka, 1980).

# An Anatomy of the U.S. Foreign Assistance Program

Ernest H. Preeg

This chapter is principally a descriptive presentation of U.S. economic and other forms of official economic support to developing countries from 1970 through 1987. It summarizes quantitative flows of aid in terms of overall levels, geographic distribution, and functional concentrations. It also elaborates on some of the qualitative factors that affect the impact of economic aid on the development goals of recipient countries. The presentation begins with that part of U.S. economic assistance to developing countries classified as official development assistance (ODA), which is defined as financial assistance provided by the U.S. government on concessional terms in support of development objectives of the recipient developing country.[1] ODA is a fairly clear concept in economic terms and is even more clearly distinguished in U.S. thinking by its direct budgetary cost to the taxpayer; every year, it is presented to Congress as part of the international affairs account in the President's annual budget, and it is one of the most exhaustively debated sections of the budget.

The terms of reference for this chapter also call for the discussion of other areas of economic support for developing countries: "other official flows" (principally export credits), debt relief, and commodity agreements and other trade measures. These categories of support can constitute important support for developing countries, but they all come with significant qualifications and therefore have less impact than ODA on development objectives. Their non-comparability with ODA is indeed highlighted, and *no attempt is made to construct aggregate figures for ODA and non-ODA support.*

These various elements of economic support for development are brought together in a more analytical context toward the end of the chapter, which closes with a broader commentary on economic relations with developing countries.

# Official Development Assistance

A quantitative presentation of ODA flows involves a number of technical definitions, some of which have an important bearing on the significance of the figures presented. Except where specifically cited otherwise, the definitions used throughout this chapter are those adopted by the Development Assistance Committee (DAC) of the Organisation for Economic Co-operation and Development (OECD).[2]

A central definitional question is whether figures are presented on the basis of *disbursements* or *commitments*. Figures presented here are generally on a net disbursement basis—namely, the actual flow of financial or in-kind support during the period stated, net of repayments by the recipient country of earlier ODA loans.[3] This is the relevant measure of financial assistance actually received from year to year and is a far more concrete measure of economic assistance than "new commitments." Commitments can be for projects that get bogged down in implementation or get canceled for a number of reasons, such as poor design at the outset or the inability of either the recipient or the donor country to comply fully with the provisions of the original commitment. A fairly frequent problem for both multilateral and bilateral donors is that a large number of project commitments get backed up in the "pipeline" and are unlikely to be implemented.

Another definitional question relates to the classification of recipients as "developing" countries. There are various definitions of a developing country, and they are complicated by the transition to "industrialized" status currently under way or achieved by the most advanced developing countries. For example, the Republic of Korea and Singapore are now more industrialized by virtually any objective criteria (such as industrial infrastructure, rapid growth of a technology-oriented labor force, and export competitiveness in manufactured products) than are the lower tier of OECD countries and some East European countries. Israel, the largest recipient of U.S. economic aid, has also achieved advanced status in many respects. The U.N. system's classification of developing countries to some extent reflects the political orientation of membership in the "Group of 77," while the World Bank's criteria for "graduation" from "developing" status emphasize per capita income and the ability to borrow in commercial capital markets. The definition used here is that adopted by the DAC, which is a broad interpretation that includes recipients of bilateral economic aid that are not clearly established industrialized countries or centrally planned socialist countries.[4] Other definitional questions, particularly relating to *qualitative* aspects of ODA, are discussed in the following sections.

## Overall ODA Levels

Table 1 presents levels of U.S. ODA from 1970 through 1987. Total ODA increased from $3.4 billion annually in 1970–72 to $8.9 billion in 1987. This represents a 162 per cent increase in current dollars, but the increase is less than 15 per cent when adjusted for inflation. ODA as a share of GNP declined steadily—from 0.32 per cent in 1970–72 to about 0.25 per cent in the late 1970s-early 1980s, and then to 0.20 per cent in 1987. The overall DAC average in 1987 was 0.35 per cent, and the United States ranked seventeenth among the eighteen member countries, with only Austria at a lower percentage share of GNP. This relatively low share reflects both budget constraints and a lack of public support for the aid program.

### Multilateral versus Bilateral Assistance

Table 1 also separates U.S. ODA into bilateral and multilateral assistance, and then again into principal subcategories. The bilateral share of total ODA was 81 per cent in 1970–72; it then dropped to about 68 per cent in 1974–84, before rising again to almost 80 per cent in 1986–87. Single-year variations in the bilateral/multilateral mix can be misleading, since contributions to multilateral development banks (line B.2), in particular, can be "lumpy," depending on replenishment schedules, which in the case of the United States have been accentuated by arrearages followed by large catch-up payments.[5] Nevertheless, the dip in the percentage share for bilateral assistance in the middle years of Table 1 (1974–1984) followed by a rise again in the mid-1980s, does reflect a deliberate policy in the 1970s to give greater emphasis to multilateral ODA, while very large bilateral programs in Southeast Asia wound down. This was followed by an equally striking buildup of bilateral ODA in the early 1980s—from $4 billion annually in 1978–80 to $7-$8 billion in 1985–87.

Within the bilateral assistance category, there was a more striking trend in favor of grant assistance, mostly fast-disbursing budget or balance-of-payments support (line A.1.d), which increased

## Table 1.    U.S. Official Development Assistance to Developing Countries and Multilateral Agencies, Net Disbursements ($ millions and percentages)

| | 1970–72[a] | 1974–76[a] | 1978–80[a] | 1982–84[a] | 1985 | 1986 | 1987 |
|---|---|---|---|---|---|---|---|
| **Total Official Development Assistance** | **3,408** | **4,065** | **5,829** | **8,331** | **9,403** | **9,564** | **8,945** |
| *(ODA as percentage of GNP)* | *0.32* | *0.26* | *0.25* | *0.25* | *0.24* | *0.23* | *0.20* |
| **A. Bilateral ODA** | **2,757** | **2,778** | **3,972** | **5,627** | **8,182** | **7,602** | **7,007** |
| *(percentage of total ODA)* | *80.9* | *68.3* | *68.1* | *67.5* | *87.0* | *79.5* | *78.3* |
| 1. Grants and Grant-Like Contributions | 1,506 | 1,710 | 2,496 | 4,658 | 7,310 | 7,033 | 6,688 |
| *(percentage of total ODA)* | *44.2* | *42.1* | *42.8* | *55.9* | *77.6* | *73.5* | *74.8* |
| a. Technical Assistance | 561 | 532 | 562 | 1,372 | 1,458 | 1,506 | 1,749 |
| b. Food Aid | 364 | 393 | 492 | 532 | 781 | 640 | 808 |
| c. Administrative Costs | 0 | 0 | 0 | 412 | 468 | 475 | 486 |
| d. Other[b] | 580 | 785 | 1,482 | 2,342 | 4,603 | 4,412 | 3,645 |
| 2. Development Lending and Capital | 1,251 | 1,068 | 1,476 | 969 | 872 | 569 | 319 |
| *(percentage of total ODA)* | *36.7* | *26.3* | *25.3* | *11.6* | *9.3* | *5.9* | *3.6* |
| a. New Development Lending | 822 | 357 | 744 | 246 | (63) | (226) | (287) |
| b. Food Aid Loans | 308 | 600 | 690 | 672 | 898 | 742 | (584) |
| c. Other[c] | 121 | 110 | 42 | 50 | 37 | 53 | 48 |

| | 1970–72[a] | 1974–76[a] | 1978–80[a] | 1982–84[a] | 1985 | 1986 | 1987 |
|---|---|---|---|---|---|---|---|
| **B. Contributions to Multilateral Institutions** *(percentage of total ODA)* | **651** *19.1* | **1,287** *31.7* | **1,857** *31.9* | **2,704** *32.5* | **1,221** *13.0* | **1,962** *20.5* | **1,938** *21.7* |
| 1. Grants *(percentage of total ODA)* | 233 *6.8* | 383 *9.4* | 635 *10.9* | 886 *10.6* | 973 *10.3* | 836 *8.7* | 723 *8.1* |
| a. U.N. Agencies | 207 | 324 | 463 | 692 | 758 | 631 | 590 |
| b. Other | 26 | 60 | 172 | 195 | 215 | 205 | 133 |
| 2. Capital Payments *(percentage of total ODA)* | 418 *12.3* | 904 *22.2* | 1,201 *20.6* | 1,809 *21.7* | 252 *2.7* | 1,132 *11.8* | 1,220 *13.4* |
| a. World Bank | 4 | 0 | 40 | 159 | 30 | 133 | 63 |
| b. International Development Association | 235 | 517 | 777 | 1,163 | 0 | 742 | 895 |
| c. Regional Development Banks | 178 | 387 | 372 | 487 | 222 | 257 | 262 |
| d. Other | 0 | 0 | 13 | 0 | (4) | 0 | 0 |

[a]Annual average.
[b]Includes Emergency Support Fund.
[c]Includes debt reorganization.
[d]Includes International Finance Corporation.

Source: U.S. Statistical Submissions to OECD/DAC, various years.

from $580 million annually in 1970–72 to $3.6-$4.6 billion in 1985–87, while development loans (line A.2) declined in absolute terms from $1.3 billion annually in 1970–72 to $319 million in 1987.

Two principal factors accounted for this dramatic shift. First, there was a strong tendency in the 1980s toward fast-disbursing grant assistance in support of structural adjustment/policy reform in recipient countries. Second, repayments on loans to aid "graduate" countries in Asia and Latin America tended to offset, to some extent, new loans to poorer countries. For example, new development lending in 1987 (line A.2.a) shows a figure for *net* new disbursements of minus $287 million, which reflects gross new disbursements (mostly to poorer countries) well below gross repayments of principal on earlier loans (mostly from middle-income aid graduates).

Contributions to multilateral institutions showed steady growth in grants to the United Nations and other agencies during the 1970s, with a leveling off and some decline in the 1980s. Capital payments to multilateral development banks (MDBs) (line B.2) are harder to assess, since year-to-year swings in payments were especially wide, and the low levels in 1985 were offset by larger payments, partly for arrearages, in 1986-87. The regional development banks, however, showed a clear decline relative to the World Bank/International Development Association (IDA), starting in 1986, which reflected the growing predominance of contributions to IDA, the soft-loan window of the World Bank, among all MDB contributions.

### Grants versus Loans

Another observation relating to Table 1 pertains to the quality of aid in terms of grants in contrast to loans and to the overall degree of concessionality as calculated by the DAC formula. All of Table 1 except for Development Lending and Capital (section A.2) is essentially grant assistance; if that figure is subtracted from total ODA, grant assistance in 1970–72 constituted 63 per cent of all U.S. ODA, and that figure climbed steadily to 96 per cent of net disbursements in 1987. The average overall grant element calculation of U.S. ODA was 87 per cent in 1970-72 and 96.4 per cent in 1985–86. In comparison, the grant element in 1985–86 for all DAC countries combined was 92.5 per cent.

### Tied Aid

Table 1 also gives some indication—although not a very accurate one—of the degree to which U.S. ODA is tied to U.S. exports. Tied aid has an important impact on the quality of aid, since tying aid disbursement to the exports of the donor country not only can increase the cost and reduce the choice of appropriate technology for the recipient country, but also can influence the overall structure of an aid program toward the commercial interests of the donor country rather than the development priorities of the recipient country. Indeed, pressures can develop to orient tied aid programs toward middle-income developing countries, which have a greater capacity to import capital goods and other commercially sensitive products rather than toward the poorest countries, which need fast-disbursing budget support. The U.S. program is sharply criticized by U.S. industry for not, in fact, financing large projects in the commercially sensitive power generation, transportation, and telecommunications sectors—while Japanese and Western European aid programs do so.

Despite the importance of aid tying to the quality of ODA, the United States can only roughly estimate the degree to which its aid is tied. This partly reflects the fact that U.S. Agency for International Development (USAID) procurement decisions are generally made by the field missions, and that it is difficult to keep full records on the country of origin. The figures submitted to DAC for tied procurement of U.S. ODA were 78 per cent in 1970, 73 per cent in 1980, and 44 per cent in 1986. These numbers are estimates based on samples taken some years ago, and they tend to overstate the degree of tying. For example, they do not take account of large amounts of local cost financing. They also do not reflect the discretion AID mission directors have to approve non-U.S. procurement for tied projects where the high cost of U.S. equipment or the inability to maintain it are overriding considerations. In Sub-Saharan Africa, for example, many projects in such sectors as rural health services and small-scale agriculture involve the purchase of vehicles, but since only European and Japanese vehicles can be serviced effectively in the region, U.S. procurement is generally waived on a case-by-case basis.

Another point to be noted in relation to Table 1 is that virtually all contributions to multilateral development agencies are untied, as is almost all of the fast-disbursing support (line A.1.d). Tied aid, in contrast, consists principally of food aid—from which U.S. farmers benefit directly—and a large share of technical assistance and development lending. Taking the latter categories as a share of total ODA for 1987 gives a rough estimate of 29 per cent tied aid.

### Geographic and Functional Distribution of Bilateral ODA

Table 2 presents U.S. bilateral ODA by geographic region. Some very striking changes are apparent over the period 1970-87. Four subre-

**Table 2.    U.S. Bilateral ODA, Net Disbursements, by Destination ($ millions and percentages)**

| | 1970–72[a] | | 1974–76[a] | | 1978–80[a] | | 1982–84[a] | | 1985 | | 1986 | | 1987 | |
|---|---|---|---|---|---|---|---|---|---|---|---|---|---|---|
| | $ mil. | % of Total | $ mil. | % of Total | $ mil. | % of Total | $ mil. | % of Total | $ mil. | % of Total | $ mil. | % of Total | $ mil. | % of Total |
| **Total ODA** | 2,780 | | 2,769 | | 3,972 | | 5,627 | | 8,182 | | 7,602 | | 7,007 | |
| Europe | 96 | 3.5 | (6) | — | 178 | 4.5 | 225 | 4.0 | 120 | 1.5 | 143 | 1.9 | (44) | — |
| Africa | 267 | 9.6 | 371 | 13.4 | 1,199 | 30.2 | 1,913 | 34.0 | 2,860 | 35.0 | 2,170 | 28.5 | 2,024 | 28.9 |
| North of Sahara | 76 | 2.7 | 151 | 5.5 | 722 | 18.2 | 1,112 | 19.8 | 1,459 | 17.8 | 1,216 | 16.0 | 1,155 | 16.4 |
| South of Sahara | 164 | 5.9 | 190 | 6.9 | 418 | 10.5 | 751 | 13.3 | 1,318 | 16.1 | 882 | 11.6 | 783 | 11.2 |
| Unspecified | 27 | | 30 | | 59 | | 50 | | 83 | | 72 | | 87 | |
| America | 426 | 15.3 | 312 | 11.3 | 283 | 7.1 | 916 | 16.3 | 1,465 | 17.9 | 1,318 | 17.3 | 1,437 | 20.5 |
| Central | 121 | 4.4 | 127 | 4.6 | 207 | 5.2 | 783 | 13.9 | 1,175 | 14.4 | 1,030 | 13.5 | 1,211 | 17.3 |
| South | 271 | 9.7 | 131 | 4.7 | 34 | 0.9 | 84 | 1.5 | 218 | 2.7 | 208 | 2.7 | 119 | 1.6 |
| Unspecified | 34 | | 54 | | 43 | | 49 | | 72 | | 80 | | 72 | |
| Asia | 1,680 | 60.4 | 1,626 | 58.7 | 1,654 | 41.6 | 1,817 | 32.3 | 2,705 | 33.1 | 2,940 | 38.7 | 2,058 | 29.4 |
| Middle East | 70 | 2.5 | 430 | 15.5 | 1,034 | 26.0 | 1,189 | 21.1 | 2,042 | 25.0 | 2,008 | 26.4 | 1,388 | 19.8 |
| South | 597 | 21.5 | 542 | 19.6 | 359 | 9.0 | 422 | 7.5 | 454 | 5.5 | 478 | 6.3 | 369 | 5.2 |
| Far East | 991 | 35.6 | 632 | 22.8 | 243 | 6.1 | 185 | 3.3 | 180 | 2.2 | 420 | 5.5 | 265 | 3.8 |
| Unspecified | 23 | | 23 | | 18 | | 21 | | 29 | | 34 | | 37 | |
| Oceania | 53 | 1.9 | 83 | 3.0 | 108 | 2.7 | 163 | 2.9 | 165 | 2.0 | 230 | 3.0 | 176 | 2.5 |
| Other Unspecified | 261 | | 383 | | 549 | | 593 | | 867 | | 801 | | 1,356 | |

[a] Annual average.
Source: U.S. Statistical Submissions to OECD/DAC, various years.

gions—Northern and Southern Africa, Central America, and the Middle East—showed large increases in the share of bilateral ODA, while three other subregions—South America, South Asia, and Far East Asia—showed corresponding large decreases. Increases for North Africa and the Middle East principally reflected the large increases in economic aid to Egypt and Israel stemming from the Camp David accords of 1978. These two subregions accounted for 5.2 per cent of U.S. bilateral ODA in 1970–72 and 36.2 per cent in 1987.

The increase for Sub-Saharan Africa from 5.9 per cent in 1970–72 to over 11 per cent in 1986 and 1987 reflects the growing concentration of ODA in the poorest, most needy countries, many of which are in that region. The increased share for Central America, up from 4.4 per cent in 1970–72 to 17.3 per cent in 1987, was a consequence of the Caribbean Basin Initiative announced by President Ronald Reagan in 1982, which placed higher priority on economic support to this region, including a preferential reduction of U.S. trade barriers to exports from the region, incentives for increased private investment, and a quadrupling of economic aid. The decline in the share of U.S. bilateral ODA to South America—from 9.7 per cent in 1970–72 to 1.6 per cent in 1987—reflects, in large part, the "graduation" from concessional financing of such countries as Colombia, Brazil, and Chile, which had been among the largest recipients of U.S. ODA under the Alliance for Progress aid program during the 1960s. U.S. bilateral ODA to South America in recent years has been restricted almost entirely to the poorer Andean countries—Bolivia, Ecuador, and Peru. The decline in the share for South America is also a consequence of the higher priorities given to other regions and the severe overall U.S. budget constraints since 1985.

Assistance to South Asia and Far East Asia has been similarly affected by the "graduation" or transition from major aid recipient status of the Republic of Korea, Taiwan, Malaysia, and Thailand, and by the shifting of U.S. budget priorities elsewhere. In addition, the very large economic assistance program in South Vietnam was terminated at the end of the Vietnam War. Overall, the share of U.S. bilateral ODA destined for South Asia and Far East Asia declined from 57.1 per cent in 1970–72 to as low as 7.7 per cent in 1985, before recovering to 9.0 per cent in 1987 as a result of sharply increased assistance to the Philippines government of President Corazon Aquino.

Table 3 presents U.S. bilateral ODA by function or sector. This series of data is not comparable to that used in Tables 1 and 2, in that the figures are only available beginning in 1975. In addition, the figures are based on commitments rather than disbursements, which produces a total for bilateral ODA in 1987 of $7.4 billion in

**Table 3.  U.S. Bilateral ODA Commitments, by Sector and Purpose ($ millions)**

| | 1975–76[a] | | 1978–80[a] | | 1982–84[a] | | 1985 | | 1986 | | 1987 | |
|---|---|---|---|---|---|---|---|---|---|---|---|---|
| | $ mil. | % of Total | $ mil. | % of Total | $ mil. | % of Total | $ mil. | % of Total | $ mil. | % of Total | $ mil. | % of Total |
| **Total ODA** | 4,431 | | 5,080 | | 7,038 | | 9,157 | | 8,746 | | 7,412 | |
| **Contributions Allocable by Sector** | 1,239 | 28.0 | 2,442 | 48.1 | 4,136 | 58.8 | 3,856 | 42.1 | 3,770 | 43.1 | 3,071 | 41.4 |
| Planning and Public Administration | 18 | 0.4 | 43 | 0.8 | 85 | 1.2 | 133 | 1.5 | 114 | 1.3 | — | — |
| Public Utilities | 154 | 3.5 | 406 | 8.0 | 407 | 5.8 | 219 | 2.4 | 262 | 3.0 | — | — |
| Agriculture | 377 | 8.5 | 835 | 16.4 | 859 | 12.2 | 1,037 | 11.3 | 968 | 11.1 | — | — |
| Industry, Mining, Construction | 149 | 3.4 | 78 | 1.5 | 19 | 0.3 | 18 | 0.2 | 32 | 0.4 | — | — |
| Trade, Banking, Tourism, Services | 43 | 1.0 | 16 | 0.3 | 273 | 3.9 | 369 | 4.0 | 338 | 3.9 | — | — |
| Education | 84 | 1.9 | 211 | 4.2 | 332 | 4.7 | 357 | 3.9 | 320 | 3.7 | — | — |
| Health | 179 | 4.0 | 346 | 6.8 | 426 | 6.1 | 629 | 6.9 | 609 | 7.0 | — | — |
| Social Infrastructure and Welfare | 74 | 1.7 | 85 | 1.7 | 330 | 4.7 | 492 | 5.4 | 418 | 4.8 | — | — |
| Multisector and Unspecified | 161 | 3.6 | 422 | 8.3 | 1,405 | 20.0 | 602 | 6.6 | 709 | 8.1 | — | — |

| Contributions Not Allocable by Sector | 3,192 | 72.0 | 2,638 | 51.9 | 2,902 | 41.2 | 5,301 | 57.9 | 4,976 | 56.9 | 4,341 | 58.6 |
|---|---|---|---|---|---|---|---|---|---|---|---|---|
| Financing for Current Imports | 2,625 | 59.2 | 1,623 | 31.9 | 1,617 | 22.9 | 1,727 | 18.9 | 1,507 | 17.2 | — | — |
| Contributions Not Directly Linked to Imports | 407 | 9.2 | 789 | 15.5 | 1,147 | 16.3 | 3,317 | 36.2 | 3,220 | 36.8 | — | — |
| Emergency and Distress Relief (non-food) | 74 | 1.7 | 116 | 2.3 | 138 | 2.0 | 215 | 2.3 | 197 | 2.3 | — | — |
| Other | 86 | 1.9 | 110 | 2.2 | 0 | | 6 | 0.1 | 0 | | — | — |

*Note:* Sector classifications were redefined in 1987.

[a] Annual Average.

Source: U.S. Statistical Submissions to OECD/DAC, various years.

commitments, as compared with the $7.0 billion figure for disbursements in Tables 1 and 2. Nevertheless, Table 3 gives a fairly clear breakdown in relative terms of bilateral ODA by sector.

The most striking aspect of Table 3 is the large share—generally over half of bilateral ODA—that is not allocated by sector. This consists principally of commodity import programs and direct budget support to finance immediate import needs, which took on even greater prominence in 1985–87 (57–59 per cent of the total) than in the early 1980s. Of the sector-specific programs, agriculture and health consistently have been the largest recipients of ODA (11.1 per cent and 7.0 per cent, respectively, in 1986), while more modest shares went to education (3.7 per cent) and social infrastructure/welfare (4.8 per cent). Public utilities and industry/mining/construction have received very small shares of U.S. bilateral ODA in recent years.

### Toward a Development Strategy of Structural Adjustment

The foregoing quantitative discussion of U.S. development assistance cannot be understood fully without a more integrated commentary on overall development strategy and public attitudes about economic aid in the United States.

Particularly since the mid-1980s, the strategy pursued by the United States in concert with other donors, as well as by most developing-country aid recipients, has centered on the need for each recipient developing country to undertake a fundamental restructuring of its own economy, so as to establish appropriate incentives for increased productivity and job creation. The strategy of structural adjustment is also referred to as a strategy of market-oriented policy reform. This is because in the large majority of cases, the existing circumstances in the developing country are characterized by excessive government regulation and control, a somewhat arbitrary and inefficient allocation of investment capital, and a protectionist trade policy with strong disincentives for the export sector. The direction of needed policy reform, as agreed between the recipient country and the aid donor community, is to give decisive influence to market-oriented prices and allocation procedures. More specifically, the reform process involves a decentralization of power away from overstaffed ministries, the rationalization or privatization of public-sector entities, market-oriented prices for farmers and private businesses, and a more open trading system, with foreign exchange allocated largely through a convertible national currency.

This development strategy has increasingly involved a high

degree of formal coordination between the host-country government and principal aid donors, both bilateral and multilateral. The World Bank has come to play a central role in coordinating donor efforts in support of policy reform and structural adjustment in the recipient country.

Structural adjustment can bring immediate gains to many people in the poorer segments of society, through private-sector job creation and higher prices to small farmers. There is growing recognition, however, that such adjustment can involve a difficult transition for those segments of the population adversely affected by policy change, and that there is a corresponding need for targeted support for foreign aid programs for such segments of the population.

ODA in support of structural adjustment is, therefore, directed toward three principal objectives:

1. *Fast-disbursing balance-of-payments support.* The restructuring of macroeconomic policy can best be undertaken in the context of overall economic growth, which often requires a large increase in fast-disbursing foreign exchange in the short run to pay for imports associated with economic growth targets.

2. *Targeted assistance to adversely affected segments of society.* The poorest segments of society, in particular, need to be protected from the adverse transitional effects of structural adjustment, through emphasis on such programs as health delivery systems, primary education, and direct support for small-scale agriculture and small to medium-size private sector firms. Emphasis on this dimension of economic assistance is associated with the theme, "structural adjustment with a human face."

3. *Direct support to the private sector.* Such programs involve technical assistance, the strengthening of financial institutions that provide credit at reasonable rates to the private sector, and vocational or other training to supply the human resource needs of private-sector growth.

This, in brief terms, is the strategy for development that has evolved during the 1980s (for a fuller discussion, see chapter by Elliot Berg in this volume). It explains, to some extent, the increased share of U.S. assistance provided as fast-disbursing, balance-of-payments support. In some cases, it has influenced the country levels of assistance. For example, balance-of-payments assistance to Zambia was halted in 1987, when that country reversed previously adopted reform measures, while Cameroon was treated more favorably because it had a successful adjustment program under way.

However, although this broad strategy for economic development receives widespread support in the United States in conceptual terms, the actual U.S. bilateral economic aid program is frequently criticized and does not have strong public support. There are four basic reasons for this lack of support:

*First,* most of the aid goes to a relatively few countries of high foreign policy interest to the United States. Almost 40 per cent goes to Israel and Egypt; another 30 per cent goes to Central America, Pakistan, and the Philippines. This aid is criticized for having short-term political objectives rather than being more fully in support of longer-term economic development.

*Second,* there is widespread skepticism that aid programs in fact produce the desired results. Many recipient governments are viewed as corrupt or incapable of implementing sound economic policies. In such circumstances, financial support can provide the means to postpone difficult reform decisions and to maintain corrupt bureaucrats in power.

*Third,* the implementation of projects is heavily encumbered by many detailed provisions and restrictions in U.S. aid legislation. There are narrowly defined and, at times, conflicting objectives spread throughout hundreds of pages of legislation. These encumbrances have accumulated over the years largely as a result of the Congress trying to impose its priorities on programs administered by the Executive Branch of the government.

*Fourth,* economic aid has been caught up in the overall budget reduction program of the past several years and does not generally receive as high a priority as the defense budget and domestic programs.

The various criticisms of the U.S. foreign aid program came to a head with the publication of two critical assessments in early 1989—one a report by a Task Force of the U.S. House Foreign Affairs Committee, and the other by Alan Woods, then Administrator of the U.S. Agency for International Development.[6] Both reports were supportive of the underlying structural adjustment development strategy but critical of the way the existing bilateral program was implemented. They called for more clearly stated objectives, a greater emphasis on development criteria, and a basic reorganization to simplify procedures and eliminate bureaucratic inefficiency.

# Other Elements of Support for Developing Countries

Three other categories of support for developing countries are discussed in this chapter: Other Official Flows (OOF), debt relief, and commodity agreements and other trade measures. Each of these categories can provide assistance to individual or groups of developing countries, but there are important qualifications to be made in virtually all specific circumstances—both with respect to the impact on national development goals and to the actual financial benefits that accrue. In almost all cases, these categories of support are of less direct economic benefit than ODA, and therefore no attempt is made to add together ODA and non-ODA support to obtain an aggregate support figure.

### Other Official Flows

Other Official Flows consist largely of export financing at commercial or near-commercial rates, as distinct from ODA, which, by definition, involves a minimum degree of grant element (25 per cent for untied and 35 per cent for tied credits according to DAC definitions).[7] The United States has two basic facilities for such official export credits: the Export-Import Bank, which provides export financing where private-sector export financing is not readily available, and the Commodity Credit Corporation (CCC), which provides similar financing for agricultural commodities. Table 4 presents recent figures for these categories of Other Official Flows for developing countries during the period 1980–86.

The development impact of official export credits is hard to assess, since for many donor countries most export credit is provided by the private sector, and official credit is restricted to the role of a supplemental facility. For the United States in 1986, for example, total exports to developing countries were $74 billion, of which only $2.2 billion, or 3 per cent, was financed officially. In contrast, the socialist countries, with no private banking sector in their economies, have financed all or almost all exports to developing countries through official credits. It should also be emphasized that such official credits do not provide direct financial benefits to developing countries—except for the extent to which the terms of such credit are slightly better than commercial rates.

The principal benefit is that official credits can finance exports to developing countries that would not otherwise take place, but even this benefit is more limited than it might appear, since many developing countries are constrained as to how much additional debt they can realistically service at commercial rates. Such a constraint can be explicit in an International Monetary Fund financial stabilization program or a World Bank structural adjustment loan. In such cases, official export credits provided by one donor country merely substitute for those provided by another donor country, and the principal impact is among competing exporters to the developing coun-

## Table 4.   Selected U.S. Other Official Flows to Developing Countries ($ millions)

| | 1980 | 1981 | 1982 | 1983 | 1984 | 1985 | 1986 |
|---|---|---|---|---|---|---|---|
| **Gross Official Export Credits** | 2,452 | 2,417 | 1,892 | 2,079 | 1,623 | 1,032 | 405 |
| Export-Import Bank | 2,302 | 2,400 | 1,892 | 1,858 | 1,464 | 1,022 | 399 |
| Commodity Credit Corporation | 150 | 18 | — | 221 | 159 | 11 | 7 |
| **Net Official Export Credits** | 815 | 761 | 494 | 721 | −74 | −898 | −1,787 |

Sources: Agency detail from U.S. Department of Commerce, Bureau of Economic Affairs, which also compiles Other Official Flows, gross and net, as published in OECD Development Assistance Committee (DAC), *Development Co-operation* (Paris: OECD, various years), Flow of Resources Table.

try. For this reason, the United States considers the Export-Import Bank a support for U.S. commercial interests and not a development assistance agency.

As shown in Table 4, U.S. official export credits declined sharply during the 1980s. Gross credits declined from $2,452 million in 1980 to $405 million in 1986; net credits declined from *plus* $815 million to *minus* $1,787 million over the same period. This decrease resulted mainly from a reduction in the number of large investment projects financed at commercial rates—which is the core of Export-Import Bank lending—in developing countries faced with fiscal austerity and debt-servicing problems. Such projects increasingly have been financed with ODA and with longer-term financing from the multilateral development banks (MDBs). The even sharper decline in net lending reflects the relatively short term of loans that entail a high level of repayment that led to a net negative credit level beginning in 1984.

### Debt Relief

External debt obligations have reached huge proportions for developing countries, and in some cases the projected debt-servicing burden is unsustainable. Debt relief to help resolve the debt-servicing problem can take three forms: debt rescheduling, which spreads out repayment over a longer period of time; debt restructuring, which provides softer terms; and debt forgiveness, which simply extinguishes existing debt. Debt relief also must be considered in terms of three distinct categories of creditors—namely, the international financial institutions (i.e., the International Monetary Fund and the MDBs), commercial banks, and governments (official bilateral debt).

The international financial institutions as a matter of policy insist on full payment, on schedule, of their loans, but for countries faced with severe financing problems, they generally attempt to provide new financing that more than offsets repayment.

The debt of commercial banks has often been rescheduled, and, through 1988, small amounts have been sold off at a discount, which amounts to partial forgiveness. In March 1989, the United States proposed reduction of commercial bank debt on a much larger scale, with possible inducements to the banks, such as official purchase of or guarantee on part of the debt, to help the process. To the extent that such inducements involve financial contributions by governments, debt reduction would constitute additional official support for development comparable to ODA.

With respect to official bilateral debt, the United States has generally not provided debt forgiveness. Such actions could require budget allocations to compensate the U.S. Treasury, and since the overall budget allocation for foreign assistance has a firm ceiling, budget allocations to forgive or restructure outstanding credits to developing countries could lead to a corresponding reduction in new aid flows, with no net benefits to developing countries.

Debt relief in the form of debt rescheduling is carried out in a substantial way for U.S. bilateral official credits when developing countries are in severe financial difficulties and a program of policy adjustment is likely to lead to eventual creditworthiness. These reschedulings take place within the context of the "Paris Club," wherein the large majority of bilateral creditors agree to rescheduling on comparable terms. During 1987, such rescheduling became more generous, with a maximum of thirty years' repayment with ten years' grace. Such rescheduling usually involves all repayment of principal and most interest payments as well. Reschedulings also can include interest payments from previous reschedulings. The net result, therefore, can be an almost total relief of debt payments coming due over an extended period. In 1984–86, U.S. rescheduling of official debt totaled $1.2 billion in each year—a sharp increase from the $200–$300 million level of 1982–83. This reflected the debt crisis in many developing countries that led to Paris Club rescheduling. U.S. reschedulings consist primarily of official credits at commercial rates, of the Export-Import Bank, the Foreign Military Sales Program, and the Commodity Credit Corporation. Relatively little ODA is involved, since ODA is either grant assistance or loans on very soft terms.

The question of how such debt rescheduling compares with ODA or debt forgiveness depends on whether the debt is ultimately repaid. Although debt-rescheduling agreements always specify the intent of full repayment, the outlook for repayment by some developing countries, at this stage, is questionable at best.

### Commodity Agreements and Other Trade Measures

Commodity agreements and other special trading arrangements can provide financial benefits to certain developing countries, but they are generally undertaken in a context of restricted market access and trade-distorting impact on world markets, which tend to reduce immediate benefits and raise broader questions about longer-term export markets for developing countries. The most striking example is the policy on sugar imports from developing countries as administered by the consuming countries, principally the United States, the European Community, and the Soviet Union. In 1987, the United States paid a very high price for imported sugar, about 22 cents per pound, as compared to a world price of only 7 cents per pound. The high import price, however, was adopted primarily to provide high support prices for domestic producers of sugar which, in turn, is leading to a higher degree of self-sufficiency in sugar for the United States. As a consequence, while the presumed subsidy payment to developing countries in 1987 was $463 million (the difference between 7 cents and 22 cents per pound for imports of 1.4 million tons), the volume of U.S. imports of sugar from developing countries has declined steadily—from 3.5 million tons in 1980 to 1.4 million tons in 1987. Moreover, the use of the world market price for sugar as a benchmark for calculating financial benefit to developing countries currently overstates the benefit, since the world market price is artificially low as a result of protectionist import regimes. The world market price represents a volatile residual market, which does not reflect the longer-term balance between demand and the cost of production.

Another example of what might be interpreted as benefits to developing countries through special trading arrangements is the international Multi-Fibre Agreement on textiles. An elaborate system of country quotas restricts U.S. imports of textiles, while at the same time resulting in much higher prices for textiles to the U.S. consumer. To some extent, these subsidies constitute a financial gain for developing countries, since the textile agreement is administered primarily on the basis of quota allocations to the exporting country, which can thus obtain very large windfall profits. The question of net benefit to developing countries, however, depends on the balance between higher prices received on existing exports and the potentially higher level of textile exports in the absence of the quota arrangement. Moreover, such net benefits vary greatly among developing countries, which has led to mixed attitudes on their part. Some less efficient producers of textiles prefer restrictive quotas and higher prices, which hold back more efficient competition from other developing-country exporters. On balance, most observers consider the textile arrangement as having a net adverse effect on developing-country exports as well as on industrialized-country consumers.

A third example of presumed benefits to developing countries from special trading arrangements is the generalized system of tariff preferences (GSP), which provides duty-free entry for a large range of products from developing countries. At a minimum, this provides a revenue transfer of forgone tariff payments and, in addition, presumably some increase in exports at the expense of competing industrialized-country exporters. In 1986, $13.9 billion of U.S. imports benefited from GSP, with a direct financial gain in terms of tariff payments of approximately $500 million. However, the large majority of GSP benefits have gone to a relatively few of the most advanced, newly industrialized developing countries. In 1986, for example, 58 per cent of total U.S. GSP benefits went to four East Asian exporters: the Republic of Korea, Taiwan, Singapore, and Hong Kong. Another 20 per cent went to Mexico and Brazil.

These examples illustrate both the potential scope and the limitations of developing-country benefits from commodity and other special trading arrangements.

# Concluding Comment

This chapter has presented a summary of U.S. ODA and other forms of U.S. financial support to developing countries and has also discussed a number of qualitative considerations. These programs, however, constitute only one part of the overall economic relationship between the United States and developing countries. Total economic support for development can be expressed in terms of aggregate need for foreign exchange by developing countries to finance given levels of imports and investment. Principal categories of such financing are ODA, other official flows, private flows (such as foreign direct investment and commercial credits), grants by private voluntary agencies, debt reorganization, and U.S. imports from developing countries. A summary of these sources of foreign exchange, as provided by the United States, and by DAC countries as a group, in 1986, is presented in Table 5.

The principal conclusion that emerges from Table 5 is the preponderant weight of developing-country exports as a means of financing development and the corresponding importance of access to industrialized countries' markets for developing-country exports. For the United States, 88 per cent of total payments to developing countries was for imports. Another fundamental aspect of the developing-country relationship is the great diversity of interests among developing countries. The poorest countries are most heavily dependent on ODA, while the upper-tier developing countries are becoming increasingly oriented in their foreign exchange needs toward exports and foreign direct investment. The decline in commercial bank credit availability stemming from the debt buildup of the early 1980s lends even greater importance to exports and direct investment inflows to the more advanced developing countries. This divergence in developing-country interests, moreover, has been increasing in recent years. A small number of "newly industrialized" countries, such as the Republic of Korea, Singapore, Thailand, Brazil, and Mexico have taken on more and more of the characteristics of industrialized countries, while the grouping of poorest countries, particularly concentrated in Sub-Saharan Africa, has, if anything, regressed in the level of development.

This leads to the even more basic question of how much relevance the concept of a dichotomy between "developing" and "industrialized" countries retains. There has never been a clear definition of a "developing country"—and whatever it may have been formerly, it is less and less applicable as the more advanced developing countries industrialize, including, in some cases even developing internationally competitive, high technology industries. Instead of a dichotomy, there is a continuing spectrum (or overlapping spectrums) of countries at different stages of economic, social, and political development.

A full discussion of this trend is beyond the scope of this chapter. However, with respect to the provision of ODA, there is a shifting pattern, wherein highly concessional assistance in amounts large enough to have substantial impact on the development performance of recipient countries will be more and more limited to the low-income countries, principally in Sub-Saharan Africa, South Asia, and a few small Latin American countries in the Andean and Caribbean subregions. In the rest of the developing world—where the large majority of the world's people live—ODA will play a relatively small or insignificant role compared with trade, foreign direct

## Table 5.    DAC and U.S. Foreign Exchange Resources to Developing Countries, 1986 ($ millions)

|  | DAC Countries | United States |
|---|---|---|
| Official Development Assistance | 36,678 | 9,564 |
| Other Official Flows | 2,124 | −559 |
| Private Flows | 22,988 | 1,344 |
| Grants by Private Voluntary Agencies | 3,338 | 1,753 |
| Debt Reorganization | 4,478 | 1,218 |
| Imports from Developing Countries | 286,067 | 98,415 |

Sources: OECD Development Assistance Committee, *Development Co-operation, 1987 Report* (Paris, 1987); and IMF, *Direction of Trade Statistics Yearbook* (Washington, D.C.: IMF 1987).

investment, debt reduction, etc. Moreover, in this latter group, much of ODA is in the form of loans, on only modestly concessional terms, for economic infrastructure which, if tied to procurement in the donor country, have a trade-distorting impact among donor countries. This trade-aid linkage is already an issue of policy debate among industrialized donor countries. In sum, a new dichotomy among aid recipients is emerging that will require new policy thinking and revised definitions for the appropriate reshaping of development assistance.

## Notes

[1]The precise definition used by the Development Assistance Committee of the Organisation for Economic Co-operation and Development is that the resource flow is provided by an official agency; that it is administered with the promotion of the economic development and welfare of developing countries as its main objective; and that it contains a grant element of at least 25 per cent, based on a 10 per cent discount rate.

[2]Eighteen donor countries and the European Economic Community are represented on the DAC, which monitors development assistance levels and policies as well as relations between developed and developing countries.

[3]The DAC definition of disbursements is net of repayment on principal, but not interest, of past loans. In the case of the United States, such interest payments in 1986 amounted to $657 million, or 9 per cent of bilateral ODA. Some of these payments were from aid "graduates," such as South Korea, and other portions were subject to debt rescheduling in the Paris Club.

[4]The DAC list of developing countries and territories includes all countries and territories in Africa except South Africa; in North and South America except the United States and Canada; in Asia except Japan; in Oceania except Australia and New Zealand; and the following in Europe: Cyprus, Gibraltar, Greece, Malta, Portugal, Turkey, and Yugoslavia.

[5]Contributions to multilateral institutions are based on when funds are deposited with the institution rather than when disbursed to the recipient countries. For the grant payments to U.N. agencies and financing of concessional loans by the multilateral development banks, however, such contributions track closely with disbursements, at least over the one-to-three-year replenishment cycles.

[6]U.S. House of Representatives, Committee on Foreign Affairs, *Report of the Task Force on Foreign Assistance*, known as The Hamilton-Gilman Report (Washington, D.C.: U.S. Government Printing Office, 1989); and USAID, *Development and the National Interest: U.S. Economic Assistance into the 21st Century*, A Report by the Administrator, February 1989 (Washington, D.C.: USAID, 1989).

[7]Other Official Flows also includes debt refinancing, which is discussed later in the section on debt relief, and a few other relatively small accounts.

# III. Education and Training

# Cooperation and Aid for Education and Training

Margarita P. Strepetova and Leon Z. Zevin

## The Objectives and Scale of Aid

Aid to developing countries in education and personnel training is an important part of the Soviet Union's program of economic and scientific-technical cooperation. Its aim is to facilitate the development of national education and personnel training systems in developing countries, the formulation of state policy regarding the development and improvement of the labor force, and the creation of conditions for self-sufficiency in the replacement and growth of the national labor force.

The Soviet concept of cooperation with the developing countries in this sphere is based on the following premises:

1. Education contributes to the development of men and women, to their professional and business acumen, and to their ability to think. Each new stage of scientific and technological progress necessitates qualitative change in the educational and occupational skill structure of the labor force.

2. A radical, comprehensive resolution of the problem of educating and training personnel is possible only within the framework of state policy that is part of the mainstream of economic, social, and cultural progress of a given country and of international developments in these spheres. The historical experience of both developed

and developing countries shows that an economic breakthrough is invariably preceded by one in the education and personnel training system.

3. The development of all forms of education and personnel training is both an integral part of and a necessary prerequisite for scientific-technological, social, and cultural progress. The development of a modern system of general and specialized education has particular significance for the developing countries because of their need to create their own base for socio-economic development, which is impossible without skilled indigenous personnel and a system for the replacement and growth of the skilled labor force.

Cooperation in the field of education requires:

- An integrated approach to ensure the training of personnel at different levels and with different skills;
- The coordination of personnel training activities with a given developing country's strategy, plans, and programs for national development; and
- A long-term form of cooperation that is secured by bilateral governmental agreements.

The Soviet approach to cooperation in this area emphasizes that personnel must mostly be trained in the developing countries themselves. Numerous kinds of aid are provided: assistance in general education reforms; in the development of teaching methods, teaching guides, and curricula; in the construction of various kinds of educational institutions and laboratories; and in the staffing and equipment of institutions and laboratories with teaching personnel and with teaching and learning aids. An infrastructure is thereby created for the development of national general education and vocational training systems.

Soviet aid in the development of education concentrates on the upper grades of general education schooling, where more sophisticated curricula and more highly qualified teaching personnel are required, and on the development of both higher and "secondary specialized" systems of education.[1] Soviet aid practice takes into account the fact that most developing countries have amassed sufficient experience to organize their primary education systems largely on their own.

Nationals of developing states also receive education and training to upgrade their skills in the Soviet Union. The combination of personnel training in the U.S.S.R. and in developing countries facilitates a more complete supply of skilled personnel for these countries.

As of the beginning of 1989, nearly 2.2 million developing-country nationals had been trained as specialists and skilled workers through various forms of training assisted by the Soviet Union (Table 1). Between 1981 and 1989, the number of trained specialists and skilled workers increased by some 54 per cent. In the period 1981–85, the developing countries on average received about 133,100 skilled persons a year as a result of cooperation with the Soviet Union, compared to about 101,000 persons a year in 1976–80—an increase of some 33 per cent.

Most specialists and workers are trained for industrial production and technical service in various branches of industry and agriculture; roughly 90 per cent of the trainees acquire a technical occupation. By the beginning of 1989, the great majority of indigenous personnel trained with Soviet assistance were taught in the developing countries: 53 per cent were trained at building sites; 37 per cent at vocational training centers that function at these sites and train personnel at their request; and some 10 per cent at institutions of higher and secondary specialized learning built with Soviet aid.

The numbers graduating from these training centers, secondary specialized institutions, and institutions of higher learning (universities, technical institutes, etc.) in the developing countries increased more than twofold in the 1980s. The number graduating from higher and secondary specialized institutions in the Soviet Union during the same period rose by 60 per cent.

From the cited data, it is clear that priority was given to the training of personnel at facilities built in developing countries with joint U.S.S.R. and national efforts. This form of assistance will be discussed later in greater detail; here we shall only note some of its advantages. First, conditions are created for using the production base of the construction project and the Soviet specialists working there to train personnel—which reduces the developing countries' personnel training costs. Second, it makes it possible to provide a facility with skilled workers and foremen in the most common occupations in a short period of time. Finally, training is carried out under local conditions with which the worker is familiar, without the need for additional costs and loss of time that workers require to adapt when trained overseas.

# Programs in the Developing Countries

Cooperation within the framework of programs in the developing countries themselves is carried out in three principal channels.

## Table 1.　Specialists and Skilled Workers (Nationals of Developing Countries) Trained with Soviet Assistance (thousands of persons)

|  | As of beginning of 1981 | of which: 1976–80 | 1981–85 | As of beginning of 1989[a] |
|---|---|---|---|---|
| **Total** | 1,412.9 | 504.9[b] | 665.5 | 2,180.1 |
| **Trained in the Developing Countries** |  |  |  |  |
| On-the-job training at the building sites | 817.3 | 271.9 | 243.7 | 1,047.5 |
| At vocational production training centers | 353.5 | 160.3 | 249.5 | 729.0 |
| At institutions of higher and secondary specialized learning | 67.8 | 34.2 | 69.2 | 204.9 |
| **Trained in the U.S.S.R.** |  |  |  |  |
| Vocational and technical training upgrade skills | 111.8 | 38.5 | 59.6 | 115.6 |
| At institutions of higher and secondary specialized learning in the U.S.S.R. | 52.0 | — | 38.0[c] | 83.1 |
| In cooperation with international organizations | 10.5 | — | 5.5[c] | — |

[a]Preliminary data.
[b]Not including graduates from higher institutions and secondary technical institutions in the U.S.S.R. receiving scholarships from international organizations.
[c]Authors' estimate.

Sources: Calculations based on I. N. Grekov, A. I. Kachanov, D. I. Sukhoparov, T. V. Teodorovich, *Ekonomicheskoe i tekhnicheskoe sodeistvie SSSR zarubezhnym stranam* [U.S.S.R. Economic and Technical Assistance to Foreign Countries], Moscow, 1987, p. 145; *Intellektual'nyi potentsial razvivaiushchikhsia stran* [The Intellectual Potential of the Developing Countries], Moscow, 1984, p. 119; *MEiMO* [*Mezhdunarodnaia ekonomika i mezhdunarodnye otnosheniia*], No. 11, 1985, p. 119; *Ekonomicheskoe sotrudnichestvo stran-chlenov SEV* [Economic Cooperation of CMEA Member Nations], No. 9, 1984, p. 59.

### On-the-Job Training at Building Sites
### Constructed with Soviet Aid

In most developing countries, the first steps taken by the Soviet Union to provide economic and technical assistance encountered the very serious obstacle of a shortage of skilled workers, technicians, and foremen, and the related predictability of dragged-out construction, inferior work performance, and unsatisfactory operation of equipment. These problems made on-the-job training of workers in the most common occupations seem an urgent need. This approach was particularly effective in the initial period of cooperation, especially in countries where a considerable part of the population was illiterate, where there were virtually no skilled specialists, and where the state did not yet have sufficient resources for the development of a national education system.

Training is carried out in brigades, groups, and individually. The choice depends on the complexity and scale of the project, the availability of manpower, and the literacy level of trainees. Mixed brigades of local and Soviet specialists are set up at certain enterprises. In a number of cases, continuous courses are organized for the training of specialists at various levels, and lectures are offered in specific disciplines. It is the practice to send Soviet specialists to large facilities for the purpose of providing vocational and theoretical training in complex specializations, such as thermal-power engineering, instrument making, electronics, and ferrous and nonferrous metallurgy. Individual on-the-job training is provided temporarily by the Soviet specialists directly to individual nationals assigned to them to be taught specific skills and to assume the Soviet specialists' roles when they leave.

The training of such a category of specialists was, for example, provided for the construction of a steel mill in Al Hajar, Algeria, in 1972; for the Euphrates multiple-use, hydro-development construction project in Syria; for power-generating facilities in Cuba and Iraq; for the construction of the Aswan Dam in Egypt (1960–67); and for the construction of the Bhilai Iron and Steel Plant in India (1955–61).[2]

In some cases, the U.S.S.R. has granted a developing country credits (usually as part of an intergovernmental agreement on the construction of an industrial project) to defray the costs to Soviet organizations of sending their specialists to provide technical assistance and to help in the operation of facilities. During the first half of the 1980s, the share of costs for building vocational and technical centers and for their operation averaged about 15 per cent of the entire volume of credits for building a given industrial or other national economic project, and in the case of some least developed countries, it amounted to 25–30 per cent.[3] Credits also have been granted to cover the cost of maintaining specialists of a developing country sent to the U.S.S.R. to receive training at Soviet enterprises and institutions. The salaries of Soviet specialists working under contract in the developing countries (within the framework of a credit agreement or on a commercial basis) in most cases have been substantially lower than those of similarly qualified specialists sent by Western firms.

The role of on-the-job training of workers and specialists at construction sites in the developing countries declined somewhat in recent years; in 1981–85, it was the type of training received by approximately 39 per cent of the total number of trainees—compared to 54 per cent during 1976–80. The reasons for this were a reduction in the number of new construction projects in the developing countries (although the volume of assistance grew considerably over the same period); the expansion of the network of developing-country vocational training centers, including those built with Soviet assistance; as well as an increase in the number of these countries' own engineers and technicians capable of training the local population to be skilled workers in an ever broader range of specializations.

## Vocational-Technical Training Centers and Schools

Agreements and contracts with developing countries for large construction projects funded with U.S.S.R. assistance frequently include articles regarding the creation of one or two training institutions and/or centers in a corresponding specialization as well as other specialized training measures. Such training institutions are also built without regard to any specific project—for the purpose of servicing a group of enterprises in a similar area, or an entire branch of specialization.

The number of vocational-technical training centers in the developing countries have increased rapidly, as have the areas of specialized training, and the numbers of students. We estimate that by 1988 there were over 570 training centers.

Under the agreements in effect with developing countries in 1988, the schools and centers could simultaneously train more than 200,000 people. The number of skilled workers and foremen graduated from the newly built training institutions has grown rapidly: 18,300 in 1976; 34,700 in 1980; and 72,900 in 1988. The numbers of such skilled trainees graduated by these centers in specific countries include, for example: 210,138 in Egypt; 193,336 in Cuba;

## Table 2.  Number and Regional Distribution of Vocational-Technical Training Centers and Schools in Operation or Under Construction with Soviet Assistance

|                           | 1971 | 1981 | 1986 |
|---------------------------|------|------|------|
| Total, of which:          | 108  | 371  | 526  |
| Asian countries           | 33   | 84   | 108  |
| African countries         | 71   | 96   | 133  |
| Latin American countries  | 4    | 191  | 285[a] |

[a]Cuba accounted for 185 of these centers and schools in 1980 and for 279 in 1986.

Sources: Calculations based on: I. N. Grekov, A. I. Kachanov, D. I. Sukhoparov, and T. V. Teodorovich, *Ekonomicheskoe i tekhnicheskoe sodeistvie SSSR zarubezhnym stranam* [U.S.S.R. Economic and Technical Assistance to Foreign Countries], pp. 149–54 and *Pravda*, February 26, 1987.

78,500 in Mongolia; 52,648 in Algeria; 39,173 in India; and 28,000 in Iraq. In Afghanistan, as of the mid-1980s, 10 Soviet-assisted vocational-technical training schools had trained 20,000 nationals in 146 areas of specialization. In Mozambique, 6 vocational-technical training schools are training agricultural equipment operators, workers for industry, and instructors for vocational-technical centers; these schools provide approximately 25 per cent of all skilled workers and foremen for the nation's economy. In Nicaragua, two vocational-technical centers—a power engineering center and a 900-trainee polytechnical center—have been created. And under a steel mill construction agreement between the U.S.S.R. and Nigeria, a 1,400-person training center and a 625-person specialized secondary institution have been built in Ajaokuta. Soviet specialists trained 850 skilled workers at the mill, and 648 Nigerian specialists received vocational training in the U.S.S.R.[4]

The U.S.S.R. is providing significant assistance to Cuba, Vietnam, Mongolia, Kampuchea, and Laos in the development of vocational-technical education. Some 50 per cent of the skilled workers and 25 per cent of the technicians trained in Cuba are graduates of training centers established in Cuba with the assistance of the U.S.S.R.; in Mongolia, the same is true of 75 per cent of all graduates of the country's vocational-technical training schools.

### Higher and Secondary Specialized
### Education Institutions

The unique features of the historical development of most Third World countries prompted the discrepancy that persists in many of these countries between the inadequacy of higher and secondary specialized education on the one hand and the growing needs of the national economy on the other. Soviet programs for assisting the developing countries in this sphere take into account the need to fill this gap. They include:

- Assistance in the construction and equipment of higher and secondary specialized educational institutions; and
- Providing instructional personnel to organize the educational process, present lectures, and supervise scientific/research work.

As of the beginning of 1989, the Soviet Union had agreements with developing countries to build seventy-four higher and secondary specialized education institutions (Table 3). Twenty-two of these were by that time already functioning in Asian countries, sixteen in Africa, and one in Latin America. A number of higher and secondary specialized education institutions have been built and equipped in tropical Africa; some of these are the very first educational institutions in their countries to train indigenous personnel.

In all regions, technical institutes, technical faculties at universities, and secondary specialized institutions predominate among the educational institutions that have been or are being built (see Annex I at the end of chapter); these include institutions for training various levels of agricultural personnel (see Annex II).

The estimated capacity of the educational institutions that already have been or are being built in developing countries is 53,000 students (including postgraduate students); institutions already in operation account for 44,000 of this total estimated capacity. By the beginning of 1989, graduates from these educational institutions numbered 159,900. The largest numbers of graduates were in Algeria, Afghanistan, Burma, Guinea, India, Mali, and Ethiopia.

# Programs in the Soviet Union

The training of citizens from the developing countries in the Soviet Union encompasses the three principal areas discussed in the following sections.

## Table 3. Higher and Secondary Specialized Education Institutions[a] in Developing Countries Built or Under Construction with the Assistance of the U.S.S.R.

|                            | 1971 | 1981 | 1989 |
|----------------------------|------|------|------|
| Total                      | 52   | 60   | 74   |
| Asian countries            | 30   | 22   | 42   |
| African countries          | 22   | 38   | 31   |
| Latin American countries   | —    | —    | 1    |

[a]In operation or under construction at beginning of indicated year. Including new faculties at already operational educational institutions. (An illustrative list of these institutions is provided in Annex I).

Sources: I. N. Grekov, A. I. Kachanov, D. I. Sukhoparov, and T. V. Teodorovich, *Ekonomicheskoe i tekhnicheskoe sodeistvie SSSR zarubezhnym stranam*, [U.S.S.R. Economic and Technical Assistance to Foreign Countries], Moscow, 1987, p. 149. Figures for 1989 are authors' estimate.

### Vocational and Technical Training Programs and the Upgrading of Skills

These forms of training engineers, technicians, and workers are practiced at enterprises and industrial associations, in design and scientific research institutes, on state farms, and at vocational and technical education institutions. Some specialists and workers receive technical training in connection with deliveries of machinery and equipment and the construction of national economic facilities with the participation of Soviet organizations.

Individual, group, or course training at enterprises and in institutions are common forms of vocational and technical training and internship for citizens from developing countries. Training is based on the syllabi and curricula of Soviet educational institutions, with due regard for the general educational and skill level of the interns and the particular educational conditions in their country. A number of Soviet enterprises operate permanent training bases that have the necessary learning aids, technical literature, equipment, and films. Interns receive their training at leading Soviet industrial enterprises.

Between the mid-1950s and early 1989, more than 115,000 persons went through vocational and technical production training and internship in the Soviet Union. At present, as many as 10,000 persons a year receive production practice and internship in the Soviet Union. Most of the specialists coming to the Soviet Union for such training in recent years have been from Vietnam, Mongolia, Afghanistan, India, Iraq, Algeria, Pakistan, and the People's Democratic Republic of Yemen.

### Training in Higher and Secondary Specialized Education Institutions and Scientific Internships

The Soviet Union has developed a broad system for the training of foreign specialists—including those from developing countries—with higher qualifications (Table 4). This system takes into account the specific requirements and unique circumstances of developing countries. In the mid-1980s, some 7,900 students from Afghanistan, 4,300 from Syria, 3,000 from Ethiopia, 2,000 from Jordan, 1,700 from Nicaragua, 1,500 from Algeria, and 1,200 from the People's Republic of Yemen were among those attending Soviet institutions of higher and secondary specialized education.

The developing countries' growing demand for specialists in engineering-technical fields and in the natural sciences in large measure determines the structure of personnel training for these countries (Table 5). In the 1986/87 school year, 42,600 foreign students were being trained in technical occupations in the Soviet Union; 17,000 in pedagogical occupations; 17,000 in medicine; 4,300 in agriculture; and 4,200 in other disciplines. The principal specializations in which students from the developing countries receive training in the Soviet Union are: geology and prospecting for minerals, power engineering, metallurgy, machine building and instrument making, electronic engineering, electrical instrument making and automated systems, technology of food production, geodesy and cartography, agriculture and forestry, health care and physical culture, pedagogy, and cinematography.

In the 1987/88 school year, the number of students and postgraduates was 110,000. By the beginning of 1989, approximately 83,000 specialists from the developing countries had been graduated from higher and secondary specialized education institutions in the U.S.S.R.. The increase in admissions of students in recent years (see Table 4) ensures increased numbers of graduates from these institutions in the next few years.

Students and postgraduates are receiving training in 300 specializations at more than 300 higher and secondary specialized education institutions in the U.S.S.R. Among these are the Moscow M. V. Lomonosov State University, a number of other Moscow institu-

## Table 4.  Students and Graduate Students from the Developing Countries Attending Higher and Secondary Specialized Education Institutions in the U.S.S.R. (thousands)

|  | School Years | | | | |
|---|---|---|---|---|---|
|  | 1960–61[a] | 1970–71[a] | 1975–76 | 1980–81 | 1986–87 |
| Total | 2.5 | 13.5 | 33.2 | 78.9 | 85.1 |
| of which from: |  |  |  |  |  |
| Asia | 1.4 | 5.7 | 15.8 | 40.5 | 43.0 |
| Africa | 0.9 | 6.3 | 10.3 | 17.1 | 24.0 |
| Latin America | 0.2 | 1.5 | 6.1 | 21.3 | 18.1 |

[a]Excluding the Korean People's Democratic Republic, Cuba, Laos, Mongolia, and Vietnam.

Sources: O. K. Dreier, *Kul'turnye preobrazovaniia v razvivaiushchikhsia stranakh* [Cultural Reform in the Developing Countries], Moscow, 1972, p. 67; A. E. Shirinskii, *Problemy obrazovaniia v razvivaiushchikhsia stranakh* [Educational Problems in the Developing Countries], Moscow, 1985, p. 195.

## Table 5.  Training of Specialists from Developing Countries with Higher and Secondary Specialized Education Qualifications, Mid-1980s (percentages)

| | |
|---|---|
| Technical disciplines | 50% |
| Agricultural disciplines[a] | 5 |
| Medical personnel | 20 |
| Pedagogy and other humanistic disciplines | 20 |
| Other disciplines | 5 |
| Total | 100 |

[a]Agricultural occupations here include agronomers, plant breeders, livestock specialists, etc. Engineering-technical personnel training for agriculture are classified under technical disciplines.

Sources: *Nauka, tekhnika i obrazovanie—perspektivnyye oblasti sotrudnichestva sotsialisticheskikh i razvivaiushchikhsia stran* [Science, Technology and Education—Promising Areas of Cooperation of Socialist and Developing Countries], Moscow, 1986, p. 80.

tions of higher learning, and institutes in the cities of Odessa, Leningrad, Kiev, Minsk, Tashkent, and other university centers in the nation.

The Patrice Lumumba University of Peoples' Friendship in Moscow has a special place in the training of personnel with higher qualifications. The establishment of such an institution of higher learning expressly for the training of specialists for the Third World is without parallel in world practice. The university was founded in 1960 by the All-Union Central Council of Trade Unions, the Soviet Committee for Solidarity of Asian and African Countries, and the Union of Soviet Societies of Friendship and Cultural Relations with Foreign Countries. In its first twenty-five years, the university graduated 13,000 specialists, including 9,000 for the developing countries. Its current enrollment is 6,700 students, approximately two-thirds of whom are young men and women from the developing countries, while one-third are from the U.S.S.R.; this structure makes it easier for foreign students to adapt to local conditions and to master the Russian language, and it is instrumental in maintaining the country's generally accepted standard for teaching, scientific work, and technical equipment of laboratories and departments.

The Patrice Lumumba University's curricula and scientific research programs are geared to the specific conditions of the developing countries (the university is attended by students from 110 countries) and to their socio-economic problems. This is evidenced by the professional distribution of the specialists graduated: engineers, 40 per cent; physicians, 24 per cent; agronomists and livestock specialists, 18 per cent; pedagogy, cultural fields, and other specializations, 18 per cent.[5]

A UNIDO-financed seminar/practice program for engineer-machine builders from the developing countries is in operation at the university. There are ongoing advanced training courses for that institution's alumni, annual seminars for Russian language teachers, and a summer school in comparative and international law at the scientific center of the International Association of Democratic Lawyers. Over 300 citizens from the developing countries are enrolled in postgraduate studies. Some 150–200 specialists are admitted to internship every year.

In addition to the Patrice Lumumba University, there is also a special faculty of tropical and sub-tropical agriculture at the Kuban Agricultural Institute (Krasnodar), a faculty of international law and international relations at Kiev State University, and a special journalism department at Belorussian State University.

Foreign students spend one year studying Russian in special preparatory faculties to assure that the level of their knowledge meets the standards of the Soviet higher school. Special courses, seminars, and electives are incorporated into the educational process so that the specifics of the developing countries can be taken into account. Courses and diploma work are chosen with a view to using the results in the economic, scientific, and cultural life of the students' home countries. The syllabi of almost 100 specializations at engineering-technical, medical, and agricultural institutes of higher learning, universities, and pedagogical institutes include one hundred and twenty-three special courses.

The majority of students from the developing countries receive training in the Soviet Union free of charge and enjoy the same benefits and advantages as Soviet trainees, as well as a number of other special benefits: higher scholarships, dormitory accommodations, free medical care and learning aids, a clothing needs grant (for persons coming from countries with a different climate), special summer vacation conditions, etc. All students receive monthly stipends in the following amounts: students attending vocational-technical and secondary specialized educational institutions, 90 rubles; students attending institutions of higher learning, 90-110 rubles; postgraduate students, 150 rubles; and interns, 150, 250, or 300 rubles—depending on their vocational skills and practical work experience.

Because of more complicated curricula, higher prices, inflation, and other factors, the cost of education in the Soviet Union is rising. That is why higher education institutions are now allowed to accept foreign students from both developing and developed countries on a contract basis. Average annual tuition fees range from $2,500 to $6,500—depending on the chosen profession. This contingent of students will be accepted in addition to students who get their education free of charge in accordance with inter-governmental agreements and agreements between various organizations of partner countries.

In recent years, it has become common practice to send students to the U.S.S.R. for higher education under a special program that assigns graduates to jobs at facilities being built (or already built) with the economic and technical assistance of the U.S.S.R.. As of 1980, only 623 specialists had been trained under this program, but by 1989, they already numbered 1,350. This is a promising form of training that meets the current requirements of both the developing nations and the Soviet Union.

Developing-country nationals also receive training in the form of postgraduate studies and scientific internships in the Soviet Union. These two types of training are leading forms of preparation of scientific and pedagogical research personnel for the developing countries. As of 1985, 1,150 foreign postgraduate students—mostly from developing countries—had successfully defended candidate dissertations at the University of Peoples' Friendship alone.[6]

Internships for foreign specialists in Soviet institutions of higher learning usually last from several weeks to two years. Interns arrive in the U.S.S.R. with individual, previously specified programs. Their training includes theoretical preparation and consultations in the specialization at various institutions of higher learning and scientific research institutes, as well as practice or teaching practice.

### Contributions to Multilateral Assistance for Personnel Training

According to incomplete data, as of 1985, 16,000 U.N. scholarship students from more than one hundred developing countries had received training in the U.S.S.R. The funding of these activities is mostly provided by the U.S.S.R. from its ruble contributions to the U.N. agencies. Every year there are as many as forty international workshops, permanently established courses, and study trips, in which some 700–800 specialists from Asian, African, and Latin American countries upgrade their qualifications. Among the various forms of group training are UNIDO seminar and practice programs that have been conducted in the U.S.S.R.; under a UNIDO-U.S.S.R. agreement, these programs have acquired standing-program status. Moreover, the regional U.N. Economic Commission for Africa (ECA), the regional Economic and Social Commission for Asia and the Pacific (ESCAP), the U.N. Conference for Trade and Development (UNCTAD), the International Maritime Organization (IMO), the U.N. Environment Programme (UNEP), and other U.N.-system organizations account for the largest volume in the implementation of one-time seminars, workshops, study trips, and conferences providing group training for specialists from the developing countries in the U.S.S.R.

The Soviet Union also took the initiative of training specialists in the management of a system of training of indigenous personnel that was supported by international organizations. In cooperation with UNIDO, a number of such seminars were conducted with the participation of indigenous personnel from developing countries. Starting in 1984, a working group of U.N. experts, using demography courses at the Moscow M. V. Lomonosov State University as their base, held sessions that formulated tasks and made practical recommendations on the training of personnel in the field of demography.

Personnel are also trained in cooperation with international organizations through independent study programs for individuals that are formulated by an organization in a developing country and approved by the accepting institution in the Soviet Union. Such training programs vary in length from 3–4 days to 2–3 years. Funding for such programs is provided by Soviet institutions and international organizations.

Soviet aid to developing countries in personnel training is also provided on a multilateral basis through the Scholarship Fund of CMEA member countries. This fund has been in operation since the 1973/74 school year. In 1985, it funded the studies of more than 5,500 persons from sixty developing countries at institutions of higher learning in CMEA countries. By that time, more than 1,700 persons had already completed their studies or upgraded their qualifications.[7]

Soviet educational institutions training specialists from the developing countries maintain contacts with them even after they return home. Direct ties are also maintained between institutions of higher learning in the Soviet Union and the developing countries; approximately 60 Soviet institutions of higher learning and more than 90 educational institutions in the developing countries take part in the cooperation between institutions of higher learning. This form of cooperation provides graduates of Soviet institutions of higher learning with information about the latest developments in their field of work.

# Prospects for Cooperation in the Context of *Perestroika*

Despite the generally recognized positive results of Soviet cooperation with the developing countries in the formation of national systems for the education and training of skilled personnel, a number of problems in this sphere of interaction must be noted. These relate in part to the training of personnel specifically for facilities built through joint efforts in a developing country. They also relate to a broader range of concerns about improvement of the actual process of cooperation in educating and training indigenous personnel.

Almost nine-tenths of the total number of specialists and skilled workers completed their training or received training directly in the developing countries themselves, and a little over one-tenth were trained at educational institutions or at enterprises in the Soviet Union. This ratio has been influenced by, among other factors, the volume and structure of cooperation, the state of public education and personnel training systems in the developing nations that are partners in the cooperation, and the material and financial potential of the parties. Changes presently taking place in the nature of economic cooperation between the Soviet Union and the developing countries, the increase in the number of subjects covered, structural diversification, and the attempt to organize relations at the micro-level (notably, between industrial enterprises), will inevitably also generate a need for increased interaction in education. In particular, new forms of personnel training will be developed related to the establishment of direct links between enterprises and organizations of the Soviet Union and the developing countries, to the creation of joint ventures of different types, and to the use of trilateral cooperation involving the participation of firms in particular developing, capitalist, and socialist countries.

In the past, economic and scientific-technical cooperation has been carried out primarily within the framework of inter-governmental agreements. But relations at the macro-level are now beginning to be supplemented by relations at the micro-level, and this necessitates the organization of a system for the professional training of personnel for the servicing of these new forms of economic and scientific-technical interaction. There is now also a need for specialists who know the microeconomic, legal, and other norms of their own country and the partner nation as well as international economic law. Recently, Soviet universities and other institutions of higher education gained the right to establish direct contacts and links on an independent contract basis with analogous institutions in the developing countries to educate nationals of those countries. This innovation may expand the volume of cooperation in this field both quantitatively and qualitatively.

One of the substantive elements in the restructuring of Soviet society is the increased integration of the system of general and specialized education with science and production. Enterprises and industrial associations on the one hand and higher and secondary specialized education institutions on the other are making the transition to a new type of interaction based on contractual obligations. It is becoming more common practice to transfer part of the education process to production by creating branch production training centers within large enterprises, associations, and scientific research and design organizations. This process is reflected in the establishment of a single state body that organizes and manages both general and specialized education in the nation; this role was previously played (without effective coordination) by two agencies: the Ministry of Higher and Secondary Specialized Education and the State Committee for Vocational-Technical Training. The newly created State Committee for Public Education coordinates its personnel training activity for developing countries with associations of the Ministry of Foreign Economic Relations and branch ministries participating in the provision of economic and technical assistance to developing countries.

Education reforms in the U.S.S.R. are designed to raise secondary specialized and higher education to a qualitatively new level; to make extensive use of modern teaching methods; to train active, highly qualified specialists who are capable of confidently finding their bearings under conditions of regulated market relations and who are receptive to progress in science and technology. The education and training of personnel in the U.S.S.R. is also to an ever greater degree becoming *continuous* in character—prompting close ties between secondary and higher education and subsequent training to take into account changes in production, science, management, etc.

These reforms expand the prospects for substantially larger enrollment from developing countries in terms of both the numbers of persons trained and the selection of specializations. They also relate to the need to train skilled specialists at all levels for efficient work in joint ventures involving Soviet organizations and enterprises and those of developing countries as well as in other new forms of economic cooperation.

In the 1980s, the developing countries increasingly have felt the shortage of instructors, technical training teachers, persons specializing in technical maintenance and operation of enterprises, managerial and administrative personnel, and personnel for planning bodies. This will obviously influence the training of such specialists in the Soviet Union for these countries. The concentration will be on the training of personnel in the most complex and technically sophisticated occupations. There will be an increase in the admission of persons from developing countries to postgraduate studies and internship programs in order to upgrade the qualifications of specialists who have already acquired an education in the U.S.S.R.; teaching methods and familiarization measures will be developed jointly with international organizations.

The attainment of a dynamic balance between the availability and structure of the skilled labor force and the actual demand for them on the part of the national economy, the system of state management, and the service sector is one of the most complex problems relating to cooperation in the education and training of personnel. Considering the general scarcity of specialists in the Third World, the development of the system of higher and secondary specialized education must, in the long-term perspective, be more rapid than the economic growth rate. While this naturally places an additional load on society, the skilled workers, foremen, and technical experts will have a stimulating influence on the process of development and will promote the more effective use of available resources.

The effective operation of joint construction projects is an urgent problem within the framework of economic and technical cooperation of the U.S.S.R. with the developing countries. Maintaining equipment in operating condition through scheduled repairs and tuneups is of the utmost importance. The problem is of course greatest in countries where the economy is backward, where the level of development of general education and vocational training of personnel is low, and where manpower is unskilled while imported machinery is sophisticated. According to the U.N. Industrial Organisation (UNIDO), the service life of basic equipment in the developing countries is on the average shortened by 30 per cent[8] because of the dramatic deterioration of maintenance. Many studies show that the effectiveness of enterprises built with foreign aid in the developing countries is often low; that the enterprises do not attain projected indicators; and that they are unreceptive to innovation. These problems are now receiving special attention in Soviet aid to developing countries.

A phenomenon that may be called an "internal brain drain" must also be highlighted. Discrepancies between conditions confronting the work force at cooperative projects in the *public* sector compared with analogous enterprises in the private sector—conditions relating to wages, housing, other forms of incentives—are responsible for the "internal migration" of labor between the two sectors of the national economy. This shift primarily involves "higher" and "middle" management and the most highly qualified engineers. Many such "migrants" are persons who received education or training in the Soviet educational institutions and were expected to work at the projects built with Soviet assistance.

Virtually all of those from developing countries who receive training in the Soviet Union return home—so that there is no "brain drain" in the usual sense. But some graduates of education institutions who return home after receiving training with Soviet assistance at the first opportunity transfer to (generally better paying) jobs at enterprises in the private sector. This phenomenon weakens the position of the public sector while simultaneously promoting the development of private enterprise. This is particularly undesirable in branches where the public sector's functioning is important to the general national interest. This tendency also affects public sector enterprises built with the assistance of the Soviet Union. So far the cooperating parties have found no effective way to deal with this problem.

The unresolved problem of reciprocal recognition of higher education diplomas between the U.S.S.R. and many developing countries is a stumbling block to the expansion of cooperation. While citizens from more than 100 developing countries are presently being trained in the Soviet Union, there are agreements on the reciprocal recognition of such diplomas with only about half of these countries. An increase in the number of such agreements would stimulate an increase in the number of persons sent to study at Soviet institutions.

The prospects for cooperation between the U.S.S.R. and the developing countries are directly and primarily linked to ways in which the *perestroika* process manifests itself in the reform of the Soviet public education and personnel training system. With the implementation of the reform, new and more effective forms of this cooperation are appearing and will continue to emerge.

## Notes

[1]In the Soviet education system, "secondary specialized education" refers to schools (some are called "technicums") in which students in grades 8 to 11 obtain training for a technical profession alongside the general education curriculum.

[2]See respectively, *Vneshniaia torgovlia [Foreign Trade]*, No. 9 (1982), p. 6; Ibid., No. 1 (1985), p. 29; *Bulleten inostrannoy kommercheskoy informacii* [Bulletin of Foreign Commercial Information], Vol. 11, No. 5 (1970), and O. Riulle, *Khleb dlya shesti milliardov*, [Bread for Six Billion], Moscow, 1965, p. 265.

[3]*Tiers Monde*, Vol. XXIV, No. 95, July-September 1983, p. 163.

[4]I. N. Grekov and A. I. Kachanov, D. I. Sukhoparov, and T. V. Teodorovich, *Ekonomicheskoe i nauchno-technicheskoe sodeistvie SSSR zarubezhnym stranam* [U.S.S.R. Economic and Technical Assistance to Foreign Countries], Moscow, 1987, pp. 153, 255, 260, 287.

[5]V.F. Stanis, *Universitet vo imia mira i druzhby* [University in the Name of Peace and Friendship], Moscow, 1985.

[6]Ibid., p. 14.

[7]*Ekonomicheskoe sotrudnichestvo stran-chlenov SEV* [Economic Cooperation of CMEA Member Nations], No. 6 (1985), p. 61.

[8]*Razvitie liudskikh resursov dlia obespecheniia effektivnogo tekhnicheskogo obsluzhivaniia na urovne predpriatiia* [Development of Human Resources for Effective Maintenance at the Enterprise Level], ID/WG, 469/5/SPEC/20, July 1987, p. 4.

## Annex I. Illustrative List of Higher and Secondary Specialized Education Institutions Built or Under Construction in Developing Countries With Soviet Assistance

| Type of Institution | City, Country | Planned Annual Capacity |
|---|---|---|
| | | (persons) |
| **ASIA** | | |
| Polytechnical institute | Kabul, Afghanistan | 2,000 |
| Auto-mechanics technicum | Kabul, Afghanistan | 1,000 |
| Training technicum | Kabul, Afghanistan | |
| Mining and petroleum technicum | Afghanistan | 500 |
| Social sciences institute | Kabul, Afghanistan | |
| Technological institute | Rangoon, Burma | 1,050 |
| Polytechnical institute | Hanoi, Vietnam | 2,400 |
| Polytechnical institute | Conakry, Guinea | 4,000 |
| Technological Institute | Bombay, India | 1,500 |
| Autonomous faculties in India | | |
| —Metallurgy faculty | Kharagpur | |
| —Geophysics faculty | Hyderabad | |
| —Aircraft construction | Bombay | |
| —Automation and IBM | Bangalore | |
| Machine-building technicum | Ranchi, India | |
| Polytechnicum | Baroda, India | |
| Metallurgy technicum | Durg, India | |
| Technological institute | Ambon, Indonesia | 1,000 |
| Technological institute | Phnom Penh, Cambodia | 1,000 |
| Secondary specialized education institution | Laos | |
| Higher education institution | Laos | |
| Land reclamation technicum | Mongolia | |
| **LATIN AMERICA** | | |
| Engineering faculty | Managua, Nicaragua | |

---

aThis list (gathered by the authors from the Soviet press and the press of the specific developing countries) is clearly not comprehensive; it merely indicates the types and size of institutions and programs.

## AFRICA

| | | |
|---|---|---|
| African oil and textile center, of which: | Boumerdes, Algeria | 3,000 |
| —Institute of oil, gas, and chemistry | | 500 |
| —Petroleum technicum | | |
| —Institute of light industry | | 2,500 |
| —Textile technicum | | |
| Annaba University | Annaba, Algeria | 3,000 |
| Mining-metallurgy technicum | Annaba, Algeria | |
| Hydrotechnology and land reclamation institute | Blida, Algeria | |
| Institute of applied mathematics and industrial chemistry | Algeria | |
| Higher school of veterinary medicine | Algeria | |
| Mining and metallurgy institute | El Tabbin, Egypt | 150 |
| Training technicum | Huambo, Angola | 600 |
| Polytechnic institute | Canakry, Guinea | 600 |
| Engineering faculty | Lusaka, Zambia | |
| Medical faculty | Lusaka, Zambia | |
| University center | Dganga, Cameroon | 650 |
| Higher school of administration | Bamako, Mali | 250 |
| Agricultural institute | Bamako, Mali | 300 |
| Training technicum | Mozambique | |
| Technical faculties of university | Congo, People's Dem. Rep. | |
| Institute of fisheries | Aden, People's Dem. Rep. of Yemen | |
| Mining and metallurgy technicum | Ajaokuta, Nigeria | 625 |
| Higher engineering school | Tunis, Tunisia | 700 |
| Polytechnic institute | Bahr-Dar, Ethiopia | 1,000 |
| Institute of water technology | Ethiopia | |

## Annex II.  Illustrative List of Agricultural and Scientific-Technical Institutions in Developing Countries Built or Under Contruction with Soviet Assistance[a]

### ASIA

| | |
|---|---|
| Afghanistan | Agricultural crop/pest and disease control laboratory |
| | Animal disease control laboratory |
| | Several veterinary polyclinics |
| Laos | Experimental crop production and animal husbandry laboratory |
| Syria | Scientific research station for irrigated and non-irrigated agriculture and for forestry |
| | Truck and tractor training center |

### AFRICA/NEAR EAST

| | |
|---|---|
| Algeria | Hydrotechnology and land reclamation institute |
| | Refrigeration training center |
| | Five agricultural training centers |
| | Five experimental stations for the study of agricultural crop production on irrigated land |
| | Higher school of veterinary medicine |
| Angola | Three technical production training centers for the training of agricultural equipment operators |
| Arab Republic of Egypt | Training centers for the training of desert-development equipment operators |
| Ghana | Agronomy training school |
| Iraq | Training center for the Iraqi "Tartar Project" organization |
| | Water management and irrigation planning institute |

[a]The list is based on incomplete data (in the Soviet press) and thus illustrative only.

Sources: N. A. Ushakova, *Strany SEV i razvivaiushchiesia gosudarstva sotsialisticheskoi orientatsii: ekonomicheskoe sotrudnichestvo* [CMEA Countries and Developing Countries With a Socialist Orientation: Economic Cooperation], Moscow, 1980, pp. 71, 107, 128, and 148.

| | |
|---|---|
| Cameroon | National agricultural institute |
| | Timber industry school |
| | Agricultural experimental stations |
| | Veterinary medicine laboratory |
| | Expansion of agricultural school |
| | Vocational-technical center for training agricultural equipment operators (in Brazzaville) |
| Madagascar | Vocational-technical school for training agricultural equipment operators |
| | Veterinary station |
| Mozambique | Three technical production schools for training agricultural specialists |
| Mali | Agricultural institute |
| People's Dem. Rep. of Yemen | Animal husbandry and veterinary medicine section at a research station |
| | Scientific research institute for fish-breeding |
| | Agricultural training center |
| Sudan | Agricultural research laboratory |
| | Central veterinary medicine research laboratory |
| Tanzania | Six regional veterinary medicine centers |
| | Secondary education agricultural institution |
| Uganda | Organization of national agricultural mechanization college |
| Ethiopia | Phytopathology laboratory |

# Education, Training, and Technical Assistance

Gerald M. Meier

Foreign assistance programs display a mixture of humanitarian, political, and economic objectives. If, however, programs are to be evaluated by their contribution to the development and utilization of human resources, it is the economic objective that should matter the most. The need for human resource development is now firmly established in the mainstream of Western development economics.

## Economic Rationale

Human resources are the ultimate basis of the wealth of nations. From this perspective, the goals of development are the maximum possible utilization of human beings in productive activity and the fullest possible development of the skills, knowledge, and capacities of the labor force. If these goals are pursued, then others—such as economic growth, higher levels of living, and more equitable distribution of income—are thought to be the likely consequences.[1]

Many empirical studies of economic growth confirm the importance of non-material investment. Historical investigations demonstrate that output in the presently rich countries increased at a higher rate than can be explained by only an increase in the inputs of capital, labor, and natural resources. A doubling of inputs, for example, has led to more than a doubling of total output. The "residual" difference between the rate of increase in output and the rate of increase in physical inputs represents "total factor productivity" (TFP). An increase in TFP encompasses many "unidentified factors," but a prominent element is the improvement in the quality of inputs.

Although some of this progress may be incorporated in physical capital, the improvements in intangible human qualities are more significant. Long ago, the economist Alfred Marshall observed that nature may be subject to diminishing returns, but man is subject to increasing returns. If an economy's development is characterized by increasing returns, then it is essential to improve the quality of human beings as productive agents.

For purposes of measurement, investment or capital formation is usually identified with fixed physical capital and working capital. But the capital stock should be interpreted more broadly to include the body of knowledge possessed by the population and the capacity and training of the population to use it effectively. Expenditures on education and training, improvement of health, and research contribute to productivity by raising the quality of the population as economic agents, and these outlays yield a continuing return in the future.

The essence of regarding something as "capital" is that it yields a stream of income over time, and the income is the product of the capital. From this point of view, all categories of income describe yields on various forms of capital and can be expressed as rates of interest or return on the corresponding items of capital. Alternatively, all forms of income-yielding assets can be given an equivalent capital value by capitalizing the income they yield at an appropriate rate of interest. By extension, the growth of income that defines economic development is necessarily the result of the accumulation of capital, or of "investment." But "investment" in this context must be defined to include such diverse activities as adding to material capital; improving the health, discipline, skill, and education of the population; moving labor into more productive locations; and applying existing knowledge—or discovering and applying new knowledge—to increasing the efficiency of productive processes. All such activities incur costs in the form of the use of current resources. Investment in them is therefore socially worthwhile if the rate of return over cost exceeds the general rate of interest, or if the capital value of the additional income they yield exceeds the cost of obtaining it. More generally, from the perspective of promoting economic development, efficient development involves allocation of investment resources according to priorities set by the relative rates of return on alternative investments.[2]

Although investment in human beings has been a major source

of growth in the richer countries, the small amount of human investment in poor countries has done little to extend the capacity of the people to meet the challenge of accelerated development. The characteristic of "economic backwardness" is still manifested in several particular forms: low labor efficiency, factor immobility, limited specialization in occupations and in trade, a deficient supply of entrepreneurship, and customary values and traditions of social institutions that minimize the incentives for economic change.

The slow growth in knowledge is an especially severe restraint to economic progress. The economic quality of the population remains low when there is little knowledge of the natural resources available, the alternative production techniques that are possible, the skills that are necessary, the existing market conditions and opportunities, and the institutions that might be created to favor economizing efforts and economic rationality. Improvement in the quality of the "human factor" is then as essential as investment in physical capital. Advance in knowledge and the diffusion of new ideas and objectives are necessary to instill the human abilities and motivations that are more favorable to economic achievement. Although investment in material capital may indirectly achieve some lessening of the economic backwardness of human resources, the direct and more decisive means is through investment in human beings. Moreover, in many newly developing countries, the absorptive capacity for physical capital has proved to be low, because the extension of human capabilities has failed to keep pace with the accumulation of physical capital.[3]

With these considerations in mind, it is not surprising that, when asked why the whole world is not developed, many would answer that development is a function of the rate of technological change, and the transfer of technological change is an educational process.[4] The spread of development depends on the growth of science and the diffusion of modern education. The diffusion of modern education in turn depends on an incentive structure and new political conditions and ideological forces. Historically, the development of formal schooling led to a secular, rationalistic, and materialistic trend in intellectual thought that promoted development.

Historical experience attests to the value of education and training. So do recent studies of the rate of return of earnings derived from education. Econometric studies based on the hypothesis that education contributes to productivity and that earnings are linked to productivity present high estimates of the social as well as the private returns to education.[5] Moreover, there is a tendency for these returns to be higher at the primary level and substantially lower for higher education. Estimated private rates of return, however, have tended to be large for all levels of education. Less evidence is available for technical education, but here, too, satisfactory returns frequently have been reported.

Although historical experience and human capital theory indicate a high potential for human resources development, the realization of this potential is being thwarted by pervasive deficiencies in the actual educational systems in poor countries. Statistics convey some of the problems:

- During the past year, 100 million children were born in the world, but 60 per cent of them were born into households where income per head is lower than $350 a year.

- Some 1.6 billion people in the world are under 15 years old, but most of them—1.3 billion—live in the developing countries. And in these countries, the majority of children are in households at the bottom of the income scale.

- More than 250,000 children die every week in the developing world from frequent infection and prolonged malnutrition. The consequences of infant malnutrition endure even after the period of undernourishment is past. Malnutrition stunts growth, and there is medical evidence that it can retard intellectual development and limit the individual's learning abilities and educational achievement.

- About 33 per cent of the children of primary school age in the developing countries are not enrolled in school. Of those who enter school, 60 per cent will not complete more than three years of primary school.

- The poor child is often a working child—far removed from the classroom. The International Labor Organisation estimates that 75 million children under 15 years of age are working at a fixed job. Some 17 million Indian children have gone straight from "swaddling clothes into working gear." Child labor is by its nature in low productivity jobs that yield only an irregular and inadequate income.[6]

- Approximately 600 million adults in the less developed countries cannot read or do simple calculation.

- Educational opportunities are poorly distributed, with children in the rural areas, the urban poor, and girls and women having the least opportunity to learn. Because of high rates of drop-out and grade repetition, fewer than half the children complete the four years necessary to obtain and retain basic skills.

These statistics—and many others that could be cited —indicate that it is becoming increasingly difficult for developing countries to keep up—financially, logistically, and otherwise—with the growing demands that are being placed on their education and training systems. Unless considerable progress can be made in improving the efficiency of primary and secondary schooling, vocational education, and technical training, the goals of enabling most people to obtain at least a basic education and of meeting labor market demands for trained manpower will remain unobtainable for the less developed countries. Therefore, a priority task is to ensure that available resources are fully mobilized and efficiently employed.

With this wide gap between the actual and the potential recognized, we can now examine how U.S. assistance attempts to reduce that gap.

## U.S. Bilateral Aid for Education

Ever since President Harry Truman enunciated his "Point Four" program for Technical Assistance in 1949, a major objective of the U.S. foreign assistance effort has been to promote education, training, and technical assistance. The primary means for doing this is through the bilateral programs of the Agency for International Development (USAID).

The U.S. government also participates in multilateral programs for human resources development through the World Bank Group, the multilateral regional development banks, and United Nations agencies (UNICEF, UNDP, ILO, and WHO). There is also non-official U.S. assistance for education from private foundations, religious organizations, and voluntary groups.

This chapter, however, concentrates on only the activities of USAID. The discussion focuses on the nature and scope of USAID's programs.

In recent congressional presentations, USAID has stated its policy objectives with respect to education and human resources (EHR) development as seeking to improve:

- Basic schooling opportunities for children 6–14, with particular attention to strengthening analytical, planning, and management capacities of the education system;

- Skills training for adolescents and adults—with particular attention to training for self-employment and employment in small and medium-size enterprises;

- Scientific, technical, administrative, and managerial training—as needed in support of USAID programs in each sector.[7]

USAID also underwrites project-related training efforts and supports labor development and other aspects of human resources development. Of special significance is USAID's participant training program, which provides education or training in the United States or third-country institutions for students from developing countries.

Although USAID's education assistance is directed first toward improving the efficiency of existing education systems—both formal and non-formal—the ultimate goal is to increase the availability and improve the quality of basic formal education and training opportunities. An essential element of USAID's education program is strengthening the capacities of less developed countries to identify inadequacies in existing education systems, test technical and strategic options for overcoming inadequacies, and implement cost-effective new programs.

To fulfill these objectives, both USAID and the host country must resolve a number of issues. What enrollment targets are financially, physically, and administratively feasible within a reasonable period of time? Under what assumptions would faster progress or more complete coverage be feasible? What changes in education policy or administrative practices will contribute to meeting these goals?

# Basic Education Programs

U.S. assistance has attempted to expand and improve primary education systems. The improvement of primary education is given priority in USAID assistance (a) when fewer than two-thirds of the eligible age group are completing at least the first four years of primary school, and (b) when there is a country policy commitment to improving internal efficiency. It is readily obvious that countries that have fewer than two-thirds of the eligible age group completing at least the first four years of primary school can be expected to have a significant nationwide problem with basic numeracy and literacy. Moreover, complementary efforts by USAID in its agriculture, health, and population programs can expect significantly less than optimal progress in the absence of improvements in the primary school systems of these countries.

USAID has recently adopted the following guidelines[8] for assistance to basic education programs:

### Support for Comprehensive Education Reform

• *Help countries mobilize, allocate, and manage their own resources more effectively.* . . . A.I.D. can assist most effectively by helping countries use available public resources more efficiently and identify and mobilize other resources for education. The latter includes private-sector resources, privately managed schools, and more effective ways to utilize local revenue and local administrative capacities.

Any education sector assessments, planning exercises, or institutional strengthening activity supported by A.I.D. should include components focused on education financing, financing mechanisms, and financing management.

• *Emphasize sector analysis as the basis for improving systems management as well as for initiating dialogue at all levels on reform and restructuring of education systems.* . . .

• *Assist countries to develop indigenous monitoring and evaluation capacity in support of sector reform.* . . . In support of education reform, A.I.D. will assist developing countries to improve existing monitoring and evaluation capacity and work in conjunction with other donors to establish baseline data and indicators of quality enhancement, capacity growth, and other reform objectives.

### Support for Multiple Assistance Modalities

• *Expand collaborative and coordinated education assistance activities with other major donors.* A.I.D. has approached donor collaboration and coordination with the intent of leveraging or leading other donors. Where appropriate and cost-effective, the Agency must also be able to cooperate on sound initiatives on which other donors have taken the lead. The key considerations must be the degree to which the USAID effort supports and facilitates education sector improvements, expansion, and reform. Whether A.I.D. has the lead role or is contributing to major innovations is a secondary consideration.

• *Expand central/regional bureau field support services to facilitate pre-investment planning and feasibility studies.*

• *Increase use of non-project assistance, especially where A.I.D. is working with other donors on national reform efforts.* For more effective use of limited resources, A.I.D. will employ alternatives to the conventional bilateral project and develop USAID assistance within a broader framework of multi-donor support. Increasing use will be made of program assistance, of program-project hybrid assistance, of commodity assistance and local currencies generated by commodity import and other programs, and buy-ins to centrally managed projects. These mechanisms will be used to provide missions with a broad range of analytic services, access to technical assistance and training of educators, as well as direct budget support to education reform programs.

Bilateral projects will continue to be a major mode of assistance for education sector activities. However, project activity should only be initiated after determining its consistency with national education reform goals and the system's capacity to absorb the assistance productively and to sustain the activity beyond donor participation.

### Support for a Wider Range of Countries

- *Concentrate on a basic set of educational inputs for countries with low enrollment and completion rates.* In general, this would include countries below the threshold of 80 per cent *net* enrollment and 70 per cent primary school completion rate, e.g., most of Sub-Saharan Africa and South Asia. These countries have not yet achieved a sustainable broad-based school system, have not developed the means to achieve full and equitable enrollment, and generally have avoided difficult policy reform choices, particularly on education finance and delegation of administrative authority.

  Education assistance to these countries should be concentrated upon improvements in system quality, access, equity, and internal and external efficiency. To enhance quality, A.I.D. should concentrate on a basic set of instructional materials and teacher training, using technology as appropriate. To increase system capacity and improve access, A.I.D. should focus on the logistical, personnel, and financial management problems of the school systems. Equity and efficiency are directly enhanced by quality improvement and broadened access.

- *Maintain technical assistance relationships in countries that exceed basic education enrollment and completion rate thresholds.* For these countries, A.I.D. should have different technical priorities, focusing on second generation problems such as sustainability, enhancing quality, monitoring system performance, broadening participation to include parents and private-sector entities, strengthening national education institutes, and improving systems management.

  More emphasis should be given to joint research, counterpart collaboration, and technical cooperation rather than resource transfer and external coordination of assistance packages.

In addition, these are countries in which A.I.D. can appropriately assist adult education programs; experiment with various non-formal education approaches, such as service agencies; develop and implement instructional innovations; and introduce planning models for marginal resource allocation.

- *Develop new modalities for cooperation with advanced developing countries (ADCs).* In differentiating among countries at different levels of education and economic achievement, A.I.D. must create new programs and program support capacities for advanced developing countries that are more appropriate for technical cooperation relationships than are the typical concessional assistance and resource transfer programs. These programs should begin to address educational problems beyond the scope of basic education and this strategy.

Curriculum reform, teacher training, use of educational technology, and non-formal education methodology may all enter into a basic education project. But there is an attempt to integrate these components more explicitly and completely into the developing country's effort to achieve reform, increase systems efficiency, and produce an impact on employment and overall national development over the long term.

Assistance to Costa Rica provides a notable example of USAID's educational support. Activities there include: support for a Ministry of Education initiative to produce and distribute textbooks to all Costa Rican schoolchildren at the primary and secondary levels; improvement of the quality of teaching in the nation's one-room schools; and repairing and refurbishing the nation's one-room schools.

In Africa, programs in Botswana, Lesotho, Mali, Swaziland, and other countries focus on upgrading teacher skills, training new teachers, and developing curricula to suit the needs of particular countries.

In Mali, for example, USAID is part of a multi-donor, $56-million effort to restructure the education sector. The two other key donors are the World Bank and France. USAID is contributing $3 million to a total of $12 million quick-disbursing monies to reward Ministry of Education reforms, which in general decrease resources to secondary and higher levels and increase those for primary schooling. In addition, USAID is contributing $7 million in project support to build systems for using primary resources more equitably and efficiently. Assistance targets include: in-service pedagogical and management training for primary school personnel; monitoring and evaluation systems for measuring the impact of classroom inputs; management information systems for optimizing education personnel; and measures to increase the supply and demand for primary schooling, especially among girls.[9]

Numerous projects with similar objectives have been sponsored by USAID in Latin America. A small number of USAID projects are also under way in Asia and the Near East. The longest-standing program is in Egypt, where USAID has provided over $200 million since 1975, including a major effort to increase primary-school enrollment through the construction of 620 schools in rural areas.

It should be also be noted that USAID recognizes a connection between education and improvement in nutrition and health programming. For this purpose, USAID has been involved in school feeding programs. It also supports some rudimentary health delivery—e.g., immunizations—via the school systems.

The rationale underlying all of AID's basic education support is the belief that, for society as a whole, basic education sufficient to make informed choices is key to non-coercive approaches to fertility and other personal decisions, to efficient functioning of market economies, and to full participation in modern social, economic, and political institutions.[10]

Although USAID's professed program for basic education has been commendable, the funding provided has been low. Moreover, the actual results have been far short of those programmed. Some of the causes of these shortfalls are discussed later in this chapter.

# Vocational Education and Technical Training

The large numbers of out-of-school adolescents, unemployed school-leavers, and self-employed in the informal sector constitute a major manpower problem. A high percentage of the adult labor force may be underemployed—engaged in low-productivity activities in the informal sector. This sector is characterized by easy entry into the labor force, reliance on indigenous resources, acquisition of skills outside the formal school system, prevalence of self-employment and labor-intensive methods of production, and small-scale activity. To reach individuals in the informal sector, USAID sponsors vocational and technical training to expand employment opportunities by helping individuals acquire a broader range of skills that will allow them to increase their productivity and income. The programs encourage non-formal approaches that involve as direct a role as possible for community organizations, local private voluntary organizations, and producer associations.

In the more formal sector of the economy, special emphasis is given to in-service training that allows a strong and direct role for employers to implement their own programs. For small- and medium-scale enterprises, USAID encourages both in-service training for the existing workforce and pre-service training for new workers and for workers needing retraining for new occupations.

USAID's basic guidelines for support to vocational and technical training programs are as follows: with adolescents and adults, USAID concentrates on vocational education and skill-training related to employment or self-employment and improving productivity in key development sectors. The skills and information provided in vocational education and technical training projects should be directly related to specific social or economic program objectives. To the maximum extent possible, participants themselves and potential employers are to be involved in the identification of training needs and the specification of training objectives. Vocational training programs are to be tailored to the skill needs of specific groups of learners. Training programs are to provide opportunities for women to participate. Preference is to be given to supporting the specific vocational and technical training initiatives of community organizations (including groups of employers). The training courses are to be as brief as possible, applicable to the specific needs of the labor market, and undertaken at the lowest possible per capita cost.

Although the programs that provide vocational education and technical training are to deal most directly with the existing under-utilization of human resources and the growing need for new occupational activities as a country develops, the methodology underlying the programs has been only rudimentary and ad hoc in character. Moreover, the scale of the programs has been very limited relative to the need, and more effort is needed to implant and build more relevant monitoring and policy-analysis institutional capacity. During the 1980s, only some 7–9 per cent of USAID's education assistance has been for vocational and technical training. And much of project funding has been earmarked for construction of training centers, training of instructors, and purchasing of equipment.

Programs have typically been guided by such broad statements as: "training should be closely related to employment needs, be practical in nature, and be coordinated with the employing industries, ministries, and local organizations. A strong role for the private voluntary organizations and for the private sector in implementing training is encouraged."[11]

A weakness in many vocational education programs, however, has been a lack of linkages with industrial sector employers. Projects tend to be concentrated in urban rather than rural areas. Although there has been growing participation by women, men are still the major recipients of training. Moreover, little assessment has been carried out on how well the participants acquire the intended technical, mechanical, construction, or commercial skills. Nor has there been systematic evaluation of how well the programs have succeeded in fulfilling manpower requirements for specific labor markets.

## Participant Training

Participant training for the purpose of human resource development has been a major activity of U.S. foreign assistance since before the establishment of the Marshall Plan in 1947. Approximately 250,000 participants have been trained in the United States and in developing countries by USAID and predecessor agencies during the last four decades.

"Participant training" refers to USAID-sponsored training of developing-country nationals in the United States, in their own countries, or in other countries. The program emphasizes the training of developing-country scientists, administrators, managers, and technicians, as well as the improvement of specialized training capacities in developing countries. The objectives of participant training are: staff development for USAID-assisted projects, strengthening of key development institutions, and the establishment of local training capacities.

USAID policy does not encourage general participant training that is not linked to specific development objectives. Nor does it encourage the training of teaching faculties in technical fields or disciplines not considered to be of development priority; USAID policy discourages the use of participant training programs as general scholarship funds. All participant training programs are expected to provide opportunities for women. Moreover, to avoid an external "brain drain," it is emphasized that USAID-sponsored trainees should return to work in their home countries, in positions in which their training is utilized effectively.

Table 1 summarizes recent participant training trends. Over the period 1982–1990, the number of participants in U.S. institutions more than doubled. Slightly more than half of the participants were in non-degree technical programs, and slightly less than half studied for academic degrees. The major subject area was agriculture, followed by industry/energy, and public administration. In FY1987, participant training represented an annual investment of over $200 million.

Since 1982, USAID has placed greater emphasis on participant training. As a result, the numbers have grown significantly, reaching approximately 19,000 annually in 1990. The Latin America and Caribbean region significantly increased its percentage—from 13 per cent in 1982 to 42 per cent in 1989. The shares of Asia and the Near East and of Africa declined during the years 1982–86.

Most of the training—whether short- or long-term—is directed toward the effective implementation and institutionalization of USAID-supported projects. The participants are primarily mid-level career managers and technicians from the public and private sectors who are selected jointly by USAID and the host country. In the Latin American and Caribbean region, there has been special emphasis on training for the socially and economically disadvantaged, with much of this training at the undergraduate level.

Training that is provided to strengthen key private and public institutions may be furnished as a general participant training program, as a training program focused on a specific sector, or as a component of a project supporting a specific institution. To expand local training capacities, USAID supports the training of teaching faculty, although other personnel, such as administrators and curriculum technicians, also may be included.

Training in the United States for nationals of a particular country is limited to fields in which training is not available in that country and for which U.S. training is cost-effective. Preference is given to training in nearby third-country institutions before relatively expensive training in U.S. institutions is recommended. Most of the long-term training for non-teaching managers and technicians is at the Master's level. Training for the Ph.D. degree is limited to teaching faculty, researchers, scientists, and key administrators of programs for institutions that employ scientists and researchers. USAID support for academic training in U.S. institutions is limited to three calendar years.

Some examples of training programs that have contributed to the increase in USAID participant training are as follows:

- In 1983, as part of the step-up in the scale of U.S. aid to Pakistan, a $400-million Pakistan development support training project was initiated. Its primary goal was to upgrade the management and technical expertise of Pakistanis in the federal and provincial governments as well as in the private sector who are involved in the implementation of Pakistan's social and eco-

**Table 1.  Summary of Trends in Participant Training in United States, 1982–1990 (numbers of participants and percentages)**

| | 1982 | 1983 | 1984 | 1985 | 1986 | 1987 | 1988 | 1989 | 1990 |
|---|---|---|---|---|---|---|---|---|---|
| **Total Number of Participants in U.S. Training** | 8,364 | 9,636 | 11,225 | 12,837 | 15,658 | 17,632 | 17,373 | 18,855 | 18,957[a] |
| **General Demographics** | | | | | (percentages) | | | | |
| Technical (non-degree) | 48 | 52 | 53 | 52 | 54 | 55 | 49 | 50 | 50 |
| Academic (degree) | 52 | 48 | 47 | 48 | 46 | 45 | 51 | 50 | 50 |
| Male | 82 | 82 | 82 | 80 | 79 | 75 | 75 | 73 | 73 |
| Female | 18 | 18 | 18 | 20 | 21 | 25 | 25 | 27 | 27 |
| **Participants by Subject Area** | | | | | (percentages) | | | | |
| Agriculture | 31 | 31 | 29 | 28 | 27 | 23 | 26 | 24 | 25 |
| Industry/Energy | 15 | 20 | 20 | 22 | 22 | 21 | 23 | 23 | 22 |
| Public Administration | 14 | 14 | 16 | 18 | 18 | 20 | 21 | 23 | 23 |
| Health/Family Planning | 17 | 16 | 16 | 15 | 15 | 13 | 11 | 11 | 11 |
| Education | 9 | 7 | 7 | 6 | 7 | 9 | 9 | 9 | 9 |
| Labor Support | 7 | 5 | 5 | 4 | 4 | 3 | 3 | 2 | 2 |
| Housing/Community Development | 4 | 4 | 3 | 3 | 3 | 6 | 3 | 4 | 4 |
| Transportation | 1 | 1 | 1 | 1 | 1 | 1 | 1 | 1 | 1 |
| Miscellaneous | 2 | 2 | 3 | 3 | 3 | 4 | 3 | 4 | 4 |

**Participants by Region**

*(percentages)*

| | | | | | | | | | |
|---|---|---|---|---|---|---|---|---|---|
| Africa | 38 | 37 | 32 | 26 | 23 | 20 | 19 | 19 | 19 |
| Asia/Near East | 49 | 48 | 49 | 45 | 41 | 40 | 41 | 39 | 37 |
| Asia | (17) | (16) | (15) | (15) | (16) | (19) | (20) | (19) | (18) |
| Near East | (32) | (32) | (34) | (30) | (25) | (21) | (21) | (20) | (19) |
| Latin America/Caribbean | 13 | 15 | 19 | 29 | 36 | 40 | 40 | 42 | 43 |

[a]Incomplete.

Source: USAID Office of International Training database.

nomic development programs. This upgrading effort involves a combination of long- and short-term training programs for 3,250 participants in the United States, 3,000 in Pakistan, and 778 in third countries.

- Indonesia's General Participant Training Project II was originally approved in 1983 and amended in 1986 to a total of $29 million. The purposes of the project are: to finance training in the United States at the graduate level or in short-term technical training in critical development areas; to help establish a new capability within the government of Indonesia to plan and administer overseas training programs for its citizens; to make available experts of various types to conduct training-related studies and to help with the design of training courses in Indonesia; to develop an English-language capability; and to implement an effective follow-up program for participants after their return home. Some 785 participants received financing for U.S. training under this project: 275 for the Master's degree, 75 for the Ph.D degree, and 435 for short-term training.

- In FY1986, the USAID program in Egypt accounted for the largest number of USAID-financed participants (1,460) attending short-term technical and academic degree training programs in the United States. The Peace Fellowship Program represents the single largest participation program in Egypt, with a total of $60 million programmed over the life of the program (1980–88) to finance both academic and non-academic technical training in the United States for approximately 2,100 Egyptians.

- The Caribbean and Latin American Scholarship Program will have trained approximately 13,450 participants between 1984 and 1993. Valued at $225 million, the program will provide an increased focus on the socially and economically disadvantaged, on undergraduate training, and on training for women and minority groups.

- The African Manpower Development Project II covers 26 countries. The $45-million, 5-year project provides both academic and technical training in fields critical to African development goals. About 900 participants are being trained in the United States, 268 in third countries, and 2,000 in their own countries. The African Graduate Fellowship Program III, a $42-million project, awards academic scholarships to high-caliber participants from 41 countries. A $38-million project to train South Africans has brought to the United States an average of 100 graduates and undergraduates each year.

Recently, USAID has not only increased the number of participants in training in the United States and the percentage of participants who are women but has also given major attention to private-sector training and to English-language training for USAID participants.

Moreover, in support of private-sector development, USAID is using private industry more frequently to conduct specialized training—often in conjunction with academic programs. Many of the participants receive training in laboratories, offices, and agricultural or industrial settings, where they become familiar with and use American methods, technologies, and equipment. New programs are being considered to expand training for the indigenous private sector and to take advantage of the training capabilities of U.S. firms.

A large number of private-sector enterprises, universities, and international organizations provide training services to USAID. In FY1986, for example, more than 150 contractors, grantees, and other private groups managed programs for participants under more than 300 separate contracts and grants funded by USAID.

Although participant training is the major means of assisting the development of high-level skills and institutional leadership, other support is given through local technical assistance projects.

There are also agreements with the U.S. Departments of Labor, Agriculture, Commerce, and Transportation that allow USAID participants to utilize the unique training capabilities of these government agencies. The Department of Labor, for instance, provides expertise to developing countries requiring assistance in labor and employment-related fields. Funding comes from USAID, multilateral development banks, or one of the U.N. specialized agencies. Activities include manpower planning models, an international labor statistics program, a technological exchange program, informational seminars on small training programs, and transfer of new learning technologies for vocational and technical training.

The Department of Agriculture plays an important role in providing technical assistance and training projects for the agricultural sector in developing countries. Training courses and degree programs in agriculture are offered for students from nearly 100 countries. Since the early 1950s, more than 85,000 students have participated in training activities sponsored by the Department, which tailors individualized training in U.S. universities, the private sector, or at the Department for about 2,000 agriculturalists a year. USAID pays for about 70 per cent of the training costs and the U.N. Food and Agriculture Organization (FAO) for about 25 per cent. Instructors have also been provided for overseas courses in more than a dozen countries in Asia, Africa, and South America. The

Department of Agriculture has also helped USAID organize and staff agricultural task forces for Honduras, Peru, Liberia, and Thailand. Funded by local currencies, some 150 research projects are also being undertaken on a collaborative basis between U.S. researchers and colleagues in India, Pakistan, Egypt, Costa Rica, and Yugoslavia.

The Department of Agriculture also cooperates with USAID and international organizations in supporting technical assistance activities. These help developing countries to become more self-reliant in producing food and fiber from limited resources and to improve their food-processing and food-distribution systems. The assistance is provided on a reimbursable basis.

Since participant training is USAID's priority program, the evaluation of its efficacy is especially important. USAID's policy guidelines state that all participant training programs must be justified by needs assessments and economic analyses and that participant training programs must include efforts to place the trainees in appropriate positions within their home countries. USAID has contracted with private consultants for outside reviews of its activities,[12] and it gives frequent accountings of training programs and outcomes to Congress.

Virtually all participants do return home—most to predetermined jobs in key development fields—to work for a stipulated length of service. There has been some internal drain—from the public to the private sector, but this is not contrary to USAID's recent emphasis on support of the private sector.

Equitable access has been promoted, but more emphasis still needs to be given to the recruitment of women for the program. English-language training also remains a problem for some participants.

Although USAID emphasizes the private sector in developing countries, its involvement of U.S. private industry in education and training has not yet been very extensive. It still relies mainly on formal education and training in U.S. educational institutions. This is not surprising, in that the extensive and diverse U.S. university system offers a wide range of expertise as well as the most accessible institutional context in which to operate.

USAID has undertaken significant reviews of the short-term impact of training programs for specific projects as well as of the provision of trained local staff to carry on after USAID withdraws support from a project. But more should be done to ascertain the longer-term effectiveness of projects in strengthening key private and public institutions and in developing local training activities. As will be discussed in the final section of this chapter, it is necessary to weigh the relative importance given to participant training programs and to basic education or vocational training.

# Funding of Education Programs

A useful comparison of annual EHR funding since 1960 is not possible, as there have been changes in the data base, in category designations, and in the definitions of projects. Nonetheless, the statistics in this section provide an approximate summary and indication of trends.

USAID's appropriations request to Congress for FY1991 is $134.2 million for education and human resources development (Section 105)—exclusive of approximately $70 million of education and human resources (EHR) activities in the African region, which are funded under the Development Fund for Africa appropriations. This compares with $122.3 million requested for EHR in FY1988 (also exclusive of EHR activities in Africa). In 1988, Participant Training for administrators, managers, scientists, and technicians was about 50 per cent of the total program. About 25 per cent supports elementary, secondary, and adult education; and 7–9 per cent, vocational and technical training. The balance goes to labor support programs, private voluntary organizations (PVOs), women-in-development programs, and a range of activities related to human resources development—such as narcotics education, legal system and election reform, local government improvement, and private enterprise development.

About 53 per cent of the FY1989 request for Section 105 will support programs in Latin America and the Caribbean, where there is a major emphasis on participant training as well as increased attention to strengthening basic schooling and skills training systems. Approximately 39 per cent will support participant training, education, labor, and PVO activities in Asia and the Near East. The remainder of the request, about 8 per cent, will support central bureau research and development, administration of participant training, and labor, women-in-development, and PVO programs.

Table 2 shows the allocation by education subcategories under Section 105 of the Foreign Assistance Act for FY1985 through FY1988 requests. Changes in project accounting and classification systems make it highly misleading to compare Section 105 EHR programs since the mid-1970s with the funding levels or program emphases for the projects classified as education in the prior years. Since 1988, with the dissolution of the Development Fund for the Sahel and the creation of the Development Fund for Africa (DFA),

## Table 2.   Education and Human Resources, DA Section 105, Obligations ($ millions and percentages)

| Subcategories[a] | FY1985 | FY1986 | FY1987[a] | FY1988[a] |
|---|---|---|---|---|
| | | *($ millions)* | | |
| Elementary Secondary, Adult/Community | 52.2 | 48.3 | 33.1 | 43.1 |
| Vocational/Technical | 18.3 | 6.2 | 4.3 | 15.3 |
| Administrative/Management, Professional/ Scientific | 78.7 | 88.7 | 73.4 | 72.2 |
| Labor Support | 16.9 | 16.6 | 14.3 | 15.4 |
| Private Voluntary Agencies | 8.2 | 6.8 | 8.8 | 8.0 |
| Planning/Analysis, Research, Other | 12.3 | 15.3 | 16.8 | 17.9 |
| **Total Section 105** | 186.6 | 181.9 | 150.7 | 171.9 |
| **Sahel** | | | | |
| Administrative/Management, Professional/Scientific | 5.1 | 4.2 | 4.3 | |
| **Total DA EHR (including Sahel)** | **191.7** | **186.1** | **155.0** | **171.9** |

**Total DA EHR Activity (Including Sahel), as Percentage of Total**

| | | *(percentages)* | | |
|---|---|---|---|---|
| Elemenary/Secondary, Adult/Community | 27 | 26 | 21 | 25 |
| Vocational/Technical | 10 | 3 | 3 | 9 |
| Administrative/Management, Professional/ Scientific | 44 | 50 | 50 | 42 |
| Labor Support | 9 | 9 | 9 | 9 |
| Private Voluntary Agencies | 4 | 4 | 6 | 5 |
| Planning/Analysis, Research, Other | 6 | 8 | 11 | 10 |

[a]Subcategories have been redefined.
   Source: Creative Associates, *Aid Policies and Programming in Education*, Washington, D.C., 1986, and (1987 and 1988) USAID Bureau for Program and Policy Coordination.

Section 105 appropriations no longer include African activities and thus make comparisons difficult.

USAID's budgetary allocations to education and training activities are not, however, appropriated only from the Development Assistance education and human resources sector functional account (Section 105). Allocations are also made from the Economic Support Fund (ESF), the Sahel Development Program (since 1988), and the Development Fund for Africa (since 1988). Total expenditures for education and training activities, including all funding accounts, have been in the range of $300 million annually (see Table 3 below).

From 1980 to 1988, the proportion of EHR allocated for programs supporting basic education has been declining. Africa accounted for about 30 per cent of the total allocation for basic education from 1980 through 1985 (involving mainly activities in Southern Africa (Botswana, Zimbabwe, Swaziland, and Lesotho). There was essentially no support for basic education in the Sahel countries (where France has provided most of the aid to education). Latin America and the Caribbean accounted for another third, with relatively large projects in Central America and the Caribbean. Basic education in Asia and the Near East was assisted at relatively modest levels—about 20 per cent of the total allocation to basic education.

In Latin America and the Caribbean, USAID has supported efforts to expand and revitalize school systems in Honduras, Haiti, El Salvador, Guatemala, and Jamaica. There has been increasing attention to skills training for employment in Belize, Ecuador, Jamaica, Honduras, El Salvador, and the Caribbean region—concentrating on the training needs of the private sector and training for self-employment. Management training has been a priority throughout the region, with major programs in Bolivia, Costa Rica, Ecuador, Haiti, Honduras, Jamaica, Peru, and the Caribbean region. The largest program allocation has been for the Central and Latin American Scholarship Program (CLASP), which provides increased support for training in the United States at the undergraduate and technical levels. The CLASP program includes the Central America Peace Scholars project and the Latin America and Caribbean Training Initiative II (LAC II, the Andean Scholars Program, and the Presidential Training Initiative for the Islands Caribbean).

In Asia and the Near East, USAID in 1989 began a $280-million, five-year basic education program in Pakistan. It also has provided additional resources for the expansion of basic education in Yemen; for participant training in Morocco, Yemen, Pakistan,

**Table 3. Total Expenditures for Education and Training Activities ($ millions)**

|  | 1985 | 1986 | 1987 | 1988 | 1989 | 1990 | 1991 |
|---|---|---|---|---|---|---|---|
| DA/DFA[a] | 191.7 | 186.1 | 155.0 | 209.2 | 202.0 | 198.1 | 201.0 |
| ESF[b] | 110.3 | 115.8 | 120.5 | 91.0 | 81.2 | 67.0 | 96.8 |
| **Total** | **302.0** | **301.9** | **275.5** | **300.2** | **283.2** | **265.1** | **297.8** |

[a]Development Assistance/Development Fund for Africa.
[b]Economic Security Fund.

Source: USAID Bureau for Program and Policy Coordination.

**Table 4. Basic Education (DA/DFA[a]) Funding (Primary and Secondary Education) ($ millions)**

|  | 1988 | 1989 | 1990 | 1991 |
|---|---|---|---|---|
| Africa | 8.2 | 23.9 | 30.3 | 27.5 |
| Europe & Near East and Asia/Private Enterprise | 16.2 | 20.8 | 22.4 | 18.4 |
| Latin America/Carribean | 15.5 | 16.4 | 14.3 | 18.2 |
| Central Bureau | 4.9 | 7.7 | 4.7 | 5.8 |

[a]Development Assistance/Development Fund for Africa.

Source: USAID 1990 Annual Report to Congress.

Bangladesh, Burma, and Nepal; as well as for regional programs in the ASEAN countries and the South Pacific.

In recent years, allocations for participant training have risen rapidly, reflecting USAID's objective of 18,000 participants by FY1989 as well as the high priority given to training as part of scholarship diplomacy strategies in Central America and elsewhere. EHR funds obligated for participant training represent approximately 50 per cent of the total funds obligated.

Obligations for vocational/technical training have fluctuated greatly over the decade but in general have declined over the last half of the 1980s. Four large projects accounted for 80 per cent of this subcategory in both FY1988 and FY1989: training for private-sector development in El Salvador and Guatemala, the Botswana workforce and skills training project, and similar training assistance in South Africa.

Table 5 shows the allocation of Section 105 education expenditures to Africa, Asia/Near East, and Latin America/Caribbean. A comparison of the 1980 and 1987 amounts in Africa shows that the most significant changes were in labor support, which declined by two-thirds, while basic education almost doubled in percentage share. Because of a funding pattern that concentrated on only a few relatively large projects, the support for basic education in Africa fluctuated widely.

Asia and the Near East received little support for basic education and vocational/technical training. Section 105 account expenditures were relatively small in this area, but considerably more was spent on participant training (manpower training in Table 5).

The Latin America/Caribbean region received the largest increases in total appropriations during the period 1980–87. The percentage allocated for basic education declined, however, while participant training increased substantially.

If an attempt is made to include for the period of 1960–1970 those activities that approximate the current Section 105 EHR program, then the African region received assistance during 1960–1970 amounting to $2.3 million; Asia, $104.5 million; the Near East, $125.9 million; and Latin America, $193.5 million.[13] During 1960–1970, the share committed to higher education, public administration, and general participant training was 40 to 45 per cent of the total program, and basic education activities received about 15 per cent.

A comprehensive study of USAID education and training activities across all sectors and all sources of funds estimates total assistance to have been about $3.8 billion for the period 1969–1979.[14] This was more than three times the amount obligated as technical or capital assistance to education under all USAID assistance pro-

**Table 5.   U.S. Bilateral Appropriations for Education Sub-Sectors (Section 105 Account) in the 1980s, by Region ($ millions and percentages)**

| | 1980 | 1981 | 1982 | 1983 | 1984 | 1985 | 1986 | 1987 |
|---|---|---|---|---|---|---|---|---|
| **AFRICA** | | | | | | | | |
| **Total Appropriations** | $30.3 | $25.1 | $35.8 | $29.3 | $35.8 | $35.4 | $47.6 | $36.9 |
| | | | | *($ millions)* | | | | |
| | | | | *(percentages)* | | | | |
| Basic Education | 15.9% | 13.7% | 3.8% | 5.6% | 23.3% | 26.8% | 35.5% | 30.4% |
| Manpower Training | 39.2 | 38.0 | 56.1 | 43.3 | 46.5 | 44.7 | 38.2 | 39.1 |
| Vocational/Technical Education | 12.1 | 8.4 | 28.4 | 36.8 | 16.2 | 8.5 | 8.1 | 9.0 |
| Labor Support | 28.4 | 30.2 | 8.4 | 10.2 | 8.4 | 11.9 | 7.1 | 9.2 |
| Other | 4.4 | 9.7 | 3.3 | 4.1 | 5.6 | 8.1 | 11.3 | 12.4 |
| **ASIA/NEAR EAST** | | | | | | | | |
| **Total Appropriations** | $23.9 | $29.8 | $25.9 | $38.5 | $38.3 | $26.5 | $20.9 | $31.1 |
| | | | | *($ millions)* | | | | |
| | | | | *(percentages)* | | | | |
| Basic Education | 28.8% | 24.5% | 8.1% | 11.2% | 13.4% | 8.2% | 3.5% | 2.4% |
| Manpower Training | 29.6 | 36.0 | 60.8 | 68.5 | 42.3 | 36.2 | 55.3 | 78.0 |

| | | | | | | | | |
|---|---|---|---|---|---|---|---|---|
| Vocational/Technical Education | 2.1 | 7.4 | 2.8 | 0.9 | 1.5 | 1.8 | 2.2 | 0.5 |
| Labor Support | 16.3 | 13.8 | 15.9 | 10.7 | 10.7 | 15.5 | 18.6 | 12.5 |
| Other | 23.2 | 18.3 | 12.4 | 8.7 | 32.1 | 20.6 | 20.4 | 6.6 |
| | | | | *($ millions)* | | | | |
| **LATIN AMERICA/CARIBBEAN** | | | | | | | | |
| **Total Appropriations** | **$30.1** | **$36.1** | **$33.4** | **$37.0** | **$36.2** | **$107.8** | **$83.5** | **$101.4** |
| | | | | *(percentages)* | | | | |
| Basic Education | 37.2% | 33.2% | 22.1% | 9.8% | 20.8% | 21.4% | 7.6% | 14.4% |
| Manpower Training | 14.7 | 15.7 | 32.0 | 37.3 | 34.8 | 45.5 | 48.6 | 51.5 |
| Vocational/Technical Education | 6.1 | 18.6 | 5.0 | 20.0 | 12.8 | 7.3 | 3.1 | 7.6 |
| Labor Support | 27.9 | 21.6 | 24.0 | 21.6 | 22.1 | 7.4 | 9.2 | 7.8 |
| Other | 14.1 | 10.9 | 16.9 | 11.3 | 9.5 | 18.2 | 31.5 | 18.7 |

Source: Creative Associates, *Aid Policies and Programming in Education*, Washington, D.C. 1986, and (1987) USAID Bureau for Program and Coordination.

grams over this period. With education sector and program lending, local currency funding of education sector activities, and support to American schools abroad included, the total of all activities classified as being within the education sector amounted to approximately $2.4 billion. About $1.4 billion of additional assistance is estimated to have come from other programs and projects of an educational nature (such as agricultural universities and general participant programs), and from the manpower training, technical training, and extension education components of programs that are not exclusively educational (such as the training included in the health, nutrition, and population programs). In this broader classification, it is estimated that there has been approximately half as much again in educational activities outside the education sector as within the sector narrowly defined.

From 1960 to 1980, most of USAID's educational assistance went to Latin America, Asia, and the Near East; relatively little went to Africa. In the 1960s and early 1970s, assistance was concentrated on a set of countries different from those currently receiving assistance. Many countries that received assistance in the earlier period later became ineligible for concessional assistance either because they were defined by USAID as "graduate countries" (e.g., Brazil, Colombia, South Korea) or because political relationships precluded a U.S. assistance program (e.g., Ethiopia, Afghanistan, Vietnam). Just over one-third of total Section 105 obligations since 1977 have been for projects in Latin America and the Caribbean. Recently, however, the emphasis has shifted to the Near East and Africa.

# Evaluation

The need for education and training assistance is now particularly acute in Sub-Saharan Africa, where enrollment has stagnated, educational quality has eroded, and the burden on public budgets has intensified. The inability to fulfill education and training targets also remains serious in Latin America and other developing regions where balance-of-payments deficits and the external debt problem have led to the imposition of conditionality by the International Monetary Fund and the World Bank with respect to structural adjustment loans. Indeed, a recent study by UNICEF calls for "adjustment with a human face": the human implications of an adjustment policy must be made an integral part of adjustment policy as a whole.[15] As expressed by the former Managing Director of the International Monetary Fund: "Adjustment that pays attention to the health, nutrition, and educational requirements of the most vulnerable groups is going to protect the human condition better than adjustment which ignores them."[16]

In its study of ten countries over the 1980s, UNICEF found a substantial decline in access to or use of educational services as well as a decline in educational attainment. Real government expenditure per capita in the social sector declined in six of the countries. In many other poor countries, the evidence is clear that primary-school enrollment rates have declined, drop-out rates have increased, and there has been a massive decline in the numbers of qualified teachers.[17] In many countries, there have been marked reductions in government expenditures on health and education per capita in the 1980s—with a notable deceleration in growth in expenditure per capita on average in Africa, Latin America, the Caribbean, and the Middle East. The decreases in expenditure per capita on health and education have been more widespread in Latin America than in Africa, as a higher proportion of Latin American countries reduced the share of expenditures going to these sectors. Typically, Latin American countries cut education expenditures more, while African countries cut health more.[18]

Given the constraints of adjustment policy, it is now all the more essential to provide foreign assistance for health and education programs and to ensure the effective use of the limited resources that remain committed to education. What is needed is the political commitment and administrative creativity to sustain and expand the education sector despite financial limitations.[19] This calls for a considerable rethinking of options for achieving better education and training results without increasing total expenditures. This means working out how education goals can be achieved by adapting institutions and practices to achieve them rather than by altering the goals.

In practice, countries typically have maintained teachers' salaries and have instead drastically cut expenditures on building and equipment maintenance, books, and teaching supplies. Efforts to maintain or increase education budgets must ensure that priority is given to the basic minimum requirements for instructional *quality*. USAID has moved away from the emphasis of the 1960s and 1970s on least-cost assistance of specific institutions and capacities such as teacher training to provide more support for research and experimentation in areas such as curriculum reform and the development of low-cost instructional technologies. Increasingly, USAID assistance has been linked to budgetary reallocations and management reforms intended to ensure the availability of essential instructional materials and to improve the physical quality of local schools.

Because of the intangible nature of education and training, it is difficult to estimate the true economic value of activities supported by USAID funds.[20] A number of studies in the literature attest to the fact that the returns on investment in human capital—as calculated by effects on productivity, rate of return, or lifetime earnings of individual workers—are generally high.[21] Education also has favorable effects on lowering fertility rates and improving health and nutrition. There is no reason to believe that the returns on USAID's programs—especially participant training—are not similar in showing creditable positive returns. There is, however, a sharp disjunction between studies that indicate high social and private rates of return for primary education[22] and USAID's relative neglect of this level of education.

Only a few long-term studies of individual education projects are available. But it appears that the quality of individual projects has been high, except when assistance has been provided for too short a period or when local costs of maintenance and replacement have not been adequately anticipated or provided for. Typically, most education projects have been successful in terms of physical outputs—numbers of schools built, students enrolled, textbooks provided.

Many projects have resulted in high unit costs, however, and the recipient governments have had trouble in financing the recurrent costs. USAID now emphasizes systems efficiency as well as the management of total costs, and it measures systems efficiency in terms of achievement and cost per completer as well as initial access and coverage. Most USAID programs now include sector assessment and other analytic activities designed to help countries identify options for using available measures more efficiently and to explore the feasibility of various new policy options for financing education—including selective user charges, student loans, decentralization of management, and encouragement of community and private schools.[23]

It has been much easier for USAID to assess the internal efficiency of its programs than their external efficiency. True, internal efficiency must be promoted so as to make more productive use of inputs in the educational process. USAID projects have been generally successful from this standpoint. But external efficiency must also be sought if education and training are to be relevant to the development efforts of the recipient nations—especially as countries attempt to address the dual problem of removing shortages of critical skills and providing employment opportunities for surplus labor.[24] More critical assessment of USAID's programs in relation to the world of work needs to be undertaken.[25] Through Gresham's Law analysis, the easier analysis has driven out the more difficult, and a balance should be restored.

Although the quality of U.S. education and training assistance generally has been high, its quantity has diminished. The level of assistance is now about the same in current dollars as it was in the late 1960s, but the dollar's purchasing power is now much lower. With fiscal restraints, assistance has necessarily been selective, and priorities may be questioned. During the 1980s, appropriations for education and human resources approximately doubled, but most of the increase went to participant training; assistance for vocational and technical education was also at a low level. In FY1980, basic education was 30 per cent of the total education budget; in FY1989, even with the inclusion of the Development Fund for Africa (DFA), it was still only 34 per cent of the much larger EHR program. Although there have been numerous policy statements in favor of improving basic education (particularly for women, the poor, and rural children), training has in practice maintained its dominance of the EHR portfolio over the past seven-year period. In FY1986, training obligations inclusive of the Sahel Fund were $92.9 million, or approximately 50 per cent of the account. In FY1989, DA/DFA training represented $116.7 million (57.7 per cent) out of a total account of $202 million. Considering that advanced and specialized training is also provided under other funding accounts (such as those for agriculture and health)—perhaps doubling the training provided under the education and human resources development program—it is clear that training, not basic education, has been the USAID program priority.

For one who has not been privy to the decisionmaking process, it is difficult to discern the reasons why participant training programs have gained such prominence compared with other subsectors of education. Why has basic education not grown more, and why is attention to literacy and numeracy of adults and vocational training at a standstill?

USAID's policy statements express strong support for basic education and vocational training as well as participant training. Indeed, they enunciate an overabundance of priorities. When it comes to actual funding and programming, however, the priorities have been quite different from the policy statements. The differences result in large part from the politics of the funding process through the Congress. In the United States, there is no general public constituency for education in developing countries. At the same time, the support for participant training has come in large part from the U.S. university community, which favors higher education in general and participant training in the United States in particular. It also reflects the fact that participant training is favored by USAID management. Standardized training procedures and scholarship or fellowship awards are much easier to implement than are efforts to improve basic education.

The actual determination of funding is the responsibility of Congress. USAID submits requests to the Office of Management and Budget, which determines levels of funding. After a renegotiation with USAID, the budget is sent to Congress, where it is reviewed by authorizing committees in the House and Senate, the appropriations committees of the House and Senate, and the budget committees of the House and Senate. An authorizing bill passed by Congress determines the funding level by authorization category (functional accounts). The funding that emerges from this process may be quite different from that which was requested and typically is burdened with restrictions and earmarks that make it difficult to allocate according to the policy statements issued by USAID. This is particularily true in terms of the allocation by country and region. USAID often is faced with an identified education project in a country for which it does not have sufficient funding allocated.

Given that the need has intensified at the same time that the real amount of foreign assistance has declined, it is essential that measures be taken to increase the flow of resources for and improve the efficiency of education and training programs. In addition, there is a need for the United States and other donor nations to coordinate their assistance efforts. A World Bank study has proposed that the international donor community should offer three related kinds of support for the design of national education policies:

(1) *Seed money to cover both the local and foreign costs of developing policies and improving management.* The willingness of international donors to bear a part of these extraordinary expenses, perhaps on a matching basis, would provide an important incentive for governments in developing countries to review their educational policies.

(2) *Ready access to other countries' experiences in formulating and implementing policy reform.* Intensive collaboration and much wider sharing of accumulated experience among countries should pay high dividends as countries grapple with common issues.

(3) *The establishment and financing of a source of high-quality specialized technical expertise without direct financial or political ties to any government or international donor.* Governments in developing countries could then call on this expertise for

help in formulating policies at the outset, as well as in monitoring, evaluating, and correcting them during implementation.[26]

The increased coordination of assistance activities among donor nations would offer benefits through the sharing of experience, and it could help establish a better balance between the public and private sectors and provide more equitable access to education. Duplication of effort might be avoided and less strain placed on the capacity of recipients to select and design programs. Moreover, better donor coordination might reduce the pressure of interest groups and the political elements in national assistance programs. At a time when tight fiscal constraints prevent increases in the amount of assistance for education, it is all the more imperative to make the most effective use of the resources at hand.

## Notes

[1]See Frederick H. Harbeson, *Human Resources as the Wealth of Nations* (New York: Oxford University Press, 1973).

[2]Harry G. Johnson, "Towards a Generalized Capital Accumulation Approach to Economic Development," reprinted in Gerald M. Meier, *Leading Issues in Economic Development*, fifth edition (New York: Oxford University Press, 1989), pp. 461-62.

[3]To treat human beings as a form of capital may seem to some individuals contrary to democratic political philosophy. This reaction, however, involves a confusion of analytical approach and normative recommendations. To recognize that important areas of socioeconomic policy involve decisions analytically identical with decisions about investing in machines is not at all to imply that people should be regarded as no different from machines; on the contrary, refusal to recognize the investment character of a problem because people are involved may result in people receiving worse treatment than machines. One might hazard the generalization that democratic free enterprise economies tend to make wasteful use of their human resources precisely because people are not sufficiently regarded as socially productive assets. Johnson, "Towards a Generalized," op cit., p. 462.

[4]For such an answer, see Richard Easterlin, "Why Isn't the Whole World Developed?" Presidential address to the Economic History Association, *Journal of Economic History Review*, March 1981.

[5]Mark Blaug, "The Empirical Status of Human Capital Theory," *Journal of Economic Literature*, Vol. 14, No. 3, September 1976, pp. 827–55; Christopher Colclough, "The Impact of Primary Schooling on Economic Development: A Review of the Evidence," *World Development*, Vol. 10, No. 3, March 1982, pp. 167–85; George Psacharopoulos, "Education, Employment, and Inequality in LDCs," *World Development*, Vol. 9, No. 1, January 1981, pp. 37–54.

[6]See references in Meier, *Leading Issues*, op. cit., p. 444.

[7]USAID, FY1988 *Congressional Presentation*, main volume, p. 68.

[8]USAID, "Basic Education Strategy," 1990. Italics added.

[9]USAID, Bureau for Program and Policy Coordination.

[10]USAID, *FY1988 Congressional Presentation*, main volume, p. 66.

[11]USAID, Report to House Foreign Affairs Committee on AID Policy and Priorities for Education Programs, February 1982, p. 13.

[12]See, for example, Creative Associates, Inc., "Aid Policies and Programming in Education," Vols. I-III, Washington, D.C., April 1986.

[13]USAID, Report to House Affairs Committee, op. cit. p. 18.

[14]Creative Associates, Inc., *Aid Policies*, op. cit., p. 9.

[15]Giovanni Andrea Cornia et al., *Adjustment with a Human Face: Protecting the Vulnerable and Promoting Growth, A Study by UNICEF* (Oxford: Clarendon Press, 1987), pp. 2, 3.

[16]Loc. cit.

[17]Cornia et al., *Adjustment with a Human Face*, op. cit., pp. 23–26, 33–34, 73–83.

[18]Ibid., p. 80.

[19]Ibid., p. 240. This plea is admirably discussed by Richard Jolly in Chapter 12.

[20]This section draws heavily on Creative Associates, "Aid Policies and Programming in Education," op. cit. For a more detailed evaluation by sub-category of program and region, see especially Volume II.

[21]See G. Psacharopoulos, "Returns to Education: A Further International Update and Implications," *Journal of Human Resources*, Vol. 20, 1985, pp. 584–604.

[22]See numerous such studies listed in World Bank, Education and Training Department, *Education Research and Policy Studies at the World Bank: A Bibliography*, Report No. EDT 23 (Washington, D.C.: World Bank, April 1987).

[23]For discussion of various policy options, see World Bank *Financing Education in Developing Countries* (Washington, D.C.: World Bank, 1986), especially Chapters 3–4.

[24]See Philip H. Coombs, *The World Crisis in Education* (New York: Oxford University Press, 1985), Chapters 3 and 6.

[25]One USAID study of vocational education projects for women showed that job training projects often failed because salaried employment was not available and the trainees lacked capital to establish a business; Alice Stewart Carboni, "Lessons Learned from 1982–1985: The Importance of Gender for AID Projects," draft (Washington, D.C.: USAID, 1985.

[26]Ibid., p. 6 and Chapter 9.

# IV. U.S.S.R. Concluding Comment

# U.S.S.R.
# Concluding
# Comment

Ratchik M. Avakov

Beneficial changes are taking place in the world. The atmosphere of international relations is improving. There is a better chance of creating a new, more acceptable world in which all people can attain well-being in civilized society. Such a world must not be divided into those who need aid and those who provide it. Aid that becomes a permanent pattern in international relations, especially if it is politicized, is essentially a social phenomenon—an indicator of the imperfections of the world and the fallaciousness of its foundations. Aid can be considered an acceptable form of relationship only if it fosters conditions under which countries seek development not through permanent dependence on aid but through mutually advantageous partnership between equals. To make it the goal of aid to free a country of the constant need for aid is the only reliable basis for imparting a humanistic basis to aid and increasing its effectiveness and efficiency. The challenge is to achieve the affirmation of such an approach in an imperfect world.

Our book is an attempt to make a modest contribution to the process of change—to the restructuring of the code of conduct in international relations. It is also the *result* of such change. Not so long ago—it is even possible to indicate the precise date: before April 1985—it would have been impossible to even dream of preparing and publishing a joint Soviet-American book on such a burning political topic.

Aid emerged in relations between the developed and developing countries at a time when former colonies were casting off their colonial fetters and striving for independence. They found that they were deprived of everything they needed for their development under the new conditions, and that they needed everything. They certainly needed aid to get started. But this was also a time of new, unprecedented confrontation of two world systems and two superpowers—a confrontation that literally permeated all spheres of international life, including aid. Aid strategy was therefore articulated from the very beginning in accordance with the goals of confrontation. Humanistic considerations were pushed more and more into the background. Confrontation emphasized selfish interests and intensified contradictions in the actual goals and essence of aid. In this setting, aid—formulated and introduced under the conditions of confrontation between world socialism and world capitalism—was increasingly ideological and itself became one of the channels of this confrontation.

The spirit of ideological opposition and rivalry determined both the similarities and the differences in strategies, principles, goals, and directions of aid initially endorsed by the United States and the Soviet Union. From the very beginning, both powers based their aid strategies on their dichotomous visions of the world community—with the basic difference that each of them was oriented toward the path of Third World development consistent with its own sociopolitical and economic structure and ideology. Thus, until recently, Soviet aid strategy was obviously interested in the movement of the developing countries along the path of socialist economic reforms and in strengthening in their economies the principles connected with public ownership of the means of production and collectivist principles of production and distribution.

The United States rejected such an approach not only on a scientific, conceptual plane, but also in its practical aid strategy. U.S. criticism insisted that the socialist orientation was ineffective and that it did not correspond to the conditions in the developing countries. American aid was oriented toward stimulating the development of capitalist relations in Third World countries. All strategy of U.S. relations with these countries adhered to this orientation.

In Soviet and American aid strategies, two different attitudes toward the state and private sectors in the developing countries have been quite clearly discernible. Soviet aid strategy was primarily focused on the state sector in these countries. This was determined by the state character of the Soviet Union's own economy and by the advancement of the state sector and its entrepreneurial activity as the principal agent of economic development in both scientific-theoretical research and practice. This thrust of strategy did not, however, remain unchanged. Exaggerated views of the potential of the state sector and its ability to perform leadership functions in the development process gradually gave way to more realistic assessments. A positive evolution also took place in perceptions of the significance of the private capitalist sector and market relations. This was expressed in the gradual abandonment of the restrained attitude toward this type of entrepreneurial activity in favor of its support and more intensive business relations with it. These new trends were incorporated in the model of the U.S.S.R.'s foreign economic relations that was developed in the course of *perestroika* and that is beginning to be put into practice.

U.S. aid strategy also went through an important evolution— but in the opposite direction. From the U.S. point of view, the business class of the developing countries was from the very beginning the principal agent of economic development. As for the state sector, it was called upon to create the general preconditions for the development of production. In other words, aid to the state was to serve as the channel for the development of private capitalist activity and market relations.

The limitations of such an approach inevitably made themselves known in a variety of ways. First, the position of private capitalism in the economies of many developing countries is weak, or even in an embryonic state. Its development requires an "intermediary" in the form of the state. Second, in those developing countries in which private capitalist activity does assume wide scope, the role of the state does not necessarily diminish and may even increase: it has to take upon itself many tasks that are associated with scientific-technological progress with a number of other production conditions that private capital prefers to shift to the state. These considerations contributed to the increased attention that the state sector received in the United States in the 1980s.

As a result of the noted policy trends, there is quite a clearly defined convergence between attitudes vis-à-vis private and state capital in U.S. and Soviet aid to developing countries. The differences of course remain considerable, even fundamental. Nevertheless, these trends can in general be interpreted as a positive phenomenon attesting to a better understanding of the problems of Third World development—and consequently to the broader possibility of improving the quality of both U.S. and Soviet aid to the developing countries.

This unique convergence can also be seen in the sectoral structure of Soviet and U.S. aid to the Third World. The United States has directed the bulk of its aid allocations in the developing countries to *agriculture.* In this connection, in the opinion of U.S. specialists, this sector is the basis for the development of market relations. The Soviet Union, on the other hand, has preferred the opposite approach—emphasizing *industrialization and the development of industry (especially heavy industry)* in the developing countries. Soviet aid strategy has obviously reflected its internal experience of economic development, in which a key role was assigned to industrialization.

But that is how it was in the past. More recently, U.S. aid strategy has tended to reassess the place of industrialization and industrial production—including the manufacturing industry—in Third World development. As for Soviet aid, it is increasingly attracted to the agrarian sphere. The evolution of Soviet domestic economic policy is also clearly felt in this respect. Thus, in the American as in the Soviet approach, a point of view is prevailing that is more realistic and responsive to the interests of the developing countries: It is important to be guided not by the priority of one or the other sphere of the economy but by the need for *balance* between them. The new approach seems promising regardless of whether it leads to the formulation and implementation of joint Soviet-American aid projects for developing countries, or whether the United States and the U.S.S.R. continue to act in parallel, as in the past.

Although our book contains quite a large amount of material characterizing the common directions, principles, and specifics of the aid extended by both superpowers, it is not possible to compare many indicators and questions without excessive generalization. This is first of all because of different definitions of the concept of aid, as well as different practices, that have historically evolved in each of the two countries. Without going into fine points, it should be noted that the Soviet Union uses the broadest interpretation, including a number of elements of economic cooperation and trade relations in the content of aid that the United States does not include in the aid category in its "pure" form—and therefore does not include in its calculations of aid amounts and levels. Clearly the methods used in the calculations are completely different.

Another difficulty is that neither the American nor the Soviet methods offer the practical possibility of attaining complete or even significant comparability—i.e., of excluding from Soviet aid elements that are not represented in U.S. aid or of including them in the latter. It should be noted that the Soviet specialists contributing to this volume have made efforts in this regard, but the problem is admittedly complex and these initial results cannot satisfy all parties. Joint efforts are obviously needed in this area.

But comparability should not be the most important consideration. Ultimately, general views of the volume of aid to the developing countries can also be compared on the basis of data processed on the basis of modern comparative analysis. The most important aspect of the quality of foreign aid to the developing countries is the degree of its usefulness and positive effect, the degree to which it promotes the solution of their vitally important problems—especially the degree to which it helps overcome their backwardness and raise the living standard and well-being of hundreds of millions of people barely surviving in poverty, suffering from hunger, malnutrition, and disease, and deprived of the opportunity to enjoy the fruits of science, education, and culture. How effective have U.S. and Soviet aid to the Third World been viewed specifically from this point of view? The question is all the more appropriate if we consider that these are the very goals that have been proclaimed in the two superpowers' official declarations.

Clearly, resources valued in the billions have been transferred from the United States and U.S.S.R. to the developing countries. These resources have made it possible for these countries to build thousands of industrial enterprises, schools, institutes, and sports facilities, as well as to assist in raising agricultural production and in developing science and educational systems, etc., in poorer countries. Foreign aid has frequently helped out in critical situations; it has helped to raise the level of economic development; and it has facilitated entrée into world markets. This is of course one side of the reality and should not be ignored.

There is, however, another side—one that invites more troubling reflections. A serious problem is that in all too many cases, the more external resources a country has received in the form of aid, the more outside resources it has needed. Statistics confirm this trend. We do not refer to the usual increases in the breadth and depth of foreign economic relations that are a phenomenon without which the normal development of any country is impossible. The point here is about something else—about the fact that foreign aid has become a spontaneously growing phenomenon. The negative consequences of this tendency are no secret to anyone. Its "sins" include the following:

- Even though the enormous indebtedness of the developing countries and its growth are due to many factors, foreign aid bears its share of the blame.

- The growth of aid generated feelings of dependency on the part of many developing countries that only hope that foreign aid will continue to be a permanent item in their budgets and national development. The result is an increase in the number of countries whose development without foreign aid is inconceivable.

In this connection, the world community now faces a serious dilemma. It must:

- Reexamine the aid problem and its fundamental goals with a view to promoting the creation of a self-regulating national economy functioning on its own basis in each developing country—not as an autarkic entity, but as an economically solvent and equal partner in the international division of labor with its own well-organized economic mechanism; or

- Admit that the world economy will henceforth have to reckon with the existence of a group of countries that cannot develop into such partners without outside help.

The second "option"—which would make it necessary to create a permanent international fund to promote the survival of these countries—simply cannot be a solution to the situation. It would mean depriving a set of countries of the possibility of realizing their cherished aspirations of becoming masters of their own development and would doom them to a miserable role greatly resembling the fate of unemployed persons who receive an allowance that permits them a pitiful existence but hardly makes it possible to put an end to unemployment *per se.*

As for the first "option," no country offering aid has yet found a successful way to help make it happen. Moreover, this outcome cannot be realized through the isolated actions and programs of individual countries. The problem of Third World development is a *global* problem. This is not a slogan, but a real necessity—an imperative of modern times. The challenge can be met only at the global level through the joint actions of the entire world community and each of its members—through the total mobilization of the efforts of *all* countries.

A final remark is prompted by reflections on the essence of the problem of development in a modern world threatened by ecological catastrophe. The present extraordinary conditions demand a new approach, new guidelines based on a redefinition of values. After all, it is precisely the model of world development that dates back to the industrial revolution and that has been affirmed in the course of the scientific-technological revolution that has led humanity to a point threatening the extinction of life. The model has ultimately proved to be flawed and pernicious. It has become unacceptable and needs to be replaced. But by what kind of *new* model? This is the fundamental problem of modern times—a problem that also relates to the question of multilateral aid to the developing countries.

An idea advanced in antiquity is more and more frequently expressed again today: that man is a part of nature, which he nevertheless thoughtlessly ravages, even though he realizes that by so doing he is cutting off the branch he sits on. This simple idea means that the development of human society and of every country must today be viewed in the broad, truly superglobal context of the processes that are occurring in nature, and in relation to these processes. Man's relationship with nature developed harmoniously for a long time. But with the onslaught of the industrial revolution and its agent, capitalism, there was a break with nature. With the birth of the socialist countries, whose motto was planned development, it appeared that economy would be restored. But this did not happen. With "planned" development, the break with nature assumed greater, not lesser proportions. And it was reinforced by the scientific-technological revolution.

The affirmed "modern type" of development incorporated features that contradict the character of nature. Nature gravitates to systematic equilibrium. Unrestrained striving for the new through the destruction of the old is alien to it.

But how can the destruction of nature be halted? How can we move away from the abyss? How can development be sensibly channeled so as to restore the lost harmony between man and nature?

The new type of development should be a model of "rational, organic development," designed to promote two basic goals:

- First, to ensure the self-renewal of nature by normalizing relations between human activity and nature—by bringing the patterns of their development into line and by attaining ecological equilibrium; man must take from nature only that which will not inflict irreparable harm, will not disturb its state of equilibrium;

- Second, to harmonize the development of human society per se. In the development of human society, there came a time when it was necessary to think about the limits that it should not exceed with respect to both population size and the volume and quality of production activity. It is even possible that these limits have already been passed—so that the well-known idea of "zero growth" has profound meaning—and it is not impossible that we will have to return to it. We can hardly proceed on the assumption of limitless development—lightheartedly counting on the possibility of the development of other planets and on man's creative genius.

The movement toward an organic and rational model—toward its many variants—must of course occur in different societies along their own unique trajectories. But movement in this direction will not come through some kind of *compromise*—for example, between the group of developing countries and the group of developed countries. The general goal of attaining harmony between man and nature should serve as the reference point that indicates to human society and its different national units how—by what methods and with what allocated resources—it should act. It is clear that joint, collective actions are needed at the global level, and that these should be based on the renunciation of resort to confrontational methods to "resolve" contradictions and conflicts in favor of true international cooperation. It is in the context of a model of organic development that the essence and goals of foreign aid to developing countries must be reexamined—in the interest of these nations as well as of world development in general.

# About the Overseas Development Council

The Overseas Development Council is a private non-profit organization established in 1969 for the purpose of increasing American understanding of the economic and social problems confronting the developing countries and of how their development progress is related to U.S. interests. Toward this end, the Council functions as a center for policy research and analysis, a forum for the exchange of ideas, and a resource for public education. The Council's current program of work encompasses four major issue areas: trade and industrial policy, international finance and investment, development strategies and development cooperation, and U.S. foreign policy and the developing countries. ODC's work is used by policymakers in the Executive Branch and the Congress, journalists, and those concerned about U.S.-Third World relations in corporate and bank management, international and non-governmental organizations, universities, and educational and action groups focusing on specific development issues. ODC's program is funded by foundations, corporations, and private individuals; its policies are determined by a governing Board and Council. In selecting issues and shaping its work program, ODC is also assisted by a standing Program Advisory Committee.

John W. Sewell is President of ODC. Victor H. Palmieri is Chairman of the ODC Board and Council, and Wayne Fredericks, Stephen J. Friedman, and Ruth J. Hinerfeld are Vice Chairmen.

Overseas Development Council
1717 Massachusetts Ave., N.W.
Washington, D.C. 20036
Tel. (202) 234-8701

# ODC Program Advisory Committee

**Chairman:**
**John P. Lewis**
*Woodrow Wilson School of Public
and International Affairs
Princeton University*

**Nancy Birdsall**
*The World Bank*

**Colin I. Bradford, Jr.**
*OECD Development Centre*

**Lawrence Brainard**
*Goldman Sachs & Company*

**Shahid Javed Burki**
*The World Bank*

**Mayra Buvinic**
*International Center for
Research on Women*

**Lincoln Chen**
*Harvard University Center for
Population Studies*

**Stanley Fischer**
*Massachusetts Institute of
Technology*

**Albert Fishlow**
*University of California at Berkeley*

**James Galbraith**
*Lyndon B. Johnson School
of Public Affairs
University of Texas at Austin*

**Denis Goulet**
*University of Notre Dame*

**Davidson R. Gwatkin**
*International Health Policy Program
The World Bank*

**Catherine Gwin**
*The Rockefeller Foundation*

**Edward K. Hamilton**
*Hamilton, Rabinovitz, and
Alschuler, Inc.*

**Chandra Hardy**
*Washington, D.C.*

**G. K. Helleiner**
*University of Toronto*

**Albert Hirschman**
*Institute for Advanced Study
Princeton, New Jersey*

**Gary Horlick**
*O'Melveny and Myers*

**Michael Horowitz**
*Institute for Development Anthropology
and State University of New York
at Binghamton*

**Gary Hufbauer**
*School of Foreign Service
Georgetown University*

**Tony Killick**
*Overseas Development Institute*

**Paul R. Krugman**
*Massachusetts Institute
of Technology*

**John Mellor**
*Port Republic, Maryland*

**Theodore H. Moran**
*Landegger Program
School of Foreign Service
Georgetown University*

**Henry Nau**
*Elliott School of International
Affairs
The George Washington University*

**Maureen O'Neill**
*North-South Institute*

**Kenneth A. Oye**
*Massachusetts Institute of
Technology*

**Dwight H. Perkins**
*Harvard Institute for
International Development*

**Gustav Ranis**
*Economic Growth Center
Yale University*

**Jeffrey Sachs**
*Harvard University*

**Robert Solomon**
*The Brookings Institution*

**Lance Taylor**
*Massachusetts Institute of
Technology*

**Judith Tendler**
*Massachusetts Institute of
Technology*

**Norman Uphoff**
*Center for International Studies
Cornell University*

# The Series Editors

*From Confrontation to Cooperation? U.S. and Soviet Aid to Developing Countries*
is the fifteenth volume in the Overseas Development Council's policy book
series, U.S.–Third World Policy Perspectives. The co-editors of the series—often
collaborating with guest editors contributing to the series—are Valeriana
Kallab and Richard E. Feinberg.

**Richard E. Feinberg** is Executive Vice President and Director of Studies
of the Overseas Development Council and co-editor of the Policy Perspectives
series. Before joining ODC in 1983, he served as the Latin American specialist
on the Policy Planning Staff of the Department of State from 1977 to 1979,
prior to which he worked as an international economist in the Treasury Department and with the House Banking Committee. Dr. Feinberg has published
numerous articles and books on U.S. foreign policy, Latin American politics, and
international economics in this series as well as *The Intemperate Zone: The
Third World Challenge to U.S. Foreign Policy*; (as editor) *Central America: International Dimensions of the Crisis; Subsidizing Success: The Export-Import Bank
in the U.S. Economy*; and (as editor with Ricardo Ffrench-Davies) *Development
and External Debt in Latin America*.

**Valeriana Kallab** is Vice President and Director of Publications of the
Overseas Development Council and co-editor of the ODC'S U.S.–Third World
Policy Perspectives book series. She has been responsible for ODC's published
output since 1972. Before joining ODC, she was a research editor and a writer
on international economic issues at the Carnegie Endowment for International
Peace in New York. At ODC, she helped launch and was series editor of the
*Agenda* series (1972–1988) and has been co-editor of many studies, including:
(with John P. Lewis) *Development Strategies Reconsidered* and *Strengthening the
Poor: What Have We Learned?;* and (with Guy Erb) of *Beyond Dependency: The
Third World Speaks Out.*

# Contributing U.S.S.R. Authors

**Ratchik M. Avakov,** Director of the U.S.S.R. team's contribution to this study, is Professor of Economics, titular member of the European Academy of Sciences, Arts, and Humanities, and Head of the Department of External and Political Relations of the Developing Countries at the Institute of World Economy and International Relations of the U.S.S.R. Academy of Sciences (IMEMO). From 1964 to 1970 he worked at UNESCO as a Senior Economist, and from 1976 to 1984, he was a Project Director at the UNESCO International Institute of Educational Planning. He has authored seven books and co-authored and edited twelve books and numerous other publications on economic and political problems of the Third World and on the educational development of the U.S.S.R. Some of his many publications include the following: *Scientific and Technical Revolution and the Development of the Third World; Educators, Technical Progress, and Industrialization: Experience of the Socialist Countries; Developing Countries: Tendencies and Perspectives* (editor and co-author); *Social Thought in Developing Countries* (editor and co-author); and *Higher Education, Employment, and Technical Progress in the U.S.S.R.* (editor and co-author). Most recently, he published an article entitled "New Thinking and the Study of the Developing Countries" in the IMEMO monthly magazine.

**Elena B. Arefieva** is a Leading Research Fellow at the Institute of World Economy and International Relations (IMEMO) of the U.S.S.R. Academy of Sciences in Moscow. Before joining IMEMO in 1986, she was a Head of the Section of External Economic Relations of the Asian Countries at the Institute of Oriental Studies of the U.S.S.R. Academy of Sciences. She is the author of two books and numerous other publications and journal and newspaper articles focusing on Third World states' relations with the developed countries and on Soviet economic policy toward the Third World. Dr. Arefieva also wrote a chapter on "The Geopolitical Consequences of Reform," published in the ODC's recent book, *Economic Reform in Three Giants: U.S. Foreign Policy and the USSR, China, and India* (1990).

**Elena A. Bragina** is a Leading Research Fellow at the Institute of World Economy and International Relations (IMEMO) of the U.S.S.R. Academy of Sciences in Moscow. She is the author of books and many other publications, including journal articles, on the problems of industrialization and state policy in Third World countries. She has participated in UNIDO and ESCAP expert meetings focusing on the nature and specific characteristics of industrial change in developing countries and the influence of this process on the international industrial structure. Now her main interests are the correlation between underdevelopment and economic and political reforms and stabilization and adjustment in the Third World.

**Andrei I. Chekhutov** is the Leading Research Officer responsible for the project "Debt Problems of the Developing Countries" at the Institute of World Economy and International Relations of the U.S.S.R. Academy of Sciences. He is also the Editor-in-Chief of the information bulletin *Developing Countries: Economics and Politics,* published by the Commission of Academies of Sciences of Socialist Countries. Dr. Chekhutov has published a book entitled *The Tax System of the Chinese People's Republic* (1962), as well as numerous chapters in monographs and magazine articles on international economics, financial problems of developing countries, and economic cooperation of the U.S.S.R. with the Third World. His current research interests focus on the development of the international financial system, the debt crisis in the Third World, and Soviet economic relations with developing countries. As an expert with the Soviet delegation, he took part in UNCTAD II, IV-VII, and in other international economic forums.

**Margarita P. Strepetova** is a Senior Research Associate at the Institute for Economics of the World Socialist System of the U.S.S.R. Academy of Sciences. An expert in the field of public education and the training of specialists for national economies of the developing countries, she has participated in the series of UNIDO Consultations on the Training of Industrial Manpower. She has also published many books, including *Cooperation of the CMEA Countries with Developing Countries: Education and Personnel Training* (in Russian), Moscow, 1973; and *Scientific and Technical Cooperation of the CMEA Countries with Developing States* (in Russian), Moscow, 1987 (with S. Simanovsky).

**Nataliya A. Ushakova,** a Leading Research Associate at the Institute for Economics of the World Socialist System of the U.S.S.R. Academy of Sciences, is an analyst of the problems of cooperation between the CMEA countries and Third World states with progressive democratic regimes, especially in the Arab World. Some of her many monographs include *The Arab Republic of Egypt: Cooperation with Socialist Countries and Economic Development* (in Russian), Moscow, 1974; and *CMEA Countries and Developing States of Socialist Orientation: Economic Cooperation* (in Russian), Moscow, 1980. In addition, she has also published several chapters in collective works.

**Leon Z. Zevin** is Professor of Economics and a Leading Research Associate at the Institute for Economics of the World Socialist System of the U.S.S.R. Academy of Sciences. His field of research is international economic relations between countries with varying levels of development and differing systems of economic management. Currently, he is studying the influences of *perestroika* on Soviet relations with Third World countries. As a U.N. expert on inter-system relations, he prepared a number of investigations for UNCTAD, UNIDO, and ILO. He is the author of many books and monographs, including his latest, entitled *Differently Developed Nations in the World Economy: Problems of Economic Relations* (in Russian), Moscow, 1985; and *The Soviet Union and Developing Countries: Economic Cooperation Principles and Practices*, New Delhi, 1988 (with T. Teodorovich).

# Contributing U.S. Authors

**Elliot Berg** is Vice-President for Policy and Research at Development Alternatives, Inc. (DAI). He taught one of the first courses on African economic development while an Assistant Professor of Economics at Harvard University in the early 1960s. He has worked in Asia and the Caribbean, though most of his experience has been in Africa. Dr. Berg spent two years in Liberia as head of an advisory group in the Ministry of Planning, and five years elsewhere in Africa on shorter stays—doing research, teaching, and consulting. He was Professor of Economics at the University of Michigan between 1966 and 1983, and from 1970 to 1978 directed its Center for Research on Economic Development. He was coordinator and main author of the World Bank report, *Accelerated Development in Sub-Saharan Africa* (1981), and in 1982 was a resident scholar at the International Monetary Fund, studying privatization issues. Dr. Berg has written extensively on development and privatization issues, and has served on various advisory bodies and panels. He has been visiting professor at numerous universities, including Columbia, Georgetown, and Legon (Ghana), and is now Adjunct Professor at the University of Clermont in France.

**W. Donald Bowles** is Professor of Economics at American University in Washington, D.C., where he previously served as Chairman of the Economics Department, Dean of the College of Arts and Sciences, and Vice President for Academic Affairs. His main interests are the Soviet economy and economic development. He is editor of three books on the Soviet economy and has published articles in *International Economic Review, Soviet Studies, Slavic Review, Educational Record, World Politics, Journal of Forestry,* and *Asia and Africa Today* (Moscow). During 1983–85, he was an economist with the U.S. Agency for International Development (USAID). During 1985–89, he served as a consultant to USAID—carrying out evaluations of USAID programs in several developing countries and writing papers for USAID and the Development Assistance Committee of the OECD on, among other themes, structural adjustment, the preconditions for market-led development, and employment creation.

**Gerald M. Meier** is Konosuke Matsushita Professor of International Economics and Policy Analysis at Stanford University. Prior to coming to Stanford in 1963, he had been Chester D. Hubbard Professor of Economics at Wesleyan University, and he had taught at Williams College, Yale University, and the University of Oxford. His professional awards have included Rhodes Scholar, Guggenheim Fellow, Brookings National Research Professor, and Russell Sage Foundation Resident Fellow in Law and Social Science at Yale Law School. Dr. Meier's many books in the international economics and economic development fields include *New Political Economy and Development Policymaking* (Institute for Contemporary Studies, 1990); *Leading Issues in Economic Development* (fifth edition, 1989); *Pioneers in Development, Second Series* (1987); *Financing Asian Development* (1986); *Emerging From Poverty: The Economics That Really Matters* (1984); and *International Economics: Theory of Policy* (1980).

**Ernest H. Preeg** currently holds the William M. Acholl Chair in International Business at the Center for Strategic and International Studies. His previous career as a Foreign Service Officer included the positions of Deputy Assistant Secretary of State for International Finance and Development (1976–77), Deputy Chief of Mission in Lima, Peru (1977–80), Ambassador to Haiti (1981–83), and Chief Economist and Deputy Assistant Administrator at the U.S. Agency for International Development (1986–88). His previous published work includes: *Hard Bargaining Ahead: U.S. Trade Policy and Developing Countries* (in this same ODC series, 1985; *Economic Blocs and U.S. Foreign Policy* (The National Planning Association, 1974); *Haiti and the CBI: A Time of Change and Opportunity* (Institute of InterAmerican Studies, University of Miami, 1985); *The Tied Credit Issue: U.S. Export Competitiveness in Developing Countries* (CSIS, 1989); and *Neither Fish Nor Fowl: U.S. Economic Aid to the Philippines for Noneconomic Objectives* (CSIS, 1991).

*Forthcoming in Fall 1991:*
## POVERTY, NATURAL RESOURCES, AND PUBLIC POLICY IN CENTRAL AMERICA
*Sheldon Annis and contributors*

Rural poverty and environmental degradation are steadily worsening in Central America, undercutting the prospects for regional peace and economic recovery. Are there solutions that are both good for the poor and for the environment? What must Central Americans do? What can the United States and other donors do to help?

The volume analyzes strategies to reduce poverty and protect the environment in Central America and lays out a policy agenda for the 1990s. Specifically, it presents the latest thinking on five key challenges in the region:

(1) The equity and ecological consequences of traditional and non-traditional agricultural export strategies, with particular emphasis on market opportunities and obstacles for small farmers;

(2) Strategies for nongovernmental organizations and international agencies to promote sustainable development, and proposals for "process-oriented" development programming;

(3) The potential role of taxation for generating much-needed revenue, addressing the region's inequitable land distribution, and promoting both more efficient and more sustainable resource use;

(4) Cross-border environmental problems and the prospects for a regional system of "peace parks" to protect areas of major ecological importance and to defuse border-related tensions; and

(5) Reconciling resource conservation with multiple human uses of tropical lands.

**Contents:**

**Sheldon Annis**—Overview: Poverty, Natural Resources, and Public Policy in Central America

**James D. Nations**—Peace Parks in Central America

**Stuart K. Tucker**—Equity and the Environment in the Push for Non-Traditional Agricultural Exports

**Alvaro Umaña Quesada and Katrina Brandon**—The Consolidation of a System of Protected Areas: Lessons from the Costa Rican Experience

**Stephen B. Cox**—Feedback, Incentives, and Participation in Sustainable Development Programs

**Rafael Celis**—Land Taxation, Land Tenure, and Resource Use

**Statistical Annex**

**Sheldon Annis** is Associate Professor of Geography and Environmental Studies at Boston University and a specialist on the issues of poverty, the environment, and grassroots development. He is the author of *God and Production in a Guatemalan Town* and an editor of *Direct to the Poor: Grassroots Development in Latin America*.

U.S.-Third World Policy Perspectives, No. 17    ISBN: 1-56000-517-1 (paper) $15.95
1991, 240 pp.                                   ISBN: 1-56000-015-5 (cloth) $24.95

# AFTER THE WARS:
# RECONSTRUCTION IN AFGHANISTAN, INDOCHINA, CENTRAL AMERICA, SOUTHERN AFRICA, AND THE HORN OF AFRICA

*Anthony Lake and contributors*

After a decade or more of fighting and destruction in various regions of the world, new policies in Washington and Moscow as well as fatigue on the ground are producing openings, at least, for peace. Negotiations are at different stages regarding Afghanistan, Indochina, Central America, Southern Africa, and the Horn of Africa—but all share new possibilities for peace.

This volume analyzes the prospects for post-war reconstruction and development in these regions, tackling the difficult quandaries they face individually and collectively: Among realistic potential alternatives, what kind of new political structures can best manage post-war reconstruction/development? Which economic policies would be most effective in maintaining peace and political coalitions? Should the focus be on the reconstruction of pre-war economic life or on creating new patterns of development? What are the prospects for democracy and human rights?

The authors thus consider the relationship of economic planning and likely political realities: For example, might diplomats seeking to stitch together a fragile coalition in order to end the fighting also be creating a government that cannot make the hard economic choices necessary for sustained peace? Might economists calling for post-war economic programs which are theoretically sound but politically unsustainable threaten a tenuous peace?

**Contents:**

**Anthony Lake** is Five College Professor of International Relations at Mount Holyoke College. He was Director of Policy Planning from 1977 to 1981 at the U.S. Department of State, and before that a member of the National Security Council staff. He has also been director of the International Voluntary Services and of various projects at the Carnegie Endowment for International Peace and The Ford Foundation. Between 1963 and 1965, he served on the U.S. embassy staff in Hue and Saigon, Vietnam. His most recent book is *Somoza Falling*.

U.S.-Third World Policy Perspectives, No. 16     ISBN: 0-88738-880-9 (paper) $15.95
1990, 224 pp.                                     ISBN: 0-88738-392-0 (cloth) $24.95

# ECONOMIC REFORM IN THREE GIANTS: U.S. FOREIGN POLICY AND THE USSR, CHINA, AND INDIA

*Richard E. Feinberg, John Echeverri-Gent,*
*Friedemann Müller, and contributors*

Three of the largest and strategically most important nations in the world—the Soviet Union, China, and India—are currently in the throes of historic change. The reforms in the giants are transforming global economic and geopolitical relations. The United States must reexamine central tenets of its foreign policy if it is to seize the opportunities presented by these changes.

This pathbreaking study analyzes economic reform in the giants and its implications for U.S. foreign policy. It assesses the impact of the reforms on the livelihood of the nearly half the world's population living in their societies. Each of the giants is opening up its economy to foreign trade and investment. What consequences will this new outward orientation have for international trade, and how should U.S. policy respond to these developments? Each giant is attempting to catch up to global technological frontiers by absorbing foreign technologies; in what areas might cooperation enhance American interests, and in what areas must the U.S. protect its competitive and strategic assets? What role can key international economic institutions like the GATT, the IMF, and the World Bank play to help integrate the giants into the international economy?

Economic reform in the giants has important consequences for their political systems. What measures can and should the United States take to encourage political liberalization? How will the reforms affect the foreign policies of the giants, and what impact will this have on U.S. geopolitical interests?

The contributors suggest how U.S. foreign policy should anticipate these new circumstances in ways that enhance international cooperation and security.

---

---

**Richard E. Feinberg** is vice president of the Overseas Development Council and co-editor of the U.S.-Third World Policy Perspectives series. From 1977 to 1979, Feinberg was Latin American specialist on the policy planning staff of the U.S. Department of State.

**John Echeverri-Gent** is a visiting fellow at the Overseas Development Council and an assistant professor at the University of Virginia. His publications are in the fields of comparative public policy and the political economy of development in India.

**Friedemann Müller** is a visiting fellow at the Overseas Development Council and a senior research associate at Stiftung Wissenschaft und Politik, Ebenhausen, West Germany. His publications on the Soviet and Eastern European economies have focused on economic reform, energy policy, and East-West trade.

---

U.S.-Third World Policy Perspectives, No. 14        $24.95 (cloth)
Winter 1989, 256 pp.        $15.95 (paper)

# PULLING TOGETHER: THE INTERNATIONAL MONETARY FUND IN A MULTIPOLAR WORLD

*Catherine Gwin, Richard E. Feinberg, and contributors*

Side-stepped by the developed countries, entangled in unsuccessful programs in many Latin American and African nations, whipsawed by heavy but inconsistent pressure from commercial banks and creditor countries, and without effective leadership from its major shareholders, the IMF is losing its bearings. It needs a sharp course correction and a strong mandate from its member countries to adjust its policies on each of five criticial issues: global macroeconomic management, Third World debt, the resuscitation of development in the poorest countries, the integration of socialist nations into the global economy, and relations with its sister institution, the World Bank. In addition, the IMF needs to bolster its own bureaucratic, intellectual, and financial capacities.

In an economically interdependent but politically centrifugal world, a strong central institution is needed to help countries arrive at collective responses to complex global economic problems. But only if its member states are willing to delegate more authority to the IMF can it help pull together a multipolar world.

**Contents:**

**Catherine Gwin,** guest co-editor of this volume, is currently the Special Program Advisor at the Rockefeller Foundation. In recent years, she has worked as a consultant on international economic and political affairs for The Ford Foundation, The Rockefeller Foundation, The Asia Society, and the United Nations. In the late 1970s and the early 1980s, she was a Senior Fellow at the Council on Foreign Relations and at the Carnegie Endowment for International Peace, where she directed the Study Group on international financial cooperation and developing-country debt. During the Carter administration, she served on the staff of the International Development Cooperation Agency (IDCA). Dr. Gwin has taught at the School of International Affairs at Columbia University and has written frequently on international development cooperation, the World Bank, and the International Monetary Fund.

**Richard E. Feinberg** is Executive Vice President and Director of Studies of the Overseas Development Council. Before joining ODC in 1983, he served as the Latin American specialist on the Policy Planning Staff of the Department of State from 1977 to 1979, prior to which he worked as an international economist in the Treasury Department and with the House Banking Committee. He has published numerous articles and books on U.S. foreign policy, Latin American politics, and international economics, including *The Intemperate Zone: The Third World Challenge to U.S. Foreign Policy*; and (as editor) *Central America: International Dimensions of the Crisis* and *Subsidizing Success: The Export-Import Bank in the U.S. Economy.*

U.S.-Third World Policy Perspectives, No. 13
1989, 188 pp.

ISBN: 0-88738-313-0 (cloth) $24.95
ISBN: 0-88738-819-1 (paper) $15.95

# ENVIRONMENT AND THE POOR: DEVELOPMENT STRATEGIES FOR A COMMON AGENDA

*H. Jeffrey Leonard and contributors*

Few aspects of development are as complex and urgent as the need to reconcile anti-poverty and pro-environmental goals. Do both of these important goals—poverty alleviation and environmental sustainability—come in the same package? Or are there necessary trade-offs and must painful choices be made?

A basic premise of this volume is that environmental degradation and intractable poverty are often especially pronounced in particular ecological and social settings across the developing world. These twin crises of development and the environment can and must be addressed jointly. But they require differentiated strategies for the kinds of physical environments in which poor people live. This study explores these concerns in relation to irrigated areas, arid zones, moist tropical forests, hillside areas, urban centers, and unique ecological settings.

The overview chapter highlights recent efforts to advance land and natural resource management, and some of the real and perceived conflicts between alleviating poverty and protecting the environment in the design and implementation of development policy. The chapters that follow offer economic investment and natural resource management options for reducing poverty and maintaining ecological balance for six different areas of the developing world.

Contents:

**H. Jeffrey Leonard**—Overview

**Montague Yudelman**—Maintaining Production on Irrigated Lands

**J. Dirck Stryker**—Technology, Human Pressure, and Ecology in Arid Regions

**John O. Browder**—Agricultural Alternatives for Humid Tropical Forests

**A. John De Boer**—Sustainable Approaches to Hillside Agriculture

**Tim E. J. Campbell**—Resource Dilemmas in the Urban Environment

**Alison Jolly**—Meeting Human Needs in Unique Ecological Settings

**H. Jeffrey Leonard,** guest editor of this volume, is the vice president of the World Wildlife Fund and The Conservation Foundation and Director of the Fairfield Osborn Center for Economic Development. Dr. Leonard has been at The Foundation since 1976. He is the author of several recent books, including *Pollution and the Struggle for the World Product, Natural Resources and Economic Development in Central America,* and *Are Environmental Regulations Driving U.S. Industries Overseas?* He is also editor of *Divesting Nature's Capital: The Political Economy of Environmental Abuse in the Third World* and *Business and Environment: Toward a Common Ground.*

U.S.-Third World Policy Perspectives, No. 11
1989, 256 pp.

ISBN: 0-88738-282-7 (cloth) $24.95
ISBN: 0-88738-786-1 (paper) $15.95

# FRAGILE COALITIONS:
# THE POLITICS OF ECONOMIC ADJUSTMENT

*Joan M. Nelson and contributors*

The global economic crisis of the 1980s forced most developing nations into a simultaneous quest for short-run economic stabilization and longer-run structural reforms. Effective adjustment is at least as much a political as an economic challenge. But political dimensions of adjustment have been much less carefully analyzed than have the economic issues.

Governments in developing countries must balance pressures from external agencies seeking more rapid adjustment in return for financial support, and the demands of domestic political groups often opposing such reforms. How do internal pressures shape external bargaining? and conversely, how does external influence shape domestic political maneuvering? Growing emphasis on "adjustment with a human face" poses additional questions: Do increased equity and political acceptability go hand in hand? or do more pro-poor measures add to the political difficulties of adjustment? The capacity of the state itself to implement adjustment measures varies widely among nations. How can external agencies take such differences more fully into account? The hopeful trend toward democratic openings in many countries raises further, crucial issues: What special political risks and opportunities confront governments struggling simultaneously with adjustment and democratization?

The contributors to this volume explore these issues and their policy implications for the United States and for the international organizations that seek to promote adjustment efforts.

Contents:

**Joan M. Nelson** has been a visiting fellow at the Overseas Development Council since 1982; since mid-1986, she has directed a collegial research program on the politics of economic adjustment. She has been a consultant for the World Bank, the Agency for International Development, and for the International Monetary Fund, as well as a staff member of USAID. In the 1970s and early 1980s, she taught at the Massachusetts Institute of Technology, the Johns Hopkins University School of Advanced International Studies, and Princeton University's Woodrow Wilson School. She has published books and articles on development assistance and policy dialogue, political participation, migration and urban politics in developing nations, and the politics of economic stabilization and reform.

U.S.-Third World Policy Perspectives, No. 12    ISBN: 0-88738-283-5 (cloth) $24.95
1989, 186 pp.                                    ISBN: 0-88738-787-X (paper) $15.95

# BETWEEN TWO WORLDS:
# THE WORLD BANK'S NEXT DECADE
*Richard E. Feinberg and contributors*

In the midst of the global debt and adjustment crises, the World Bank has been challenged to become the leading agency in North-South finance and development. The many dimensions of this challenge—which must be comprehensively addressed by the Bank's new president assuming office in mid-1986—are the subject of this important volume.

As mediator between international capital markets and developing countries, the World Bank will be searching for ways to renew the flow of private credit and investment to Latin America and Africa. And as the world's premier development agency, the Bank can help formulate growth strategies appropriate to the 1990s.

The Bank's ability to design and implement a comprehensive response to these global needs is threatened by competing objectives and uncertain priorities. Can the Bank design programs attractive to private investors that also serve the very poor? Can it emphasize efficiency while transferring technologies that maximize labor absorption? Can it more aggressively condition loans on policy reforms without attracting the criticism that has accompanied IMF programs?

The contributors to this volume assess the role that the World Bank can play in the period ahead. They argue for new financial and policy initiatives and for new conceptual approaches to development, as well as for a restructuring of the Bank, as it takes on new, systemic responsibilities in the next decade.

**Contents:**

**Richard E. Feinberg** is Executive Vice President and Director of Studies of the Overseas Development Council. From 1977 to 1979, Feinberg was Latin American specialist on the policy planning staff of the U.S. Department of State. He has also served as an international economist in the U.S. Treasury Department and with the House Banking Committee. He is currently also adjunct professor of international finance at the Georgetown University School of Foreign Service. Feinberg is the author of numerous books as well as journal and newspaper articles on U.S. foreign policy, Latin American politics, and international economics.

ISBN: 0-88738-123-5 (cloth)
ISBN: 0-88738-665-2 (paper)
**June 1986**

**$19.95**
**$12.95**
208 pp.

# STRENGTHENING THE POOR: WHAT HAVE WE LEARNED?

*John P. Lewis and contributors*

**"bound to influence policymakers and make a major contribution to renewed efforts to reduce poverty"**
—B. T. G. Chidzero, Minister of Finance,
Economic Planning, and Development,
Government of Zimbabwe

**"deserves wide readership within the broader development community"**
—Barber B. Conable, President,
The World Bank

The issue of poverty alleviation—of strengthening the poor—is now being brought back toward the top of the development policy agenda.

The current refocusing on poverty is not just a matter of turning back the clock. Anti-poverty initiatives for the 1990s must respond to a developing world and a policy environment that in many ways differs dramatically from that of the 1970s and even the 1980s. Much has been accomplished during and since the last thrust of anti-poverty policy. The poor themselves have in some cases become more vocal, organized, and effective in pressing their own priorities. A great deal of policy experience has accrued. And national governments, donor agencies, and non-governmental organizations now employ a much wider range of tools for poverty alleviation.

*Strengthening the Poor* provides a timely assessment of these changes and experience. In an overview essay, John Lewis draws important policy lessons both from poverty alleviation's period of high salience in the 1970s and from its time of lowered attention in the adjustment-accentuating 1980s. An impressive cluster of U.S. and developing-country authors react to these propositions from diverse points of view.

---

**Contents:**

---

U.S.-Third World Policy Perspectives, No. 10
1988, 256 pp.

ISBN: 0-88738-267-3 (cloth) $19.95
ISBN: 0-88738-768-3 (paper) $12.95

# GROWTH, EXPORTS, AND JOBS IN A CHANGING WORLD ECONOMY: AGENDA 1988

*John W. Sewell, Stuart K. Tucker, and contributors*

> "particularly timely, as the Administration and Congress face critical decisions on the trade bill, the budget, and other issues affecting the economic future of the U.S. and countries around the globe"
> —Frank C. Carlucci, Secretary of Defense

*Agenda 1988,* the eleventh of ODC's well-known assessments of U.S. policy toward the developing countries, contributes uniquely to the ongoing debate on U.S. jobs and trade competition with other nations.

The administration that takes office in 1989 faces a situation without precedent in the post-1945 period. Like many developing countries, the United States has to balance its trade accounts, service its foreign debts, and rebuild its industrial base. The challenge is twofold.

The immediate task is to restore the international economic position of the United States by taking the lead in devising measures to support renewed *global* growth, especially rapid growth in the developing countries.

Meanwhile, however, the world is on the threshold of a Third Industrial Revolution. Rapid technological advances are radically changing the familiar economic relationships between developed and developing countries. The kinds of policies needed to adjust to these technology-driven changes—policies on education, training, research and development—generally have longer lead times than the immediate measures needed to stimulate global growth. In the next four years, the United States must therefore proceed on *both* fronts at the same time.

---

**John W. Sewell**—Overview: The Dual Challenge: Managing the Economic Crisis and Technological Change
**Manuel Castells and Laura D'Andrea Tyson**—High-Technology Choices Ahead: Restructuring Interdependence
**Jonathan D. Aronson**—The Service Industries: Growth, Trade, and Development Prospects
**Robert L. Paarlberg**—U.S. Agriculture and the Developing World: Opportunities for Joint Gains
**Raymond F. Mikesell**—The Changing Demand for Industrial Raw Materials
**Ray Marshall**—Jobs: The Shifting Structure of Global Employment
**Stuart K. Tucker**—Statistical Annexes: U.S.-Third World Interdependence, 1988

---

**John W. Sewell** has been president of the Overseas Development Council since January, 1980. From 1977 to 1979, as the Council's executive vice president, he directed ODC's programs of research and public education. Prior to joining the Council in 1971, Mr. Sewell directed the communications program of the Brookings Institution. He also served in the Foreign Service of the United States. A contributor to past *Agenda* assessments, he is co-author of *Rich Country Interests and Third World Development* and *The Ties That Bind: U.S. Interests in Third World Development.* He is a frequent author and lecturer on U.S. relations with the developing countries.

**Stuart K. Tucker** is a fellow at the Overseas Development Council. Prior to joining ODC in 1984, he was a research consultant for the Inter-American Development Bank. He has written on U.S. international trade policy, including the linkage between the debt crisis and U.S. exports and jobs. He also prepared the Statistical Annexes in ODC's *Agenda 1985-86.*

---

U.S.-Third World Policy Perspectives, No. 9
1988, 286 pp.

ISBN: 088738-196-0 (cloth) $19.95
ISBN: 0-88738-718-7 (paper) $12.95

# HARD BARGAINING AHEAD: U.S. TRADE POLICY AND DEVELOPING COUNTRIES

*Ernest H. Preeg and contributors*

U.S.-Third World trade relations are at a critical juncture. Trade conflicts are exploding as subsidies, import quotas, and "voluntary" export restraints have become commonplace. The United States is struggling with record trade and budget deficits. Developing countries, faced with unprecedented debt problems, continue to restrain imports and stimulate exports.

For both national policies and future multilateral negotiations, the current state of the North-South trade relationship presents a profound dilemma. Existing problems of debt and unemployment cannot be solved without growth in world trade. While many developing countries would prefer an export-oriented development strategy, access to industrialized-country markets will be in serious doubt if adjustment policies are not implemented. Consequently, there is an urgent need for more clearly defined mutual objectives and a strengthened policy framework for trade between the industrialized and the developing countries.

In this volume, distinguished practitioners and academics identify specific policy objectives for the United States on issues that will be prominent in the new round of GATT negotiations.

**Contents:**

**Ernest H. Preeg**—Overview: An Agenda for U.S. Trade Policy Toward Developing Countries
**William E. Brock**—Statement: U.S. Trade Policy Toward Developing Countries
**Anne O. Krueger and Constantine Michalopoulos**—Developing-Country Trade Policies and the International Economic System
**Henry R. Nau**—The NICs in a New Trade Round
**C. Michael Aho**—U.S. Labor-Market Adjustment and Import Restrictions
**John D. A. Cuddy**—Commodity Trade
**Adebayo Adedeji**—Special Measures for the Least Developed and Other Low-Income Countries
**Sidney Weintraub**—Selective Trade Liberalization and Restriction
**Stuart K. Tucker**—Statistical Annexes

**Ernest H. Preeg,** a career foreign service officer and recent visiting fellow at the Overseas Development Council, has had long experience in trade policy and North-South economic relations. He was a member of the U.S. delegation to the GATT Kennedy Round of negotiations and later wrote a history and analysis of those negotiations, *Traders and Diplomats* (The Brookings Institution, 1969). Prior to serving as American ambassador to Haiti (1981-82), he was deputy chief of mission in Lima, Peru (1977-80), and deputy secretary of state for international finance and development (1976-77).

ISBN: 0-88738-043-3 (cloth)
ISBN: 0-87855-987-6 (paper)
**1985**

**$19.95**
**$12.95**
**220 pp.**